Arsenal
in the blood

David Lemmon

Breedon Books
Publishing Company
Derby

First published in Great Britain by
The Breedon Books Publishing Company Limited
Breedon House, 44 Friar Gate, Derby, DE1 1DA.
1998

You are talking to someone who really understands the important things in
life, death and the universe. I had a relationship with someone who made sure
our social life was arranged entirely around the Arsenal fixture list.

David Reid, *Mortimer's Law* (1998)

ISBN 1 85983 130 3

Printed and bound by Butler & Tanner Ltd., Selwood Printing Works, Caxton
Road, Frome, Somerset.

Colour separations by Freelance Repro, Leicester.

Jackets printed by Lawrence-Allen, Avon.

Contents

Acknowledgements

The author wishes to give special thanks to the following for their patience, kindness and assistance. Without their co-operation this book would not have been possible: George Armstrong, Dennis Bergkamp, Liam Brady, Andy Charalambous, Iain Cook, Lee Dixon, Peter Goy, John Hazell, Don Howe, John Jensen (with Keith Lemmon), Laura Levy, Bertie Mee, Arthur Milton, Pat Rice, Laurie Scott, Alan Smith, Brian Talbot and Bob Wilson.

Introduction

THE main object of this book is to trace the developments and changes that have taken place at Arsenal Football Club in the half-century since World War Two. Inevitably, on occasions, the story reaches outside the confines of the club to embrace matters that have been common to all clubs during that period. For the most part, I have attempted to tell the story through the words of players, officials and supporters, and I am deeply grateful to them for giving of their time so readily. They all have Arsenal in their blood.

In no way is the book intended to be an autobiography, but I hope I may be forgiven for several personal intrusions. I was first taken to Arsenal Reserves in 1939, I had the fortune to meet and speak to George Allison, Wally Barnes, Ted Drake and Wilf Copping before their deaths, and my adult life spans the years which form the basis of this narrative, the years from Allison to Wenger, from Leslie Compton and Joe Mercer to Tony Adams and Dennis Bergkamp.

David Lemmon
June 1998

The Legacy

THE day that I was born, Joe Hulme and Cliff Bastin scored the goals that enabled Arsenal to beat Chelsea 2-1, a victory that gave Arsenal the League championship for the first time. I was born in University College Hospital, St Pancras, and lived off the Caledonian Road, and I was named after David Jack. Jack was a legendary figure who had moved to Arsenal from Bolton Wanderers and who had earned his place in history by being the first man to score in a Wembley Cup Final. He was my mother's favourite footballer, and she had been infected with her passion for Arsenal by her brother, but these were the days when one was born to support one's local team. One could always understand and respect that a lad born and bred in the East End of London would support West Ham United or Clapton Orient, as Leyton Orient were then called, but for a Londoner to say that he supported Manchester United, Liverpool or Leeds was unthinkable.

My father was from Tottenham, but they were in the Second Division in the Thirties, so we didn't talk about them. It was my uncle who taught me the names of the Arsenal players and who first took me to see a reserve match. In my early years, he was offered to me as a model, correct in dress, manners and reserve, but I was warned that the bogey man would come and get me if I began to respond to the fortunes of Arsenal as he did. If, as rarely happened, they were beaten on a Saturday afternoon, he would spend the evening slumped in misery, speaking to no one. There were times when the mood lasted for several days. I was too young to know what he suffered when Arsenal lost to Walsall in the Cup in 1933, but, in the Fifties, he was still telling the tale of Arsenal's defeat in the 1932 Final.

It was the tenth Final to be played at Wembley, and, in the previous nine, the side which had scored first had gone on to win. Bob John scored first for Arsenal in 1932, but Newcastle equalised controversially. Photographs clearly revealed that the ball was over the line before it was crossed for Allen to head the equaliser with Arsenal defenders standing still. Newcastle went on to claim the Cup. Twenty years on, my uncle was still shaking his head in wonder, muttering, "The referee was Harper, and I'd always thought he was a good referee before that." I never learned what punishments he would have inflicted on Mr Harper, but I know that he was adamant that an Arsenal full-back, Wills or Evans I believe it was, who had put the ball in his own net in the last minute to give the other side a draw should have his wages stopped for a fortnight.

This was the strength of the passion of the inheritance into which one was born. Childhood heroes – Black Beauty, Long John Silver, Flash Gordon, for ever saving the Purple Planet, were joined in one's consciousness by folklore figures: Dan Lewis, the goalkeeper who had let the ball through his arms to give the Cup to Cardiff City in 1927 and who, ever after, carried the totally unjust suspicion that he had done it on purpose because he was Welsh; Alex James, "the greatest footballer the game has ever seen"; and Herbert Chapman, the man who transformed Arsenal into the most famous football club in the world.

Like Alexander the Great, Chapman died at the height of his powers from what was believed to be nothing more than a common chill. Perhaps, like Alexander, he had no more worlds to conquer. Chapman died in January 1934, and Joe Shaw took over as team manager until end of the season with George Allison becoming managing director. Allison had had a career in journalism, edited the Arsenal handbook and programmes and became a director of the club in 1926. A chubby, jovial man with a shrewd business sense, he was a pioneer soccer commentator, and he has never been given due credit for all he did for Arsenal and for the game in general.

We take so much for granted today. We accept that we can see every goal scored in the Premier League on *Football Focus* or *Match of the Day* and that we can tune to Radio Five Live and listen to a commentary. We know that Sky Television will generally show us two live Premiership matches a week and that we can watch European football on ITV, Channel Five or BBC. It has not always been so.

The first Football League match to be broadcast in England was the First Division fixture between Arsenal and Sheffield United, at Highbury, on 22 January 1927. The game ended 1-1. A week later, there was commentary on the fourth-round FA Cup-tie between Newcastle United and Corinthians, the famous amateur side. The match was played at Crystal Palace, and the commentator was George Allison. He and several other Fleet Street journalists had been invited to Savoy Hill a few days earlier from where the BBC had taken them to Highbury where each was asked to give a few minutes commentary on a reserve game. After the audition Allison was asked to become the BBC's football commentator. He gained a reputation for becoming excited and shouting, "Shoot! Shoot, man, shoot! It's a goal, surely! No, no. Magnificent save by a brilliant goal-keeper, with clutching hands and a cat-like spring."

The players had neither names nor numbers on their backs at that time, which could not have made the commentator's life easy, but to make life easier for the listener the *Radio Times* would publish a chart of a football pitch divided into eight numbered squares. Derek McCulloch would sit alongside Allison and announce "square three" or "square four" as the ball passed into that area of the field. Allison made comments like, "By Jove, that was a wonderful movement!", which were most unlike anything we would hear today from John Motson, Brian Moore or Jonathan Pearce.

The FA Cup Final of 1927, the first in which Arsenal appeared, was the first to be broadcast, but, in 1929, there was a dispute between the BBC and the FA regarding the fee to be paid for allowing the broadcast. Agreement was reached for the 1930 Final when Arsenal won a major trophy for the first time, but smaller League clubs complained that their attendances were being affected by radio commentaries. In consequence, bans were imposed on the broadcasting of all soccer matches except the FA Cup Final, and subsequently, international matches.

In 1937, the Football League allowed certain matches to be broadcast on overseas wave-lengths, but arguments raged until well into the Fifties, and the massive source of revenue that

Saturday, 11 January 1930 and some of the 55,000 crowd who saw Arsenal beat Chelsea 2-0 that day, in the third round of the FA Cup, stream into a Highbury ground which had changed little since the club moved there in 1913. Redevelopment towards the magnificent stadium which would soon become the envy of other clubs began in 1931. It is interesting to note that in this picture, almost everyone is wearing a hat and there is not a female supporter in sight.

Skipper Tom Parker has a tight hold of the FA Cup after Arsenal's 2-0 win over Huddersfield Town in the 1930 Final at Wembley. Goalkeeper Charlie Preedy is just behind Parker. Bill Seddon and Joe Hulme are to his left. The victory signalled the greatest period in the Gunners' history, a period which established them as one of the most famous clubs in the world.

Herbert Chapman, the man who transformed Arsenal into the most famous football club in the world. Chapman died in 1934, at the height of his powers, after contracting nothing more than a common cold. The legacy he left is still being enjoyed and built upon over 60 years later.

Arsenal and other top clubs receive from television fees is a manifestation of the Nineties. One does well to remember that George Allison, one of the first men in sport to recognise the importance and growing power of the media, played a major part in setting soccer on the path which was to culminate in a lucrative source of income for the game long after his death. His broadcasts were immensely popular, and gramophone records were made of his commentaries on international matches.

He relinquished the post of managing director and became secretary-manager of Arsenal in June 1934. Allison was not a soccer tactician, but his business acumen, his showmanship and flair for publicity allied to diplomatic skills, all enabled him to perpetuate the Chapman tradition. He was greatly helped by the fact that he had Tom Whittaker as his right-hand man. Whittaker was appointed the Arsenal trainer in 1927 and had quickly won such respect that he became the regular trainer of the England side at home and abroad. Allison leaned upon him heavily for advice.

Arsenal were keen to sign top players to keep the side fresh and eager, and Allison first turned his attention to the south coast and to a strong, burly centre-forward named Ted Drake.

I was playing for Southampton in the Second Division, and I'd been

scoring a few goals and generally doing well. I was also playing a bit of cricket for Hampshire, and I was quite happy. I was out training one day, and when I got back to the club somebody in the office said to me, "The Arsenal have been on the phone asking about you." I went to see the boss and asked him what it was all about. He said that they'd made an enquiry so we contacted Arsenal, and I signed for them. I was George Allison's first signing after he took over as manager. I couldn't believe my luck. Everybody wanted to play for Arsenal. They had won everything, and they had some of the best players in the world. It was

wonderful to have the chance to play alongside people like Cliff Bastin and Alex James.

Three months after signing Drake, Allison signed Wilf Copping, a tough, uncompromising left-half who had already won international honours with Leeds United. Like Drake, Copping was eager to join Arsenal, and like Drake, he won Cup and League medals. Unlike Drake, he never scored a goal in 203 first-team appearances. He returned to Leeds in March 1939. He was not alone in anticipating World War Two, and he was keen to return north with his wife Joan, a teacher, and their family.

George Allison came to me and said that Leeds wanted me back and had

Ted Drake and Alex James in action against Blackburn Rovers at Highbury in October 1935. The Gunners won the First Division match 5-1 with Ray Bowden scoring a hat-trick. But it was in the FA Cup that Arsenal were to find their greatest success that season.

April 1936 and this time Ted Drake is grounded as Chelsea's Barber gets to the ball first at a Highbury ground which is undergoing further transformation. Drake, though, scored Arsenal's goal in the 1-1 draw. This game was played on a Monday evening with an early kick-off – no floodlights in those days although Herbert Chapman had advocated them some years earlier. Two days before, Arsenal had beaten Sheffield United 1-0 at Wembley to win the FA Cup again.

The 1936 Cup winners. Back row (left to right): Wilf Copping, George Male, Jack Crayston, Alex Wilson, Herbert Roberts, Ted Drake, Eddie Hapgood. Front row: George Allison (manager), Joe Hulme, Ray Bowden, Alex James, Cliff Bastin, Tom Whittaker.

Far left: Ted Drake, the Southampton centre-forward who was George Allison's first signing in his pursuit for quality players who could improve an already successful team.

Left: Cliff Bastin, a prolific scoring winger whose total of goals for the club was a record until Ian Wright overhauled it some 60 years later.

made an offer, and was I interested. I said I was. I didn't want to leave Arsenal, but we all knew a war was coming, and they had this lad Pugh coming along. He was good, and I knew he'd take over so I thought it was time to go. But they were a great club.

Sid Pugh made his one and only League appearance against Birmingham, at St Andrew's, a month after Copping's departure. He was badly injured, and war broke out in the September. Pugh joined the RAF, was commissioned as a Flying Officer and was killed on active service in 1944.

Allison's most famous signing was that of Bryn Jones for whom Arsenal paid Wolverhampton Wanderers £14,000, at the time a world record fee, in August 1938. He was 26 years old, and his career, like the careers of so many others, was ruined by the war. Laurie Scott remembers him:

You had to feel sorry for him. He was the most expensive player of his time. They wanted to keep the same system that they had had with Alex James, and they took it for granted that he was such a good player that he could do it. Unquestionably, Bryn was the best inside-forward in the country, but he couldn't do what Alex had done. So they tried him for about six or seven months and then decided that's the finish, we'll let him play his own game. We settled down to another system. Bryn was a good player.

Scott himself had been a professional footballer for less than three years when Arsenal bought him from Bradford City in February 1937, but he was to have to wait nine years before playing First Division football.

George Allison was the manager who took me from Bradford City. I was surprised because I hadn't been a professional long. I went out training one morning, and a man called Dick Ray, who used to be manager, a big, hefty man, asked me to go to the office. George Allison was there when I got there, and so was Tom Whittaker. Tom was the trainer, but he was really the boss.

When I went to Highbury, if I wanted to see George Allison, I'd have

Cliff Bastin is held back by the arm of Derby County's England centre-half Jack Barker at Highbury in February 1938. Arsenal won 3-0 in front of a crowd of 47,000 and at the end of the season were League champions for the fifth time in eight years.

Wilf Copping, a tough, uncompromising wing-half who was already an England international when he was signed from Leeds by George Allison. He won two League championship medals and an FA Cup winners' medal with the Gunners.

to make an appointment. Everything went through Tom Whittaker. If I wanted a weekend back in Sheffield, I would ask Tom Whittaker. He more or less ran it.

Right next to the dressing rooms was a treatment room, and then there was a little office, and that was the office that Tom had. He did all his work in the treatment room, but if you wanted to speak to him, you went into his little office.

George Allison was a very good business manager, but the players didn't have a lot to do with him. He only gave team talks occasionally, and Tom Whittaker did most of the talking. He'd had a lot of experience.

To get to a club like that was wonderful for me, but they already had the England full-backs, George Male and Eddie Hapgood, who was captain of both Arsenal and England, and, at the time, I was a little bit concerned that I'd be put down to Margate. Most of the youngsters went to Margate, a sort of nursery club, and

if you were sent there, you had to go and live in Margate. You were there about eighteen months, and then you were sent back to Highbury, but I wasn't sent down there.

The club was all in one, whether you were a seventeen-year-old just coming in right through to Eddie Hapgood.

When I came down from Bradford City life changed completely for me. You were treated very, very well indeed, and in return you gave all you had back. You got into a routine, and you didn't step out of line. We weren't allowed to drive a car to training. We lived out at Southgate and had season tickets on the Underground which were paid for by Arsenal. We had to be dressed in suit and collar and tie, look spick and span – no casual clothes.

When I first went there, there were polished seats, and you'd all got special hooks for your clothing when you were changing, and all your gear was laid out for you. I was given this spot, and I couldn't reach the peg to put my things on. So what do I do? I stood on the seat with my shoes on. Oh, I got a rocket. The lads picked me up, and they took me straight into the bathroom and threw me in the water. There was a permanent cold bath in there. You had to come out that way. You came out of the hot bath, and you had to jump into the cold bath. And I was thrown in with my clothes on. But there's a laundry as well at Highbury, and by the time I'd finished training, my clothes were all nice and clean and ironed out. That was the type of thing that used to happen. It was a completely different life, and it didn't take you long to join in and be part of it. Then you'd start looking after another youngster who might be doing things wrong.

If it was Whittaker who was primarily concerned with team affairs, it was Allison who constantly kept the name of Arsenal to the fore in the consciousness of the general public. He had business associations with Gaumont British, the film company, who needed little persuading to make a screen version of Leonard Gribble's novel *The Arsenal Stadium Mystery*. A thriller, it was released in 1939 and was a critical and box office success. It starred Leslie Banks, Esmond Knight and Greta Gynt. Allison himself appeared in the film as did the Arsenal football team. It was well directed by the talented Thorold Dickinson and has worn well, having had more than one television

George Allison is the plump chap on the right in this scene from the screen version of Leonard Gribble's novel *The Arsenal Stadium Mystery,* released in 1939 to critical acclaim and a box office success. Leslie Banks is standing next to Allison.

15

showing over the past few years. No other soccer side has yet attained this cinematic level.

Allison also involved Arsenal in government propaganda at the outbreak of war. He provided the narrative for a short film which showed Arsenal scoring a goal. The emphasis of the film was that it was irrelevant who scored the goal because every member of the team worked to bring about success, symbolic of the co-operation that was needed in wartime.

War brought to an end a decade which had seen thousands endure misery and hardship. Football, like those "dream palaces", the cinemas, offered comfort, joy and escape from a world in which the present was often unpalatable and the future uncertain. At a time when England had known depression and economic failure, the success of Arsenal shone like a beacon in the dark. They established records, on and off the field, which others had thought unattainable. In a period of nine years, they won the Football League championship five times and reached the FA Cup Final three times, winning the trophy twice. Seven Arsenal players had been in the England side which beat Italy at Highbury in 1934, and a year later, Arsenal became the first club to gross gate receipts in excess of £100,000. No football club had ever dreamed of the profits that Arsenal made in the 1930s, and those profits had their ultimate manifestation in the design and building of a new main stand in Avenell Road in 1936. Created by the architect Clive Ferrier, who died before its completion, the East Stand is on a par with the Hoover building in Perivale and, like that building, is officially listed as being of such architectural and historic interest

that it may be neither demolished nor altered without government consent. Sixty years on, the impact it has on anyone seeing it for the first time has not diminished. Bob Wilson remembers being invited to Highbury to meet Billy Wright, then manager of Arsenal, in the mid-Sixties.

I remember coming along Gillespie Road and not being very impressed, and then I turned into Avenell Road and saw the stadium, the steps and the entrance. I'd never seen anything like it. At Loughborough University, I was studying two subjects, Physical Education and History, and the architecture seemed way ahead of its time even though it was of the Thirties. When Billy Wright showed me over the ground I felt it was like a cathedral. I'd seen nothing like it, for Old Trafford at that time was nothing like it is today.

By 1939, Arsenal was the most famous football club in the world. None was better supported. None was more admired, albeit that the admiration in some quarters was given grudgingly. Those who brought about this pre-eminence bequeathed to those who were to follow them a legacy of unparalleled success on the field wedded to shrewd business management and creative vision in the board room. It was a demanding legacy, for it brought with it the responsibility for maintaining and developing the highest possible standards in every aspect of the game. Only men of quality and courage would attempt to carry such a burden.

Back to Basics

I N AN air of unreality, the Football League began its programme in the autumn of 1939. Arsenal drew at Wolverhampton and beat both Blackburn and Sunderland at Highbury. Ted Drake scored four times in the match against Sunderland, but war was declared the following day, and there was no time to celebrate. Arsenal Stadium was requisitioned and used as an ARP centre. It was home to a barrage-balloon, and it was damaged in the bombing of London. When the Football League organised soccer on a regional basis in October 1939, Arsenal played their "home" games at White Hart Lane, Tottenham. Within months, all their players were either in the armed forces or members of the Civil Defence. Their names would appear on the programme with their ranks prefixed – Fl Lt B. Joy, Sgt Nelson etc. Programmes were a single pink sheet and cost one old penny.

Initially, Arsenal found it possible to field eleven of their own players, for so many were stationed in or around London, but as the war went on it became more and more necessary to call upon "guest" players. When, for example, Arsenal met Preston North End in the Football League War Cup Final in May 1941, the team was made up of eleven Arsenal players. When they met Millwall in the Football League South Final in 1945, there were only five Arsenal men in the side, and Millwall had ten guest players.

On occasions, the inclusion of guest players brought spice and excitement. They were cigarette cards come to life. Alterations to the published programme were made known by letters being propped up on the barriers next to the touchline, and one remembers a steward manfully trying to spell out "7 Nieuwenhuys". "Nivvy", as he was affectionately known, was a South African who played outside-right for Liverpool. He was one of Arsenal's many guests, the most popular of whom, undoubtedly, was Stan Mortensen of Blackpool and later of England.

Winger Ian McPherson being bundled off the ball by Manchester United's Johnny Carey at Highbury in August 1948. McPherson, who was awarded a DFC and Bar during wartime service as an RAF Flying-Officer, scored 21 goals in 163 League and Cup appearances for Arsenal. Fast and tricky, McPherson was a "real talent" according to Laurie Scott, but one that could not be wholly relied upon because he was erratic "but you couldn't leave him out".

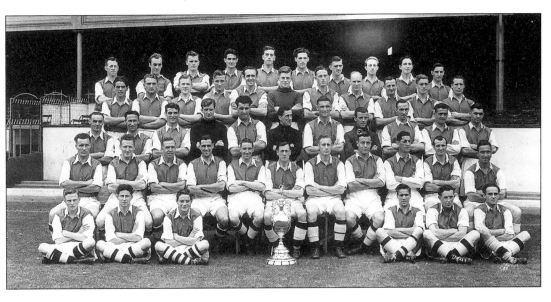

Arsenal's full-time playing staff in 1948 – some 49 players including four goalkeepers – pose proudly with the Football League championship trophy, won after the Gunners had recovered from a mediocre start to the post-war era. Many consider that the reasons for this transformation were the signing of the inspirational Joe Mercer (seen here sitting behind the trophy) and prolific goalscorer Ronnie Rooke (seated, third from the right).

Arsenal, the defending League champions, in January 1949. Back row (left to right): Archie Macaulay, Wally Barnes, George Swindin, Billy Milne (trainer), Lionel Smith, Joe Mercer. Front row: Don Roper, Jimmy Logie, Ronnie Rooke, Doug Lishman, Ian McPherson, Leslie Compton. This is the side that lost 1-0 at Villa Park.

Mortensen's entry into the international arena was somewhat bizarre. Although substitutes were not to become a part of League football until 1965-66, they were used very occasionally in wartime internationals if a player was injured. When England beat Wales 8-3 at Wembley in September 1943, Mortensen came on as a substitute for Wales, replacing the injured Ivor Powell. Three Arsenal players were in that match, Horace Cumner, who had been capped for Wales three times before the war, Denis Compton and Laurie Scott. Like Cumner, Denis Compton was an outside-left. He had won considerable acclaim as a cricketer, scoring a century in his first Test against Australia in 1938 when he was just twenty years old. He was an automatic choice for England but declined the invitation to tour South Africa in 1938-39 because he was under contract to Arsenal. Like Joe Hulme, Ted Drake and his elder brother Leslie, Denis Compton was able to earn a living as both a professional cricketer and a professional footballer, and Arthur Milton was another who combined the two.

Before the war and for a time after the war, it was possible to be both a professional cricketer and a professional footballer, but now they play football thirteen months a year, and it must be the money because you can't come up smiling every week. There's only Willie Watson and I since the war who've played cricket and football for England, but there would have been plenty of others along the way given the opportunity.

In his youth, Denis Compton was very quick and had a powerful left foot. He was the fifth member of the great England forward line – Matthews, Carter, Lawton and Hagan were the others – who beat Scotland 8-0 at Maine Road, Manchester, in 1943, and he held a regular place in the side for two years before being posted to India. He returned to play in a "Victory" international, but he was never to win a full England cap.

Another to suffer the same fate was George Marks who had become Arsenal's first-choice goalkeeper just before the outbreak of war. Shiny black hair brushed back, immaculate in all he did, he played eight times for England between 1941 and 1942, but never again. Arsenal were rich in goalkeepers. Alex Wilson, who had played in the 1936 Cup Final, was just finishing and later became an osteopath, and George Swindin were the others. As Laurie Scott comments:

We were always well off for goalkeepers, and you had to feel sorry for the one who wasn't in the team.

George Allison was to insist, even to a young fan for whom Marks was the ultimate hero, that George Swindin was the best goalkeeper on his books. In August 1946, shortly before football returned to normal, George Marks was transferred to Blackburn Rovers.

Leslie Compton, Jack Crayston, Bernard Joy, Alf Kirchen, Eddie Hapgood and Laurie Scott were others to play for England during the war, but the first four had won caps in the Thirties and Scott was to become England's regular right-back in the immediate post-war years. When war broke out, Eddie Hapgood, England's captain, was the veteran of 30 internationals, a considerable number in a period when the number of games played by England was a fraction of the number played today. On several occasions, particularly during the early years of the war, England sides were picked on a regional basis in order to avoid excessive travel at a time when cars were used only for official business and trains were constantly packed with men in uniform. This meant that an England team playing at Newcastle would be composed primarily of footballers attached to northern clubs. In spite of this, Hapgood appeared in most internationals until 1942 when he played his thirteenth and last game. This took him past Bob Crompton's record of 42 England caps, but, sadly, Hapgood's final thirteen appearances for his country were never to be recognised as full internationals.

George Male and Eddie Hapgood were full-backs for both Arsenal and England when Laurie Scott joined the club.

They were incredibly helpful to me. Eddie Hapgood could read the game exceptionally well, and I learned a lot from him. George was completely different. He was a solid, strong, safe player. He really was a great defender but without the frills of Eddie Hapgood or Ernie Blenkinsop. When I was a kid we used to watch Ernie Blenkinsop at Sheffield Wednesday. Eddie Hapgood and George Male were really two great people for me.

Laurie Scott's international career began as Hapgood's was ending. They played together against Wales at Cardiff in May 1942, but by the time Scott became a regular fifteen months later, Eddie was no longer on the scene. Scott, very quick with a fine positional sense, formed a most reliable full-back partnership with Middlesbrough's George Hardwick, and this partnership continued into the post-war period when Scott won seventeen full caps to add to his sixteen wartime appearances. The irony of his international career is that before he first played for England in 1942 he had taken the field in only two "proper" Arsenal first-team matches.

I played two games in Copenhagen in 1937. They were my first first-team games for Arsenal, that was a great thing for me. I was still learning the game. I lost years of competitive football to the war but I played for Arsenal quite a lot because I was in the Air Force and stationed just down the road, about 30 miles away, and we played at Tottenham. We just played football. That was all that mattered. We used to have guest players, and that's when I played with Stan Matthews and Stan Mortensen.

That Arsenal continued to field teams throughout the six years of war was a remarkable achievement and was due primarily to the efforts and energies of George Allison. The average attendance in the early days at Tottenham was under 10,000, and even when the war in Europe was over and the League South came into being for a year, 1945-46, gates rarely rose much above 20,000. Arsenal remained heavily in debt from the cost of building the new East Stand and financial problems had multiplied. Allison was to remark wryly that the club belonged to the bank.

Problems were not restricted to the magnitude of the overdraft. In November 1945, Moscow Dynamo came to Britain to play four matches as a gesture of friendship between Britain and the Soviet Union and to celebrate victory in Europe. They insisted that one of their opponents should be Arsenal whom they still recognised as the greatest football club in the world. Allison protested that most of his playing staff were still on active service, the majority overseas, and that any side he turned out would neither be representative of Arsenal nor would it be capable of providing the Russians with the necessary standard of opposition. The Russians insisted that it was a condition of the tour that they play Arsenal.

In front of a crowd of 85,000, they drew

with Chelsea, who included two Fulham players in their side, and then went to Cardiff where they won 10-1. Four days later, they met Arsenal at Tottenham. In the circumstances, Allison took the only course open to him. He invited Matthews, Mortensen, Rooke, Bacuzzi, Halton and Griffiths to appear for Arsenal as guests. Griffiths was a goalkeeper on Cardiff City's books, and when he was injured he was replaced at half-time by Brown of Queen's Park Rangers. The match was played on a Wednesday afternoon, and the schools in North London were empty. Laurie Scott was Arsenal's right-back.

> I played against Moscow Dynamo in the fog, but I think the crowd saw more of it than I did. I never forget that George Drury, who wasn't with us very long, played in that one. On the field, it was terrible. You couldn't see anything, and there was a Russian referee who had two linesmen on the same line, and he ran down the other side of the field. When I got to their side I found the two linesmen standing there talking to each other. It was a farce.

So intense was the fog that most of the 54,000 who went described it as the best game they had ever heard. It did little for Anglo-Soviet relations, for the Russians were angered by the use of guest players and insisted that they had beaten "England" 4-3.

Allison was confronted by a greater problem two months later. The FA Cup was revived and Arsenal were drawn against West Ham United. For that season only, ties were played over two legs, and the first leg was at Upton Park on Saturday, 5 January, with the second leg four days later. This time there could be no recourse to guest players, and Allison was forced to include Les Henley for his one and only competitive game in an Arsenal shirt, and Joe Wade who was to appear in just thirteen League matches over the next six years before winning a regular place in 1952-53 when Wally Barnes was injured. Another in the side was Dr Kevin O'Flanagan who was to play in fourteen League games in the first season after the war. He was a tremendous enthusiast who played as an amateur and, on successive Saturdays, represented the Irish Republic at soccer and rugby. The Cup-tie at the Boleyn Ground

marked Laurie Scott's debut for Arsenal in a competitive match. Like his League debut some months later, it was to be a chastening experience.

One must be allowed, momentarily, a personal intrusion. At the outbreak of war we moved to Palmer's Green, not in any attempt to escape from the Germans but in search of more respectability. Everybody in Palmer's Green and Southgate supported Arsenal or Tottenham. We argued, but we never fought, and there were many who went to Highbury one week and White Hart Lane the next.

In those years immediately after the war, football news was far harder to come by than it is today. There was no teletext with its constantly updated scores and information, nor did the radio offer the flashes of news from grounds all over the country that are now a feature of Radio Five Live. Football was a working class game, but the BBC did not then make concessions to regional accents or to distortions of what was accepted pronunciation. We relied heavily on the London evening newspapers, *The Star*, *The Evening News* and *The Evening Standard*, only one of which survives. They printed several editions throughout the afternoon, and we eagerly scoured the stop press for the latest football news.

The Arsenal had first made me cry in May 1940, when I saw them lose to Birmingham (no City then) and I have had an irrational distaste for that club ever since. But the first time they shattered me was on 5 January 1946. I had been invited to a birthday party and caught the bus to Wood Green station where I bought an evening paper. I turned eagerly to the stop press and read, "West Ham United 6 Arsenal 0." In later life, one finds one has learned to accept life's buffets with fortitude; in one's youth, rejection by a lover or crushing defeat by West Ham are harder to bear. I was unable to believe that what I read was true. I phoned home, and my aunt answered.

"Ida," I blurted out, "it says in the paper that Arsenal lost six-nil."

"Yes, dear, don't you worry. Go and enjoy your party."

As if life could hold any joy after this.

Arsenal won the second leg 1-0, West Ham lost to Chelsea in the next round (the draw was regionalised in the early stages) and a thrilling

Derby County side won the Cup by beating Charlton after extra-time.

Derby County had thrashed Tottenham at White Hart Lane on Christmas morning, for, until the 1957-58 season, football was played on Christmas Day when Arsenal or Spurs would be at home. The side that had played away on Christmas Day would be at home on Boxing Day. It was customary for the men in the family to go to football on Christmas morning while the women stayed at home and prepared the Christmas dinner. In 1946, Arsenal were to play their first First Division Football League fixture on a Christmas Day for nine years, but before then Allison and Whittaker had to attempt to rebuild the team.

Injury had brought to an end the careers of Drake, Kirchen and Crayston. Hapgood had retired and was manager of Blackburn Rovers. Denis Compton had now turned primarily to cricket and was with England in Australia. Of those remaining on the staff, Swindin was 32, Bastin was 33 and not fully fit, Leslie Compton was 34, Bernard Joy 35, and George Male 36. Laurie Scott, who was to make his League debut against Wolverhampton Wanderers in August 1946, was already 29. There was also Reg Lewis, a most capable centre-forward who was 26 and had played a little before the war. In many ways he was ahead of his time in style. As well as Scott, Ian McPherson, a very fast and tricky forward was making his League debut for Arsenal. He had been signed from Notts

County, and Horace Cumner had gone to Meadow Lane in part-exchange. In Laurie Scott's words:

Ian McPherson, unfortunately, you couldn't rely on. He was so erratic, but he had a real talent. He really could play the game. We used to have a saying with poor old Ian. We used to roll the ball to him, and his head would go down, and two or three of us at the back used to shout, "Open the gates!"

We were playing Racing Club of Paris, and he was having a bit of trouble with his full-back. He's gone along the touchline, and he's got right to the corner flag, and he's got a player there, and he's got to beat him. He can't come to the left because he's just beaten a man who's still chasing. The other bloke has come across and cut him off. Ian did a twirl around him, and the ball has gone to the side-line, but he can't get round the man because of the corner flag. He beat the corner flag as well! There were some good players at Highbury in those days. Ian had his bad days, but you couldn't leave him out of the side.

The first post-war League game was as bad as the first post-war Cup-tie had been. Arsenal were beaten 6-1 at Wolverhampton. All the goals came in the second half. It was obvious that Arsenal needed reinforcements, and even

Laurie Scott (2) watches as Liverpool's Willie Fagan gets in a flying header at Highbury in September 1949. Joe Mercer is behind Fagan. Scott was one of many talented players who lost six years at the peak of his career to the war, but for which he would probably have tripled his tally of 115 peacetime League games. Nevertheless, he won 17 England caps and skippered the Gunners.

as the war had been drawing to its close, Allison and Whittaker were looking for players. Arthur Milton was one young man to whom their attention was drawn.

At school in Bristol, if you were any good, the local clubs were interested in signing you. Being a bit of a precocious young man, I'd made a mark. My father had played semi-pro for Trowbridge in the Western League. I can see his motor bike in the garage now, the motor bike he used to get to Trowbridge on Saturday to supplement his income. He said to me, "Well, if you're going to think about professional football, we'll get somebody from a good club to come and have a look at you.

The Arsenal had a coach called Ted Davies who'd been a goalkeeper, and he used to run a team called Coulston Sports in the Downs League. So I went along and played for them. I only played the once, and I tore the ligaments in my groin battling with the centre-half, but I suppose he'd seen enough because he took me up for a few games. I played at Maidenhead, and there were all sorts of scratch games because this was the end of the war, 1945-46. There was a game at Gillingham, and a game at Brentford where I first saw Jimmy Logie, I will never, never forget that. He played wing-half, and I played inside-right. I used to play inside-right then and, of course, we had some great days together in later years.

I always remember I was supposed to go and play for the Arsenal against Tottenham. That was when Arsenal were playing at White Hart Lane because their ground had been bombed. I twisted an ankle the week before and couldn't play, but they said, "Come up!" And I went up with dad, and we went into the dressing room, and there were these two huge blokes. They were the Bedser twins, the cricketers, who used to go along to see them play. And there was a Bristolian called Ronnie Dix who was an international who played for the Spurs.

I played at Fulham in a game with Denis Compton who'd just come back from India. That was the first time I'd met Denis. They felt that they'd seen enough of me, and they said they'd like me to come up. So, at the end of the summer 1946, I went because I had to do my National Service, and I thought I'd go and see what it was like before I joined the army.

In the October, I had to go to Brentwood – Warley Barracks. I remember walking from the station with my suitcase, and I passed a couple of ATS girls, and they started to sing to me, "You'll Get Used To It." But I never did.

It was not possible for Milton and others of his generation to begin a professional career until they were twenty years old because of the demands of National Service, but Arsenal had problems that could not wait two years to be solved. On the Wednesday following their crushing defeat at Molineux, they entertained Blackburn Rovers in their first match at Highbury for seven years. Ironically, Blackburn had Hapgood as manager and Marks in goal. The attendance for this home-coming was a disappointing 28,700, but this was in a time of austerity and before the days of floodlights and an afternoon or early evening kick-off precluded many. Three days later, when Arsenal played Sunderland, there were 60,000 people inside Highbury, and there were crowds in excess of this for the games against Derby County, Stoke City, Aston Villa and Wolves. People had been starved of sport, and there was a hunger for football evidenced by the fact that this was the era in which 40,000 people would watch Hull City play Crewe Alexandra in the old Third Division North. It is likely that these attendances were larger than officially stated, for it was not uncommon for a father, arriving at the entrance with his young son, to be asked to lift the boy over the turnstile or for the lad to crawl underneath. The gateman would be given a few pence, and both parties were happy. There is no room for such "enterprise" in an all-ticket, all-seater age.

That so many people could crowd into a ground was, of course, because the great majority were standing. People were packed in tight, and it was sometimes difficult to move one's arms. One could also have the sensation that one's trousers were being slowly drawn down, and that there was nothing one could do about it. The atmosphere could be electrifying, for people were wedged so close together that they acted and generated noise as if from one body. To see the game was not always so easy, and youngsters were often passed down to the front over the heads of the crowds so that they could get a better view. When Arsenal met Charlton Athletic at The Valley in the fifth round of the FA Cup in 1956 there were more than 71,500 people present, and those high on the terraces behind one goal could really only witness what was going on at the other end.

Laurie Scott and Arthur Milton were among those Arsenal players who were used to appearing before huge crowds. Scott remembers the influence they could have:

> The crowd makes a difference in cases like when you are running down the line and you cross a ball, and the people close to you shout, "Well done! Good cross!" And things like that. We used to get booed quite a lot when we played away because we were Arsenal, but that grows on you. You didn't let it make a lot of difference. We carried on after the Hapgood and Roberts team, and that lot had won everything and were hardly ever beaten. We had to suffer because of them.

For Arthur Milton, there was the sense of excitement:

> They were great days when I went there in 1946 because everybody was coming back from the war, and the crowds used to flock to see games because they'd been starved. I always think about it because there's a lot who didn't come back. To play in front of 60,000 was nice, but the real difference is how you would feel if they weren't there. Arsenal was full every week, and there was a buzz, and the Cockneys were wonderful, great sense of humour.

In the wake of the war, the term "Cockney" was an endearing one, encompassing, as it did, the courage and wit that had been an essential part of Londoners' survival through the Blitz rather than simply referring to anyone born within the sound of Bow Bells. In the half-

century since, in spite of *East Enders*, it has become archaic. Many born in London have moved out to settle in Hertfordshire and a native wit has gone with them. Docklands has been gentrified, and a London taxi driver who has lived in Hackney all his life can say to you: "I don't understand the place I'm living in any more. I've got a American professor moved in next door. There's a lecturer at London University over the road, and a psychiatrist three doors away."

The world has become a smaller place. In the programme for the Blackburn Rovers game, the first home match after the war, "Marksman" talks of "the older ones who stuck to the job in London through bomb and fire and rocket yet still made the long trek up to White Hart Lane to give the boys a cheer." Today, when it is commonplace to drive to Barnsley or Liverpool and back in a day, a trip down Seven Sisters Road and Tottenham High Street would hardly be described as a "long trek". But these were the days when there were few cars. It was possible to drive into Finsbury Park through the gates at Manor House and out through the gates opposite Blackstock Road, but everybody came by bus or train. If you got out at Finsbury Park Station, a dismal place in 1946, and crossed into St Thomas's Road, you were confronted by the Finsbury Park Empire. It was the most important music-hall outside the London Palladium and it was customary for the great variety acts, Jimmy James, Vic Oliver, The Western Brothers, all the leading dance bands and others, to perform at Finsbury Park before moving off to the Palladium the following week.

As you approached the Empire, a few yards from where Barclay's Bank now stands on the corner, there was a sweet shop and tobacconists which had Alex James's name above it although the great man had long since conceded any interest in the business. If you turned right out of Finsbury Park Station and walked under the bridge, you were faced by the magnificence of the Astoria, one of the great cinemas of the Thirties. It was later to become The Rainbow and house pop concerts, and it is now a religious meeting place.

Its opulence was confirmed by a large and splendid goldfish pond in the foyer, but you could still get in the back row of the stalls for 1s 9d (under 9p). Football cost no more. When

23

Arsenal played AC Sparta of Prague in October 1946, admission was 1s 3d and seats were 7s 6d and 10s 6d (52½ pence). With crowds flocking to games and grounds bulging, the players had complained that they were still being paid a pre-war wage. There was even a threat of a strike, and the maximum wage was increased to £9 a week.

In those years immediately after the war, football was a working class game, and there are many supporters, like Andy Charalambous, who contend and rue that it no longer is:

> It's become much more trendy now. Many more women go, many more middle class people. Corporate hospitality is huge. There are business people who want to be associated with the game. You don't go and get the old meat pie and cup of tea at half-time and a couple of pints of beer beforehand. It's not like that any more.

Society itself has changed, and definitions of a class structure may no longer be appropriate, but when one walked up Blackstock Road in those post-war years one was undoubtedly in a working class area. Ambler School stood firm and proud as it had done for 50 years although it did not then offer the warm and effective guidance to a multi-racial community that it does today. Opposite the school was a workingmen's café where now stands a charming Italian restaurant, Il Cavaliere. Along Avenell Road and Gillespie Road, there were no burger stalls. Meat was on ration, and, in any case, burgers had not been invented and were still called rissoles. Programmes cost two old pence. The red cover and high quality paper of pre-war years had temporarily gone, for these were days of shortage in the struggle for economic survival.

The programme itself consisted of four pages, which was, in fact, a single sheet of foolscap folded in half. On the first two pages were editor's notes including a report of the previous match. The third page showed the teams set out in the positions in which they would appear on the field.

Goalkeeper

Right-back   Left-back

Right-half   Centre-half   Left-half

Outside-right Inside-right Centre-forward Inside-left Outside-left

On the reverse of the team sheet would be a League table, notice of forthcoming matches and a single advertisement which told who was playing at the Finsbury Park Empire where there were two performances each evening except, of course, Sunday.

Also on the back of the programme was a key to half-time scores, 23 of them listed "A" to "Y". In the corner where the North Bank joins Avenell Road and in the corner diagonally opposite were boards on which these same letters were printed, and, at half-time, a man would come out of the players' tunnel and trot round to put up the scores. He would disappear into a trench, and numbers would begin to appear, home side on top, away side on the bottom. At reserve matches, which often drew crowds of between 10,000-15,000, he was the only one who could provide the information as to how the first team was faring, for transistor radios were as yet unknown. His could be a hazardous job.

When Arsenal Reserves entertained Millwall Reserves in mid-September, the League side was at Villa Park. At half-time at Highbury, the man with the scores issued forth smiling and giving the thumbs-up sign to the crowd who cheered him all the way round to his trench where he revealed Arsenal were winning 2-0. It was their first win of the season. But there were other times when he was greeted like a medieval messenger bringing bad news. He would walk to his corner huddled and miserable, booed and jeered by the crowd who sensed Arsenal were losing.

Programmes for reserve games were identical to those for First Division matches, and, in the one covering the fixture against Millwall mentioned above, the editor commented on how reports suggested that football was booming on the continent and that the challenge to English supremacy, always accepted, was greater. "Having learnt from the masters, the pupils have grown up. Will that old saloon bar topic, the European League, ever take shape, I wonder. Would it be a good or a bad thing for international sport?"

This was quite a bold question for the period when people took their holidays in Southend or Blackpool and when even a day trip to Boulogne was something that lay in the future. Not least, the continent of Europe was still suffering from the ravages of six years of war. In spite of the war, however, England remained very insular, and there was a deep suspicion of foreigners. Eddie Hapgood's "ghosted" autobiography, *Football Ambassador*, published at the time, muses on the fact that continentals did not know how to make tea and smelt of garlic, but, as Liam Brady comments, "We all eat garlic now."

In the difficult search for young players, Arsenal had invited Albert Gudmundsson, an Icelandic international, to join them. A highly gifted inside-forward with creative flair, he played as an amateur against Stoke City, the first home victory of the season, and Chelsea in the October, but he was refused a work permit and joined AC Milan. He later played in France before returning to Iceland where he became president of the Icelandic FA and served in the government as Minister of Finance.

Chelsea had acquired the services of Willi Steffen, a huge full-back who played for Switzerland. In the days when full-backs were not required to hare down the wing, he looked a very fine defender, but it seems that some of the Arsenal players were less than impressed, and there were suggestions in a Sunday newspaper that they had protested that overseas footballers should not be allowed to play for English clubs. What joys we would have missed had that attitude prevailed.

With the acquisition of foreign players not an option, and with emerging young footballers almost impossible to find, Arsenal faced a dilemma in that immediate post-war period. By the end of November 1946, they had won only four of their sixteen matches and stood only one point above Huddersfield Town who were bottom of the table. Action had to be taken, and they surprised many by paying Everton £7,000 for Joe Mercer. Two weeks later, they astonished all by signing Ronnie Rooke from Fulham.

Mercer was 31 years old. He had played left-half for England before and during the war, but, due to an old injury, he had a suspect knee. He joined Arsenal because, in his own words, "Everton think I'm a bad player, and Arsenal tell me they think I'm a good player." He made his debut against Bolton Wanderers at Highbury on a muddy pitch that resembled black treacle. Arsenal kicked-off, and the ball was pushed back to him. He tried to dribble it forward and lost it. The crowd groaned, and there were shouts of "You can't play like that on a pitch like this." But it was probably the last

Skipper Joe Mercer leads out Arsenal, followed by Don Roper. According to Laurie Scott: "Joe was wonderful, a great captain, tough as a nut ...he would have a go at people, but we accepted it."

piece of criticism he ever received from an Arsenal crowd.

There was no undersoil heating at that time, nor was there the expertise in pitch preparation that exists today. The surfaces for which Steve Braddock so rightly won the Groundsman of the Year award in 1998 would have been viewed in awe and wonder a half-century earlier when, if snow fell and did not melt, it was flattened and lines were marked in red or blue so that the game could go ahead. Arsenal beat Manchester United 6-2 on such a surface in February 1947.

Throughout the 1946-47 season, it was the senior player who captained Arsenal. When he was in the side George Male was captain, and when he was absent Leslie Compton led the team. Towards the end of the season, with both of them missing, Joe Mercer was captain. At the beginning of the following season, he continued as captain because Compton was still playing cricket for Middlesex who were in the process of winning the County Championship. By the time he returned, Arsenal had played six matches and won them all. In the dressing room before the game against Preston North End, at Deepdale, Tom Whittaker, now manager, handed the ball to Compton to lead the side out. Big Les declined and gave the ball to Mercer to carry on as

In 1950, Joe Mercer led Arsenal to a famous FA Cup Final victory when they beat Liverpool 2-0. Here, Arsenal goalkeeper George Swindin and full-back Wally Barnes watch the ball go wide after Liverpool forward Albert Stubbins tries a diving header.

Arsenal centre-forward Peter Goring is just beaten to the ball by Liverpool goalkeeper Cyril Sidlow.

captain. One thing that has not changed in 50 years is that outstanding captaincy has always been an essential ingredient in any Arsenal success, and, on the field, Joe Mercer was the greatest leader of his day. To Laurie Scott, the success came as no surprise:

> I knew Joe because I'd played with him in the England side, and even if

he never kicked a ball, he'd be out there in the middle doing a marvellous job. Joe was never satisfied until you'd run your blood to water. He could get it out of you somehow. He was a strange character. He wasn't nice and gentle with it. He was a hard nut, but you took it. Some of the lads didn't take to it at first, but I was lucky because I'd been with him in the England side, and I was used to it. He really was something, a wonderful character. There haven't been many captains and characters like him.

Arthur Milton endorses Laurie Scott's opinion:

Joe was wonderful – a great captain. He used to come on Friday because he trained mostly at home,

and he'd say, "Come on, Arty, you come with me for a run." And I'd say, "Why?" And he'd say, "Because you're the only one whose legs are as bent as mine."

We used to go and have lunch in the hotel in King's Cross, a bit of chicken or something, and then we'd go back to the ground and get changed. There'd be a bit of a team talk, and Joe would get hold of the ball and lead us up the tunnel, and he'd turn round and say, "All right, lads, forget all about that. Let's go out and enjoy ourselves." Wonderful man. I was so sad to see him go. He was a tough nut as captain, and he would have a go at people, but we accepted it.

I shall never forget the day he broke

His Majesty King George VI presents the FA Cup to Arsenal skipper Joe Mercer.

27

Joe Mercer is held aloft with the FA Cup. The other Arsenal players are (left to right): Wally Barnes, George Swindin, Laurie Scott, Alec Forbes, Leslie Compton and Jimmy Logie.

his leg. I was playing outside-right, and it happened in more or less the left-back position because Joe Wade ran into him, and I heard the leg crack like a gun going off. And I can see him now being carried off on a stretcher, and he waved as if he were saying goodbye to everybody.

The match in which Joe Mercer broke his leg and ended his career was against Liverpool at Highbury in April 1954, but by then he had led Arsenal to two League championships and to victory in the FA Cup Final in 1950 when, nearly 36 years old, he was named Footballer of the Year.

As we have mentioned, Arsenal signed Ronnie Rooke a fortnight after Mercer had joined them. Rooke, who was a week past his 35th birthday when he made his Arsenal debut, had been with Fulham, a Second Division side, for ten years, was their leading goalscorer and an immense favourite at Craven Cottage. According to Tom Whittaker's memoirs, he was offered to Arsenal by the Fulham manager Jack Peart:

We had been searching for a centre-forward, and one afternoon I got a telephone call from Jack Peart, the Fulham manager, asking me whether we would like to sign their craggy-

faced leader Ronnie Rooke. Added Jack: "For heaven's sake keep it quiet that I have approached you, because if the fans know, they'll very likely overturn your car if they see it outside the ground!"

Arsenal offered £1,000 plus two players, Dave Nelson, who had 27 League appearances to his credit, and Cyril Grant, a centre-forward who had played twice in the first team. The following Saturday, Rooke walked into the main entrance at Highbury with his boots in a brown paper parcel under his arm. Laurie Scott remembers:

The players themselves couldn't understand why they signed Rooke, but look what he did when he got there. We'd have never thought of a thing like that. He had only a couple of years, but look what he did.

There may even be some older Arsenal supporters who do not remember Ronnie Rooke. His time with the club was brief but glorious. His style of playing centre-forward was not that of a Bergkamp or a Wright, but he had the art of scoring goals, and that is a quality we should now examine.

Arsenal with the Cup, in more formal pose. Back row (left to right): Tom Whittaker (manager), Laurie Scott, George Swindin, Wally Barnes, Billy Milne (trainer). Front row: Denis Compton, Peter Goring, Alec Forbes, Joe Mercer, Reg Lewis, Leslie Compton. On ground: Jimmy Logie and Freddie Cox.

Goals and Goalscorers

THERE is a goalscoring record held by an Arsenal player which has stood for 63 years and which is likely to stand for another 100 years. On 14 December 1935, Arsenal went to Villa Park and beat Aston Villa 7-1. Ted Drake scored all seven goals, a feat unapproached since that time. Those who saw the match remain convinced that he touched the ball only eight times in scoring seven. Ted himself only half-supported that view. He was emphatic:

> I scored eight. The eighth one hit the underside of the bar and came down over the line. The ref was a friend of mine, and I turned to him and said, "That's a goal!" But he just

smiled at me and said, "For Christ's sake, Ted, you've got seven already. Play on!"

Arthur Milton remembers that Drake was still at Highbury when he joined the club:

> He was one of several older players who were a great help. He was beyond his playing days, but he used to help the youngsters. He showed us how to kick a ball, but you really have to learn yourself.

The popular opinion was that Drake had a kick "like a Spanish mule" with either foot. He was hard, very fast and strong and, like most centre-forwards of his day, "capable of running through a brick wall". In 1934-35, he established an Arsenal record with 42 goals in 41 League games, and his career record for Arsenal was 124 goals in 168 League games, a scoring rate of 73 per cent. Ronnie Rooke scored 68 goals in 88 League games for Arsenal, a scoring rate of more than 77 per cent. In all games, his scoring rate was 82 per cent. No other Arsenal striker has come close to that.

Rooke was a battering ram in an age when finesse was not the most sought after quality in a striker. The finesse was provided by the inside-forward; what was wanted in the centre-forward was strength and power. During the war, for example, Arsenal had frequently used big Leslie Compton as centre-forward. The elder of two famous brothers, "Big Head", as he was affectionately known because of his towering presence and outstanding heading ability, joined Arsenal in 1930 and served them faithfully for 23 years. In the pre-war years, he was essentially a full-back, understudying Male or Hapgood when they were on international duty. He was 34 when League football resumed after the war, and he was converted into a centre-half. Laurie Scott remembers:

Ted Drake scored all Arsenal's goals when the Gunners won 7-1 at Villa Park on 14 December 1935. Altogether he scored 136 League and Cup goals and another 86 during wartime matches and six for England in five full internationals.

February 1935 and Drake scores his second goal for "England" in their 2-2 draw against The Rest at The Hawthorns. It seems strange now, but international trials were a common occurrence and this one attracted a crowd of nearly 13,000.

Ronnie Rooke (third from left) was a battering ram in an age when finesse was less important for a goalscorer. No other Arsenal striker has come close to his scoring rate of 82 per cent.

What happened was that Alf Fields was injured. Joe Mercer did it, actually, pure accident in training. Alf had been automatic to take over when the time came, but it didn't work. He couldn't do it, and the other lad, Ray Daniel, was only a youngster and not quite ready although he turned out to be a

very good player. We thought they might have bought, but they didn't have to. They moved Les, and, of course, we had Wally Barnes. He was bought out of the army, and it worked very well.

There was only one thing wrong with Les. He was really too good a player, and we used to take advantage. When we attacked along the left Wally would go forward and I would drop back to make sure we'd got cover, and if we attacked along the right, it worked the other way. There was so much up and down that there were occasions when we didn't get back because nothing got past Les. It was dangerous really, but he was so solid. He was incredible. We got pulled up a time or two because we weren't doing this up and down business, but he was like a big rock.

Leslie Compton was 6ft 2ins tall and weighed over 13st, although when reappearing in the League side at Easter 1952, when Ray Daniel was injured he weighed considerably more than that. In 253 League games, he scored

Centre-half Leslie Compton scored only five goals – all penalties – in a League career which spanned 253 games. But his only FA Cup goal, a header, was a vital one in a semi-final, and in one wartime season, playing up front, he netted 42 goals including ten in one game.

five times, and those goals came from penalties, but, as we have noted, Arsenal played him at centre-forward in many wartime matches. He scored 42 goals in 1941-42, including ten when Arsenal beat Clapton Orient 15-1 at White Hart Lane in February that season. As a centre-half, however, he was not expected to go marauding as Tony Adams has done with frequent success in the Nineties, but there was one famous occasion, in 1950, by which time Rooke had departed to become manager of Crystal Palace and Laurie Scott was having to contend with a troublesome knee injury:

There was the Cup semi-final at Tottenham against Chelsea. We were two down, and Freddie Cox scored straight from a corner just before half-time. Coming towards the end of the game, big Les decided to go up for a corner, and Joe Mercer shouted for him to get back. I don't know whether Les heard him or not, but I think he ignored him. He made out he didn't hear him, and he went up and headed the equaliser.

It was the only goal that Leslie Compton ever scored in a Cup-tie. Arsenal went on to win the replay and the Final, and Big Les won two international caps at the age of 38. He still holds the record as being the oldest England debutant. Age seemed to matter less in those days, and it was certainly the veterans who got Arsenal out of trouble.

It all really changed in that season after the war when George Allison signed Joe Mercer and Ronnie Rooke. I know it sounds crazy, but what was happening was that we were playing some good football but nobody was finishing. Reg Lewis was the only one who was getting any goals. Jimmy Logie wasn't expected to get any. He was always ten or fifteen yards back. He was a very good player, a much better player than many people thought. I am not saying he was as good as Alex James, but, for Arsenal, he did exactly the same job, a wonderful job. It was just that we couldn't get the ball in the net. When Tom Whittaker said Ronnie Rooke was coming we thought "What the hell is going on here?" He was about 40.

And look at the difference. He was leading goalscorer when we won the championship. He was my room mate when we were away for the weekend. I remember when we were playing Grimsby, and George Tweedy was in goal, and Ronnie broke his wrist. He shot the ball, and George got across to it and pushed it round the post, but the power of it broke his wrist. The 1948 side was a good side. We'd been nearly relegated the year before, and you've got to give a lot of credit to the management for signing a player like Ronnie Rooke.

Arthur Milton endorses Laurie Scott's opinion although he only knew Rooke as an opponent and as a senior when he was still trying to win a first-team place.

Ronnie Rooke made a great difference. He played for Fulham when I played in the match there. Couldn't he hit a dead ball! He got Arsenal out of trouble. He was very dark and very strong.

Certainly Rooke's appearance suggested that he was not one with whom to pick a quarrel. His nose would not have been out of place on a boxer. His impact for Arsenal was immediate. He scored the only goal in the home victory over Charlton on his debut, and he scored six more goals in the next five matches, three of which were won and two drawn. He hit a hat-trick on the snow against Manchester United and finished the season with 21 goals from 24 games as Arsenal climbed to thirteenth in the League, first among London clubs. When Reg Lewis returned after injury the pair formed a lethal combination, and Lewis finished with 29 goals from 28 games, but he was different in style to Rooke and to most other centre-forwards of the period. As we have suggested, he was ahead of his time. His two goals which beat Liverpool in the 1950 Cup Final, for example, were when he moved smoothly on to passes from Jimmy Logie and slid the ball into the net. Arthur Milton laments that he did not play more with Reg Lewis.

I'd have loved to have played more with Reg, but they brought these big

Reg Lewis heads goalwards for the Arsenal against Everton. Lewis was "ahead of his time", different in style to Rooke and, indeed, to most other centre-forwards, but he still scored 116 goals in only 175 games for the Gunners.

fellows in. Reg was looked down on because he didn't run about very much, but he didn't have to. He was always gliding into position. He had two wonderful feet, ever so small, about size six. He used to pick his spot and in they'd go, and he was good in the air. I liked Reg.

The Arsenal side was strengthened before the start of the 1947-48 season by the signing of Macaulay and Roper, and Alec Forbes was to be bought from Sheffield United some months later. Of the first seventeen matches, twelve were won and five were drawn. The first defeat came at Derby at the end of November when little winger Reg Harrison, who had played for the Rams in the 1946 FA Cup Final, scored the only goal of the game. It was a minor blip, though, and the championship was won with ease. Arsenal were back on top. And so, too, was Ronnie Rooke. He played in all 42 League games and scored 33 goals. He was leading scorer in the First Division. Four of his goals came from penalties, and it seemed that he had a simple philosophy on penalty taking. He would drive the ball as hard as he could – and that was at frightening speed – presumably on the assumption that if the goalkeeper got in the way he would go in the net with it. There were none of the subtle placings employed by Wright or Bergkamp.

Rooke scored the first goal in a 2-1 victory over Manchester United on the first Saturday of September. He swayed to his left as he hit the ball like a rocket into the top right-hand corner. There were 62,000 at Highbury that day, which was not uncommon. When Middlesbrough came to Arsenal on Good Friday, the crowd was 60,000 and Rooke scored three as Arsenal won 7-0. One of his goals must take its place among the most opportune or most bizarre.

That day, Middlesbrough gave a debut to a 23-year-old goalkeeper named Robert Anderson who later played for Crystal Palace and both Bristol clubs. The match at Highbury was to be his one and only game for Middlesbrough. He was nervous, inexperienced and playing against the side who needed just six points from nine matches to clinch the championship. Rooke noticed that his goal-kicking was not of the strongest, and with Middlesbrough defending the goal at the

North Bank end, the Arsenal centre-forward stationed himself on the edge of the penalty area facing Anderson who was about to take a goal-kick. The ball was struck hard, but the trajectory was low and hit Rooke who had, it seemed, deflated his chest so that he could expand it on the moment of impact. The ball bounded back towards the unguarded net with the young goalkeeper frantically and unavailingly in pursuit.

Just over a month later, with the title already won, Arsenal entertained Grimsby Town, already doomed to the Second Division, in the last match of the season. Rooke had been vying with Blackpool's Stan Mortensen for the honour of being leading scorer in the First Division, but it was known that Mortensen was injured and would not play in the final game, and two goals for the Arsenal man would take him clear of his rival. In the event, he scored four, and one lives in the memory. Alec Forbes ran through an ageing and static defence, rounded goalkeeper Tweedy, placed his foot on the ball on the goal-line and walked away so that Rooke could run up and kick the ball into the empty net to become the League's leading scorer. The Arsenal spirit and commitment to each other is a quality that has remained constant over the years.

Forbes was a fiery character, a red-headed Scottish international, fiercely competitive and skilful. Laurie Scott remembers his arrival at Arsenal.

In the first place, at Highbury, your background is checked before they buy you. One that was very doubtful, and he was doubtful, was Alec Forbes. Tom Whittaker asked the elder players, about five or six of us, and then he checked on him. There was still that doubt, and eventually they said, "He's a hell of a good player and we'll bring him here and see if we can change him." Because he'd been a bit naughty at Sheffield United. He didn't alter much. He was still pretty hard.

Forbes was preferred to Archie Macaulay – "a very good player, but his defence was a bit suspect" – in the 1950 Cup Final. Macaulay took a lot of work off the full-back because he pushed forward, but Forbes was used to deal with the threat of the Liverpool winger Billy Liddell, which he did very effectively if, at

Doug Lishman, seen here with Spurs goalkeeper Ted Ditchburn diving bravely at his feet, was a class player and, for five seasons in succession, he was Arsenal's leading scorer. Indeed, until the advent of John Radford he was Arsenal's most prolific post-war scorer.

times, somewhat roughly. He was the scorer of one of the most embarrassing goals seen at Highbury. Arsenal were playing Derby County, and he committed a rather brutal foul close to the touchline in front of the West Stand. The referee ran across, intending, one felt, to take serious action, but Forbes was lying prostrate, and the official hastily summoned the trainer. These were the days when a player who left the field on a stretcher was, almost inevitably, never seen on a football field again, and the on-the-field remedies lacked the technological subtleties of today. All was cured by a bucket of cold water and a sponge, even in bleak midwinter. Forbes was restored to life by the application of this shock treatment, and, as was the custom with injured players in the days before substitutes, he was moved to play on the wing – out of harm's way. He spent five or six minutes there in ineffective isolation when suddenly a long ball was played down the right wing. Galvanised, he raced past the full-back and drove the ball into the top right-hand corner of the net. The goal was greeted with a murmur of approval and embarrassment, and Forbes trotted back to his starting position of right-half.

Arthur Milton recalled:

Forbes used to love to go down the field when he should have been giving

us the ball. Jimmy Logie used to get annoyed and say, "I wish we had Archie Macaulay." He was a good looking fellow, a very stylish man. Forbes looked a real tough character, but I think he was a bit soft underneath. He went to South Africa.

He was playing when we met Aston Villa in the League and we went three up in twenty minutes, and it was called off because of fog. We thought we were very unfortunate because we wouldn't do that again, but we played them the next week in the Cup, and we were four up in twenty minutes.

Tommy Lawton played in the first game and scored, and he also scored in the re-arranged game – his only other goal of the season. I think he came to Arsenal because Tom Whittaker had a feeling for those old players.

In my days, of course, you were allowed to stay on your wing. Don Roper was on the left when I was on the right. McPherson and Roper had been the wingers, and Roper contin-ued to play when I was in the side. There weren't too many left wingers around although we had Ben Marden. I think I took over from Mac. His problem was that he didn't loose it. I don't think he knew where he was going. He was good on the ball, and he could get past people, but he didn't know when to let it go, and that's the real top and bottom of it. He used to remind me of Bobby Mitchell who played outside-left for Newcastle.

Doug Lishman was inside-left, and Peter Goring or Cliff Holton centre-forward. They always went for these big fellows.

Cliff Holton and I had a wonderful day against West Bromwich Albion in my first full season. We beat them 6-3, and I did everything but score. Cliff got two, and Doug Lishman got three. The culmination was that I found myself somehow going through in the inside-left position, and my left foot was not that good, and Cliff's left foot was not that good either, although he could hit a ball. I looked over, and he's

Cliff Holton in familiar aerial action against Spurs. Holton played a big part in Arsenal's championship win of 1952-53, netting nineteen goals in 21 games, and overall he scored 83 in 198 League games for the Gunners.

coming up the middle, and I centred it with my left foot, and he volleyed it from about 40 yards straight in the back of the net with his left foot. He did well wherever he went.

Holton played a big part in Arsenal's championship win the following season, 1952-53, netting nineteen goals in 21 games, two of the goals came on Christmas morning. Arthur Milton got one.

We used to play three matches over the Easter in those days. If the weather was fine and the pitches were hard with not much grass on, you didn't have any legs left after three games. And we used to play on Christmas Day, but never at home. I remember playing at Bolton on Christmas morning – we always played in the morning – and I've never played in a match like it. Every time the forwards went in the other half, the ball went in the net, and we were winning 5-4, and they had a penalty. Bobby Langton, the England outside-left, missed it, and we scored again to win 6-4. What a morning! Everyone went home happy.

Earlier that season, Milton had scored in a wonderful 3-1 over Tottenham at White Hart Lane in front of a crowd of nearly 70,000. Arsenal were most apprehensive about the match. Swindin was out injured, Ted Platt was in goal, one of his last appearances before giving way to Jack Kelsey, and Chenhall was in for the injured Joe Wade at right-back. Mercer was also missing and was replaced by the then inexperienced Dave Bowen. Don Roper was still on the wing. Laurie Scott remembers him:

He was a hard worker, a wonderful crosser of the ball, and he was very much to my liking because he did a lot of my work as well. He really was a good hard worker, but he didn't have the craft of Jimmy Logie or even of Reg Lewis.

Logie was one of the greatest creative talents to have donned the red and white of Arsenal. He was in the Alex James tradition, and it is a ball-playing tradition which has passed. A year before his death, Denis Compton referred to a famous photograph of James beating three Manchester City players without touching the ball and lamented that no one in modern football was capable of such an act. Doug Insole, himself a capable footballer and Test cricketer, remarked that James would not have been able to do it in the Nineties. He would have been allowed to carry the ball forward until he met a defensive brick wall which would have left him impotent. For those who saw both, Logie was James reincarnated. In Arthur Milton's opinion:

Jimmy Logie was the best player I knew at the Arsenal. He was never out of the game. He was the sort of player who made you play. You knew if you went to the wrong place, the ball wouldn't come to you. So you went to the right place. It was no problem for you. When Tapscott played, when I used to go it was never there, and when I didn't go it was there. That was the difference. The only problem was that we didn't have anybody on the other side who had quite the ability to play as Jim did, and if he was off form or wasn't in the side, we were never as good a team without him. Some sides used to put a man just to shadow him, which made it difficult. I remember one game when we came off Jim said, "What about that then? If I'd come off to go to the lavatory, he'd have come with me.

Jimmy and I had a wonderful understanding. We had a great run in that championship season, 1952-53. That game at White Hart Lane, when we won 3-1, we were playing without several of our regulars, and John Chenhall was in. He was a Bristolian, and he'd hardly ever played before. I scored that day, and I've got photographs of the ball going in the net, but I'm not in sight. You can only see Ted Ditchburn.

Tottenham were always a lovely side to play against because they tried to play good football, but we gave them the runaround that afternoon.

In those days, nobody was very demonstrative if you scored a goal, but I think we were winning 1-0 when I got to the byline, and I pulled the ball back, and Jimmy popped it in the net.

He didn't use to score many goals, and he came running over to me and picked me up. And I said, "What's all that about, Jim?" And he said, "Well, my tailor promised me a new suit if I scored against Tottenham." He was a smart dresser.

Jimmy Logie's principal job was to create goals rather than to score them, but he still managed to find the net 76 times in 326 League and Cup games. Arsenal signed him in the summer that preceded World War Two. They bought him from Lochore Welfare in Scotland, and he cost £35. Incredibly, he played only once for Scotland, just as Arthur Milton played only once for England, and Arthur believes he was lucky.

It was quite amazing really when you think that Finney and Matthews were still around. Stan Matthews used to go in and out of favour, and Tom Finney – I was delighted to see he got knighted – was playing outside-right at the time, and he got injured, and that's why I played. I was having a good run, but I didn't have a great match. It was a bit early for me. I was lacking a bit in experience. It was in the November. We drew 2-2 with Austria. We should have won. We should have scored five in the first twenty minutes, and we didn't get one. After that it was a struggle. It always is if you don't take advantage. Tom Finney sent me a telegram. I had a few telegrams, but I'll always remember that one.

Arthur Milton's mention of Matthews and Finney is a reminder of a standard joke of the time when Tommy Lawton was England's centre-forward. One day Finney said to him, "When I centre the ball and you head a goal I notice you wince a bit, but when Stan crosses it from the other wing and you head it in the net you don't react at all. Why?" And Tommy Lawton replied, "Well, Tom, it's like this – when Stan centres the ball he always makes sure that the lace is top side up."

As a joke, this fabrication has no meaning today, but in that post-war period footballs were made of leather and, once the bladder had been pumped up, they were tied with a leather lace. In junior games, on a wet afternoon, a

Thirty-four-year-old Tommy Lawton was in the twilight of his career when he joined Arsenal in September 1953, from Brentford for £10,000. He scored 13 goals in his 35 League games for the Gunners.

heading ability of Tommy Lawton. One remembers the Welsh international full-back Wally Barnes suffering a cut head and returning to the field with his head totally swathed in bandages. He still jumped to head the ball clear, and every time he did so, the crowd shuddered.

Lawton was 34 years old when he joined Arsenal and very much in the twilight of his career. He had been among the best centre-forwards England has ever known, and although there were some moments of magic like a back heel that set up a goal against Sheffield United in a 4-0 win in the autumn of 1954, his two years with Arsenal were as somebody passing through. He never made the same impact that Rooke had made, and Arsenal were passing into less successful times. Rooke, Lewis, Logie and Milton – between them they won two international caps, for international matches were fewer in number in those days and caps were not awarded so cheaply. Nor was the League programme suspended when an international was being played. When Arsenal won the championship in 1947-48, Laurie Scott missed only three of the 42 games, and each game he missed was because he was playing for England on the same day.

George Armstrong recalls that that persisted into the Seventies.

People say I was unlucky not to get a full cap, but I never lose sleep over that. When I played for England Under-23s we played on a Saturday. You might have to report on the Friday night, but the League didn't stop because of internationals. Don Revie and one or two other managers started pulling their players out, and that's what changed things.

George Armstrong first joined Arsenal 37 years ago, and he has been with them both as player and reserve-team manager. There has been no more popular figure at Highbury, nor no sounder judge of a footballer, and he feels that it was the coming of Joe Baker that first brought about a change at Highbury in the conception of the role of what we now call "the striker". Baker was born in Liverpool, brought up in Scotland and first played for England when he was with Hibernian. He was transferred to AC Torino during that first,

football absorbed moisture and became as heavy as a cannon ball, and the lace had the habit of being above the surface of the rest of the ball and could provide a cutting edge. Boots had toe caps which were like iron and sometimes began to turn up at the end like Turkish slippers. One looked in wonder at the distance that Leslie Compton could kick a ball, the power that Ronnie Rooke imparted and the

uneasy flush of English players going to Italy, and he was with Arsenal from 1962 to 1966.

Joe Baker was a great goalscorer. I always remember when he first came in the team we had that old English way – don't pass to me if I'm marked. And Joe said to me, "Listen, you, *because* I'm marked, give me the ball!" He'd been used to Italian football so he was happy to take the marker with him. I thought Joe was a terrific player, and so was George Eastham. They use the word "great" too often today, but George was a great player. He could do anything, and he was a good help to me. We used to play one-twos together.

Many people see strikers as the glamour boys of football. It is they who put the ball in the net and who claim most of the headlines and the praise. Supporter Andy Charalambous says unashamedly:

John Radford was my favourite player because he was centre-forward, and that's what I wanted to be. And Charlie George because he scored that goal in the 1971 Final.

There are times when a striker can disappoint, does not live up to expectations. Brian Talbot thinks that his colleague Charlie Nicholas was probably a case in point.

He was a lovely character, great lad. There was nothing flashy about him in the dressing room. He came as a superstar, a young superstar, but perhaps he couldn't cope with the discipline which you need to have to be a top athlete. His feet were very quick, and he could move the ball about and he could score goals, but he lacked that yard of pace in the area which would take him past people, so they could always get back at him and get in another tackle. I liked Charlie, and I thought he was a good player and good for the club, but you've got to do it on a big stage, week in and week out. I think a manager wants a player who is going to give him 35 games a season. One who is only going to give you fifteen is no good to you.

In fairness to Charlie, he'd scored goals for Scotland and Celtic, and

Joe Baker, here ahead of Alan Skirton and Geoff Strong, hit 93 goals in 144 League games for Arsenal. "If I'm marked ...give me the ball," he used to tell team-mates.

John Radford's tally of goals was 149 in all senior competitive matches. His height, strength and power in the air meant that he was superbly equipped for the striker's role.

other clubs wanted him. Everyone thought he was a fantastic capture. He was a good ball player and the crowd loved him, but the modern game has taught them to appreciate the hard worker.

Bob Wilson cites another case, that of his friend, Bobby Gould:

My best pal in the game, Bobby Gould was brilliant at Coventry. Fantastic enthusiast, Gouldie, but never really reproduced his best form at Arsenal. He would always score goals, and the crowd loved him for his enthusiasm, but he wasn't like Joe Baker, say. Joe Baker was incredible, and Wrighty has been extraordinary.

John Jensen states it simply:

Ian Wright, pictured here shortly after joining Arsenal from Crystal Palace in September 1991 for £2.5 million. Six years later, almost to the day, Wright registered his 179th goal for the club and passed Cliff Bastin's record to become the most prolific scorer in Arsenal's history.

I think that the team we had under George Graham was such a good side that it is difficult to rank one player above another, but I will say that Ian Wright is the best finisher I have ever seen.

Striker may be the glamour role, but it is a demanding one and carries the constant burden of criticism to balance the attendant praise, a point to which George Armstrong, speaking before Ian Wright's transfer to West Ham United, is sensitive.

Ian Wright is a great goalscorer. I think we've had others at the club who've been better footballers – Joe Baker, big John Radford, Alan Smith, a tremendous player – but to be fair to Ian, he's second to nobody in scoring goals. He's a genius, and he's 34. It's phenomenal. And he's playing in the most difficult role of all. We've got Lee Dixon, Bouldie, Tony, Nigel – tremendous pros. They'll never let you down, but I think up front is difficult, and being a striker is a lot more difficult than playing where I played. Ian can only get judged on the number of goals he scores, and if he goes a month without scoring a goal, people start asking questions. I think his goalscoring record is there to prove everything he's ever done. I think he's been tremendous, but I think he could possibly do with another threat, a challenge. It does all players good to have to look over their shoulders to see who is coming up behind them. It keeps them on their toes. I always think there should be another one for your position, not quite as good, but one who take your place without the team feeling much difference.

Brian Talbot's time with Arsenal did not overlap with Ian Wright's career, but he has a high opinion of him.

I've watched him many times, and he's a great player, but he gets himself into trouble for silly things and you need him on the pitch. I like him, and over the years he's been doing brilliantly. Who else has been getting the goals for Arsenal? He's held them together on his own with his goals.

He's always very friendly, and I don't know how they're going to replace him. It's not easy to find goalscorers like him. He gets goals out of nothing, and he brings other people into the game as well.

On 13 September 1997, shortly before 3.30pm, Ian Wright tapped the ball into an empty Bolton net to register his 179th goal for Arsenal and so become the leading goalscorer in the club's history. His qualities are very different from those which brought success to Ronnie Rooke. His speed takes him clear of defenders, and he will draw his marker wide, right and left. The striker is no longer a battering ram but a rapier, yet one thing remains constant – the insatiable appetite for scoring goals. Wright will appear extrovert and demonstrative on the pitch – it is part of his self-motivation – but there is a humility beneath the bubbling surface, witness the One to One advertisement in which he speaks of Dr Martin Luther King or the contribution to BBC's *Blue Peter* regarding racial harmony. Out of the side one Saturday before a European game on the Wednesday, he lunched in Il Cavaliere. As he was leaving, one customer said to him, "Make my husband happy. Score a goal on Wednesday." "I always try," he replied. None could deny that. The striker needs the accolades, for scoring goals is his life-blood, and when he is not scoring doubts arise in everyone's mind as Alan Smith testifies.

I didn't find it any harder at the time, I think, coming from Leicester. I just went out and played. In my first year, it didn't kick-off with a bang. I got sixteen goals eventually, but the first few months I wasn't scoring regularly, and there was talk that they were going to buy Kerry Dixon. And that was after about four games, and I thought, "Oh God, what's going on?" But I think it was media talk, and that was different to Leicester. You get so much media attention at Arsenal. And I thought, "They said I was the big signing, and already they're talking of replacing me."

When I wasn't scoring goals I was trying to make them, but I didn't expect the media to explain that. I think my team mates appreciated me from day one, but when you look at the goals scored column and how many you've scored at the end of the season, I think that a player of my style, back to the goal a lot, sixteen goals is all right, but I would have hoped to have got a few more. But we ended up in the League Cup Final against Luton. We were destined not to win that one. Nigel Winterburn missed a penalty. Martin Hayes missed a chance, tapped it against the post. I missed another chance. Gus Caesar dwelt on the ball, got them back in it.

I was leading scorer in both championship seasons, and my biggest moment was at Anfield in 1989. People talk about Copenhagen, and that was obviously a big highlight, but Anfield was so unexpected, and Arsenal hadn't won the League for eighteen years. I think Liverpool thought I either didn't get a touch or was offside, and that the linesman's flag had gone up, which it didn't. I also had a hand in Thomas's goal. I made the reverse pass. That was one of my better performances, but I've always looked forward to the high pressure games. I was pleased how well I played in Copenhagen, as the lone striker really, but the Anfield game was unbelievable. Words can't describe it.

The arrival of Ian Wright made a big difference to me. I stopped scoring goals, and Arsenal started playing a different way. There was so much looking to hit Wrighty early on from midfield. We didn't have any width in attack. There were no crosses coming in, and it was quite hard for me. I didn't enjoy that period. I wasn't playing well so it was a lot different. After being a major part of the team for some years, it isn't very enjoyable to be in such a situation.

Wrighty really motivates himself. He is hyped up to score in every game, and he is always shouting for the ball so that when you had young players like Dave Hillier and Ian Selley in midfield they'd try to hit long balls to him because he was calling for it, and

In 1988-89, when Arsenal won the title, Alan Smith was the League's leading scorer with 23 goals. Two years later, when they again lifted the championship, he was once more the competition's top scorer, this time with 22.

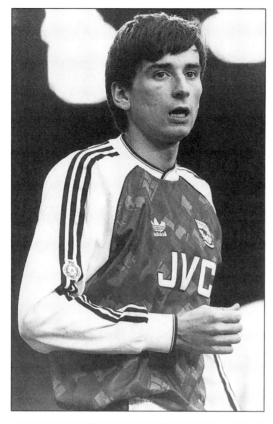

Dennis Bergkamp – "I've enjoyed it from day one with Arsenal." No wonder, as Arsène Wenger put it: "Dennis only scores best sellers." That was underlined when the Arsenal man hit the goal of the tournament for Holland in the 1998 World Cup finals in France. It put Arsenal supporters in mind of a certain effort against Leicester City in the season just ended.

if I came short to collect, the ball was going over my shoulder.

I think my best partnership was in the early days with Merson although I chopped and changed a lot. I think that was his best position. He was a good passer of the ball, and I had a good relationship with Merse.

Alan Smith and Dennis Bergkamp are linked by fond memories of games against Southampton. In 1990-91, when Arsenal were defeated only once in the League and won the title, finishing thirteen points ahead of Liverpool, Alan Smith was leading scorer with 22 League goals. He scored in the opening match, a 3-0 win at Wimbledon, but then went eleven League games without finding the net. On 17 November, Arsenal beat Southampton 4-0 at Highbury, and Smith headed two of them to end his drought. Before the start of the 1995-96 season, Arsenal signed Dennis Bergkamp for a record fee. His ball skills delighted from the start, but it was seven Premier League games before he scored, and the press were eagerly writing about "the expensive misfit".

Then came the home fixture with Southampton. Glenn Helder went down the left touchline, beat his full-back and crossed well. Bergkamp, standing just inside the penalty area in the inside-right position, hit the ball on the volley, low into the far corner. Tony Adams headed a second from a corner, but Southampton scored twice before half-time to draw level. In the second half, Bergkamp picked up the ball on the right touchline close to the players' tunnel. He controlled the ball with the outside of his right foot, twisting a defender this way and that. As he approached the penalty area he swayed as if to move inside. The defender was momentarily unbalanced, and Bergkamp hit the ball with his right foot. It struck the inside of the near post and thundered into the net. Wright added a fourth when his gyrations sent his marker dizzy on the edge of the penalty area, and Arsenal won 4-2, but it was Bergkamp's day.

I've enjoyed it from day one with Arsenal, but probably my best moment was when I scored my first two goals, against Southampton. That's when it all started for me in relation to the fans and the press, and I felt everyone started to appreciate me.

You can do good things without scoring goals, but I think, as a striker, you have to score goals. Once you are doing that, maybe not frequently, and when you score goals and play well they really appreciate you.

As Arsène Wenger remarked in a wry but memorable phrase after Bergkamp had arched the ball past the Barnsley goalkeeper Watson from the edge of the penalty area in the match at Oakwell, "Dennis only scores best-sellers." And there have been many of them – the last-minute goal in the 3-1 victory over Tottenham at Highbury when he dragged Wright's cross back inside the defender and curled the ball past Walker and inside the far post; and an almost identical goal at Leicester the following

season. He has enriched the lives of those who have watched him, and few men can say that. He has been part of a revolution that has altered our expectations of what we desire from the man up front.

Football has changed over the years so that the style of a striker in England is very different from what it used to be. Not only the foreign managers who come in are changing it, but the British managers as well. It is a good thing because it means that England is ambitious and wants to keep up with the rest of the world. It is very different in Italy, of course, but I think the level in England and Italy is not different any more.

Irish international Frank Stapleton, seen here scoring against Ipswich at Highbury in April 1976, hit 108 goals for Arsenal in 299 senior games.

Between The Sticks

"AT THE end of it all, the game of football is about putting the ball in one end and keeping it out of the other." In this, as in much else, Pat Rice agrees with Arsène Wenger. There is nothing profound in this philosophy. It is simplicity itself, but then the simplest tasks can be the most difficult to accomplish. Bob Wilson recalls that when he first arrived at Arsenal it was disaster time.

It was an Arsenal side that could score six and let in seven. Unlike the Brazilian side of 1970 which let in four but scored five, we scored four but the other lot scored five. I was hurled in. I couldn't believe it. I was a schoolteacher doing my final year. I was an amateur, getting paid my expenses only, not getting paid anything. I trained twice a week. Charlie George was there in the gym in the evening. He was the young kid that was coming through, and there was Pat Rice who nobody gave a hope in hell for. And I got hurled in against Nottingham Forest for my first League game which we won 4-2, and then I played six games on the bounce and we only lost once. That was against Chelsea, the last one, and then, I thought very cruelly, I was left out of the side. Suddenly they signed Jim Furnell. Within the League games, we'd played a Fairs Cup game, and that was against Standard Liege, Arsenal's first year in Europe.

There was a big, big do at the time about me being the first amateur to play since the Icelandic chap, Gudmundsson, and Dr Kevin O'Flanagan, the Irishman. So I'm quite proud because they didn't put the Christian names in the programme, obviously, but because I was an amateur, they had to put my initial – R.Wilson. I was quite proud of that.

Bob Wilson was always destined to be a goalkeeper. Although he was born in Chesterfield he is from a family that is most definitely Scottish, and, as well as being the first amateur to play for Arsenal for seventeen years, he was also the first "Englishman" to play for Scotland but:

I never thought of myself as an Englishman. I always wanted to be a professional footballer, certainly from the age of eight onwards although I don't think I had any idea of what being a professional footballer meant. I always wanted to be a goalkeeper, and a friend of the family, a surgeon from Sheffield whom we called Uncle Dave, gave me a blue goalkeeper's shirt for Christmas. That was important because blue was the colour for Scotland.

My first heroes were Frank Swift and Gil Merrick who wore a moustache like David Seaman. When I got into the Chesterfield Schools' side, the Derbyshire Schools' side and had a trial for England Schools, then I felt that nothing would stop me from becoming a professional. I got into the England Schools' side, and I played alongside Nobby Stiles, and the pair of us played for Manchester United juniors. I played for them for about eighteen months, and the senior players were all very friendly and most encouraging. Both Nobby and I were offered terms by United. Nobby joined, but my father said "no". He insisted that I finished my education and went to Loughborough University. I was heartbroken, but I realised later that he was right. My education came to the fore when the BBC asked me to do some work for them, and I started seeing television in terms of analysis.

While I was up at University I played against the Wolves, and we lost 5-2, but I had a blinder, and Stan Cullis asked me to join them, which I did, and I played for their reserves for a couple of seasons. Then Bertie Mee came to see me and said that Billy Wright wanted me to join Arsenal. I had met Bertie at an England Grammar Schools Football Coaching Week. I agreed to join Arsenal, but they had to pay Wolves a fee of £5,000 even though I was an amateur.

Bertie Mee was Arsenal's physiotherapist at the time of Bob Wilson's arrival, but both he and manager Billy Wright were aware that the club had a goalkeeping problem. Wright knew that Mee had met Bob Wilson and asked him to make the approach.

Traditionally, Arsenal had enjoyed the luxury of two or three top goalkeepers on their staff and Bob Wilson was to stand comparison with any of them. In the years immediately after the war, George Swindin was both a hero and a saviour. This was the age in which all League goalkeepers wore polo-neck jerseys – pullover collars which fitted the neck closely and doubled over. The jerseys worn by all League goalkeepers were coloured green except when playing for or against Plymouth Argyle. The goalkeeper would also carry a cloth cap which he wore when the sun became troublesome. The world was neither so colour-conscious nor fashion-conscious in that austerity era as it has become since.

Arguably, the goalkeeper had less protection then than he has today. He was challenged when he attempted to clear and when he had the ball in his hands and two feet on the ground he could be, and was, shoulder-charged, as Harry Gregg, the Manchester United 'keeper, discovered when Nat Lofthouse barged him into the net in the 1958 Cup Final. Like the centre-forwards of the era, the goalkeeper had to be big and strong. In many ways, George Swindin was an exception, but Arthur Milton considers that he was a great goalkeeper.

He was very good at coming out because he read the game so well. He didn't have the best time as manager. He was a bit abrasive. George Marks, who played in the war, was a class act, but George Allison reckoned Swindin was the best goalkeeper Arsenal had. If

George Swindin read the game so well, according to Arthur Milton. Swindin made almost 300 senior appearances for the Gunners and, of course, later managed the club.

Jack Kelsey and team-mate Jim Fotheringham in a scramble in front of the Arsenal goal with Tottenham's Johnny Brooks. Kelsey played over 350 times for the Arsenal first team in League and Cup games.

he'd been taller, he would have played for England.

I remember Ray Daniel putting one past him up at Newcastle. Ray was a very good player, but he used to get a bit carried away sometimes. He used to like to beat people, a footballing centre-half, and sometimes he'd lose it and give a goal away. We were up at St James's, and it was 0-0 after about half an hour. The ball had gone through, and Ray was going back, and as he got hold of the ball George called for it. Ray side-footed it, and it bobbled and he lobbed George. I think we went on to lose.

Laurie Scott had a similar experience:

We used to play Racing Club of Paris every November, one year in London, the next in Paris, and I remember on one occasion in Paris, a ball was put right down the middle past Big Les, and I'm running back to it. I saw George Swindin in goal, and the simplest thing for me to do is to push it back to him. And it all happened in a split second. I've hit the ball back, and George is not there. He is at the side of me, and that's the only time I ever scored an own-goal. That was a terrible mistake, but we could always get three or four goals against Racing Club. That's how great the difference was in those days between the continent and ourselves. They've pulled up now, of course, and probably passed us.

George Swindin was very good in

served Arsenal as a public relations officer and commercial manager. He had a nightmare debut in the First Division, being in goal when Arsenal lost 5-2 to Charlton Athletic at Highbury in February 1951. It was the game which virtually marked the end of Leslie Compton's long and illustrious career. He was opposed to the Swedish international Hans Jeppson who played for Charlton as an amateur, briefly, and scored nine goals in eleven games. Ignoring Big Les's height and strength, Jeppson exploited the slowness on the turn of the great centre-half who was then approaching his 39th birthday and was putting on weight. The ball was consistently played to Jeppson on the ground, and Jack Kelsey picked it out of the net five times. By 1953, however, with Swindin injured and ageing, Kelsey was almost claiming the regular place that was to be his until after the 1962 season when, playing for Wales against Brazil in the World Cup, he sustained a severe back injury which ended his career. It was at this point that Bob Wilson appeared on the scene.

When I arrived, Jack Kelsey had been injured, and he was finished, and there was Jack McClelland, the Northern Ireland lad, who was really going to be the one to take over; Ian McKechnie; a young lad named Tony Burns who they were trying to bring through; and another young lad named Ian Black. So I came along, and I would think that there were quite a lot of Arsenal fans at that time who believed that Jack was the best Arsenal goalie ever. There are still a lot of the older fans, obviously the older fans who saw Jack, who will argue that he was probably the greatest in so much that he was at a time when Arsenal were struggling. He won a League championship medal in his first full year because he played in more than thirteen or fourteen games. He wasn't number one always – George Swindin was still playing – but he did win a medal in his first season, and he never won anything else. But Arsenal never got relegated, and a lot of people will say that it is because of Jack Kelsey that they didn't get relegated. He was playing in a not very good side, but he

those seasons just after the war, but where I would criticise him is that whereas, for England, Frank Swift would come ten yards to pick up balls and save us work, George, because of his height, would only come six or eight yards. That was the only fault that George had. He was a very good goalkeeper, but he was only about five feet ten, and Frank was six feet three. George had some wonderful games, with great anticipation. He was halfway there before the shot came in, and he made many saves which would have been goals to any other 'keeper.

George Swindin's understudy was Ted Platt, a good goalkeeper who went to Portsmouth, but his immediate successor was Jack Kelsey, who became a Welsh international and later

Jack Kelsey in action again, diving on the ball watched by John Snedden, Gerry Ward and Len Wills. Spurs are again the visitors to Highbury.

Jack Kelsey in action again, diving on the ball watched by John Snedden, Gerry Ward and Len Wills. Spurs are again the visitors to Highbury.

was a legend, so following him was a problem.

When we did the Double in 1971 we played 42 League games and I let in 29 goals, and I had very few mistakes that season. Sadly, one was in the Final, and it could have been disastrous. I had had the best season in my career and could have ended up costing Arsenal the Double. If it had stayed at 1-0, it could have been so costly. I still think of myself in terms of Dan Lewis who cost the Arsenal the Cup in 1927 because of his shiny new jersey, but I'm a lucky guy because it turned around, and we won 2-1.

Thank goodness from my point of view in the Final, within two minutes of letting in a bad goal, I made a very important save from Brian Hall. It could have been 2-0, and within another two minutes we scored a freak equaliser. I have to say that even though I remember Peter Simpson and Frank McLintock giving me this glare after I'd let the goal in, I only gave it a fleeting thought, "Oh, I've cost Arsenal the Double!" I was lucky. I had this very important save to make,

and that was good for me and the team.

I've been coaching Arsenal goalkeepers for 22 years. The secret of coaching, the secret of one-to-one coaching, is getting inside the other person, right inside. "What makes this guy tick?" Hopefully, that individual is not just learning the tricks of the trade, as it were, but you're getting the best out of him by knowing him.

Don Howe is a great coach, but, as a goalkeeping coach, he is somewhat limited because he has never been a goalkeeper. He doesn't really understand that we do want some fitness stuff where we go bang, bang, bang – repetitive, but that my coaching, all the main exercises, is based around areas that happen in a game. What I am aiming for as a coach is to get my goalies to be fractionally one step ahead in the game. When a situation occurs they don't know exactly what is going to happen, but when somebody strikes it they know what the possibilities are, whether it's a cut-back, a cross, whatever.

The relationship between the coach

Bob Wilson, veteran of some 300 senior games for Arsenal, was always in the thick of the action. Here, he is going in where it hurts against Tottenham's 20-year-old debutant Jimmy Pearce at White Hart Lane on the opening day of the 1968-69 season.

and those he is coaching is the old basic football philosophy of respect. David Seaman, at this moment, still thinks that I'm the best goalkeeping coach in the world. I would say to most people, argue to my dying day, that currently he is the best goalkeeper in the world. I think he's better than Schmeichel in one sense – he makes fewer mistakes. Schmeichel can win you games, but he's a risky goalie. He's a bit like I played. But David Seaman, over a long period of time, will make the least number of mistakes than any goalkeeper I know. So it is all to do with respect.

Goalkeeping has changed so much. God gave me the ability to dive at people's feet and to read when they miscontrolled the ball so that, before they had the chance to hit it again, they found me head first at their feet. I had the gift to do that like my idol Bert Trautmann. But today they are even quicker than in our time, and I couldn't play like that now. I'd be sent off five or six times a season. So my style of goalkeeping, although it was

certainly adventurous, more adventurous than, say, Schmeichel's, was a very risky type of goalkeeping. And lots of things have changed.

First of all, the rules have changed dramatically in things like the back pass and hanging on to the ball for a shorter period of time. The set pieces now are like American football. Whether it is a throw-in or a long throw or a corner-kick or a free-kick, there are so many things now designed to block the goalkeeper, to create a problem for the goalkeeper. The goalkeeping role is twice as difficult as when I played, without any question.

You start with the original concept that you take a big guy and stick him between the posts, and he looks as if he can fill the goal. Even now that's the case, for guys like Schmeichel and Seaman are men with a presence. After that, you say "Who can take crosses?", and there are only a few in that area now on a consistent basis. It's nothing like it used to be, and that's because of the defences backing so much, pushing in so much. The goalkeeper

doesn't have the same sort of movement to get out there.

Dave Seaman's philosophy is different to some others, but he believes, unless it's 60/40 in his favour, don't risk it. Let somebody else clear if he's got half a chance of getting a foot in before you. Don't go where someone else might get a foot in. In other words, stay and guard your goal.

Sometimes it doesn't work like that. Sometimes you've got to risk all, but that is his philosophy. Sometimes Arsène Wenger and Pat Rice argue with me. They say, "Don't you think he should have been in this position or that position?" They're not having to weigh up the odds that you have to do when you're in there.

I can read David Seaman like a book now. I know why he stops or why he doesn't do things or why he tries to do this or whatever. He's working on percentages, and goalkeepers have always worked on percentages.

If you go out for a cross like David James in that Cup Final three or four years ago against Manchester United … He had caught everything in the area of Wembley until suddenly he went for the one he shouldn't have gone for. And who does it fall to? Cantona. And what's the final result? 1-0. Unlike me where it could have been 1-0, Steve Heighway, and we won 2-1, he's finished 1-0. And who was at fault? David James.

So goalkeeping has always been about percentages. And now you have greater problems. You've got to have a wonderful first touch. You've got to be an outfield player. You've got to get rid of the ball within four seconds. Everytime there's a rule change, it's on the goalkeeper. It will not surprise me if they start saying instead of eight yards by eight feet, the goal has got to be nine yards by nine feet. It's going that way. It's changed. I'm always going to be sticking up for the modern goalkeeper.

Arsène Wenger was acutely conscious of the importance of David Seaman in the Arsenal side. He knew how important his presence was to players and fans alike and realised that when Seaman finishes there must be somebody ready that the fans can take to immediately. In the opinion of Bob Wilson, there are two.

We've got Alex Manninger, and we've got a young boy called Stuart Taylor.

Manninger is just twenty. I had him for three days. They brought him over

from Casino Graz, and finally Arsène Wenger and David Dein said, "Look, it's up to you. Do you think he's got it?" I said, "I think he's exceptional, and John Lukic, with all his experience, thinks he's the best nineteen-year-old he's ever seen."

He made his debut against Birmingham, and he loses it. He missed his first cross. His greatest strength is his ability on crosses, and he missed his first cross, and he missed another in the second half. He got away with it, and he made a crucial save right at the end which kept us in the game before going into extra-time when we won it.

Arsène Wenger had no hesitation in playing him again. I said, "Look, you've got to get him in the first team again. It's like a crash landing." He played against Coventry, and he won the game

single-handed. He made six exceptional saves, and he got a standing ovation. His face at the end was a picture. He's twenty, and that's the way you've got to be. He was so disappointed after the Birmingham game, the first one, but he's the luckiest guy going. He's got David Seaman teaching him. He's got me teaching him. He's got John Lukic teaching him. And he wants to learn. Alex Manninger has got it made. He's just got to calm down a bit. He's quite excitable, a bit like Bert Trautmann was. Bert is German; Alex is Austrian. He's just got to calm down – a great talent.

Deputising for the injured David Seaman, Alex Manninger gave outstanding displays for Arsenal in March 1998, and was named as the winner of the Premier Player of the Month award. The fans had taken to him immediately.

One for the future – Alex Manninger, seen here celebrating Arsenal's outstanding successes, gave outstanding displays for Arsenal in March 1998 and was named Premier Player of the Month. The fans had taken to him immediately.

Comings and Goings

Arsenal's playing and coaching staff on the eve of the 1950-51 season, with the FA Cup won against Liverpool the previous April. Back row (left to right): J. Chenhall, R. Barr, D. Tilley, D. Oakes, C. Holton, R. Marden, T. Vallance. Third row: E. Stanley, D. Rossiter, W. Healey, D. Bowen, L. Davies, G. Dunkley, P. Hancock, C. Grimshaw, L. Wills, J. Gray, H. Dove, F. Grosvenor. Second row: A. James, G. Male, K. Atkinson, R. Daniel, A. Shaw, E. Platt, L. Compton, G. Swindin, A. Forbes, J. Kelsey, A. Fields, J. Wade, J. Holland, E. Collett, D. Cripps. Seated: H. Owen, J. Crayston, I. McPherson, L. Scott, D. Roper, R. Lewis, J. Mercer, T. Whittaker, W. Barnes, L. Smith, P. Goring, D. Lishman, N. Smith, W. Milne, J. Shaw. On ground: A. Milton, M. Ryan, J. Logie, F. Cox, R. Poulton, D. Bennett. Several former Arsenal stars, such as Alex James, George Male and Joe Shaw were still on the backroom staff.

DON Howe is now in his third spell with Arsenal. He has been player, coach, manager, and he is now coaching the young players. He has been associated with Arsenal, on and off, for more than 34 years, but the enthusiasm for the club and for the part he plays within the club remain undiminished.

The Arsenal is very different from other clubs. First of all, when you come in, you feel the quality of the place. You feel that you've come to the avant-garde of all football clubs. They have taken a lot of criticism, but the criticism doesn't weaken them. They're stronger for it. You do realise that you've got standards to live up to. They do expect you to conduct yourself in the right manner. I know they've had their problems with

players and in other ways over the years, and yet the standards still keep being produced; the standards of play, the standards of behaviour. It's not all been nice and perfect. We've had our testing times.

It may seem that Arsenal don't always get the credit for what they've done, but I think they do. It's hidden a lot of the time. I think people are reluctant to give us the credit because everyone in football knows the quality of the Arsenal. They know that if you go to the Arsenal, you go to a very organised place, a place that's worth coming to, to begin with, great staff, great pitch. When you go to Highbury to play Arsenal you know you're in for a hard game. There is credit out there, but a lot of it is hidden, and a lot of it

is people saying, "Oh, here they go again. They've done it again." They know it. They all know it, and the nice thing about it all is that it never affects things. And there's jealousy out there.

Of course, the salary of the players has changed since I first came here. The salaries are out of this world now, but I don't think the atmosphere in the club has changed. This club never rests on its laurels. It's as though something is pushing them on all the time to get more support and more success, and, no matter what you've done, more success. It's not that there's a stranglehold on your neck, and you're thinking "the pressure is too great – I can't handle this". No, you're given a lot of freedom to express yourself.

Arthur Milton and Laurie Scott first came to Arsenal some twenty years before Don Howe, yet they remain gripped by the same feelings. Arthur Milton played football and cricket at the top level and travelled widely, but he retains the sense of awe.

I always remember going into that place for the first time. It had been built before the war on all the success

of the Thirties. He must have been some man that Herbert Chapman. He came there from Huddersfield where he'd done the same thing. I remember going in there, and there's a bust of him, and it was just like a hospital. They really looked after you. You had digs, and they always made sure you were OK. There were about 40 on the staff. They could have put three sides in the First Division, there was so much talent, although it gradually got dissipated over the years.

And Laurie Scott:

It was a different set-up at Arsenal. I couldn't say there was nowhere like it, but I am certain there was nowhere better in discipline and everything. It even trained you so that you were prepared when you met the King and Queen. You always had to be on your best behaviour, and you were able to move into any company. It really was something, and if you go to Highbury today, it's still modern, and we're talking about somewhere that was built 70 odd years ago. It's amazing.

All the staff, the people who worked there, were so good. The boot boy – boy? he must have been 64 or 65 – laid everything out for you. You walked in and you knew what you were doing that morning from whatever you saw on the floor – running or walking, whatever it was – and it was the boot boy's job to get those out for everybody.

When you were studding and had a look at the ground, you might think "I need long studs today." So you'd go back to tell Fred, and when you got back they were already in. He knew better than we did. We didn't use to bother. We left it to him.

Arthur Milton and Laurie Scott were young men when they joined Arsenal and were just beginning their professional careers. Brian Talbot was an England international and had played in the Ipswich side which had beaten Arsenal in the FA Cup Final the year before he came to Highbury, 1979, yet even he, a seasoned campaigner, noticed a vast difference when he changed clubs.

ARSENAL IN THE BLOOD

Brian Talbot was an England international and a seasoned campaigner even before he came to Arsenal from Ipswich Town, but he still noticed a big difference between when he changed clubs.

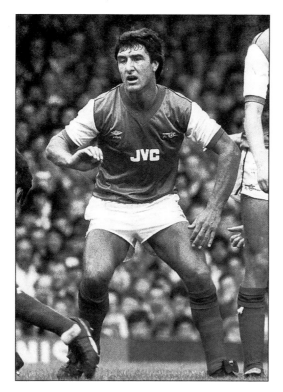

When I first arrived at the Arsenal I didn't consider myself as an expensive player but when you look back and realise how much they paid for me, £450,000, I was their most expensive signing at that time. I went to work every day and just considered myself a footballer. I was lucky enough to be in my home town and to play against all the best players of the day. You just do your best and get on with it, but when I had the chance to go to a big club I wanted to go desperately.

I found it very different when I went to Arsenal. It was strange to me, because, at the time, I had only played at Ipswich, a small club. When you look back Arsenal paid a lot of money for me, but at the time I thought, "Well, it's not my problem." When I got there I found lots of little differences, like kit. For instance, at Ipswich you had to leave your kit in the drying room and wear it again the next day. We didn't have a kit man or anything like that, but when I went to Arsenal we had clean kit every day. Tony was the kit man, and when you got on the bus he would take your bags and put them away and serve you coffee. When you finish training there's a cup of tea waiting for you,

and the floor at Arsenal is heated. We never had anything like that at Ipswich. It was little things like that when you realise you are at a big club, which probably the smaller clubs can't afford to do.

There is a greater expectancy, definitely. As a player and as a club, you've got to produce, and the players knew that. With Ipswich, when we played sides like Manchester United and Liverpool, the players would expect to win, but the actual town itself would be pleased if we got a reasonable result. At Arsenal, you had to get a result – that was the difference – and at that time we maybe weren't the best. I think Liverpool were the best, and you were always trying to be as good as them and knowing you had got to be. At Ipswich, if you come fourth, brilliant, well played. At Arsenal, they weren't like that.

A decade later, Alan Smith experienced similar feelings when he came to the club.

I found a great change when I came to the Arsenal. I think expectancy is the thing that hits you most. I was playing in the same division with Leicester, the First Division as it was then. It's just that when you walk on to the turf at Highbury you have a feeling for the history of the place. You were expected to win every home game and a large proportion of the away ones. Not like Leicester where if you played Manchester United at home and got a point, that was good. If you won, it was tremendous. The expectancy at Arsenal was very different.

Lee Dixon believes that there are players who have come to Highbury from clubs in lower divisions who have found it difficult to deal with the high expectancy and even some who have come from more established clubs who have taken time to settle.

It was a great culture shock coming to the Arsenal. I'd only been used to lower division football. I started off at Burnley and then went to Chester, Bury and Stoke, although Stoke is quite a big club, and Burnley in itself was a big club languishing in the lower

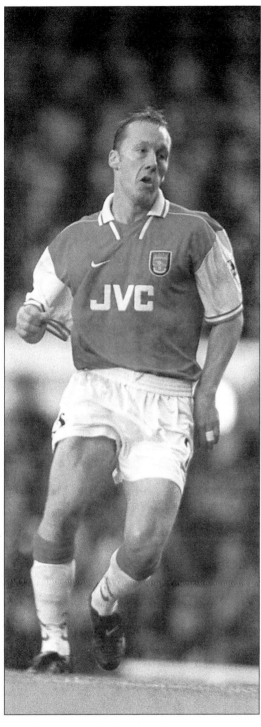

Lee Dixon, a member of one of the most successful sides in Arsenal's history but who, on his own admission, found it a great culture shock to move to the Gunners from the lower divisions. He says, "Even players from other big clubs have found it difficult to settle at Arsenal because expectations are so high."

spotlight 24 hours a day, and when Saturday comes nothing less than a win is acceptable. That pressure can get to you, and there are some players who can't quite cope with that and go under, and they're not long at the club.

I had a good introduction to the club because when I signed in the January 1988, they were still in the Coca-Cola Cup, and I was Cup-tied, so that my introduction into the first team was staggered a little bit because they were playing in the Cup every two or three weeks, and I couldn't play in those games. I wasn't going to get a big run in the team for that reason. I made my debut about a week after signing, which was nice, because it got my first game out of the way, and then I made six appearances before the end of the season. Every two or three weeks I'd get a game so the pressure wasn't on me to perform week in week out which it could have been if I'd been straight in there.

There are others, like Liam Brady, George Armstrong and Pat Rice who came to the club straight from school and for whom, like Lee Dixon, Arsenal has been a major part of their lives. Liam Brady's life has come full circle, for he now discovers players as he was once discovered.

Arsenal got in first. I was a thirteen-year-old boy in Dublin, and the representative saw me play and invited me over to come on trial, and that was the first professional club that I'd been asked to go and see. I did well on trial and never really went away. I never went on trial anywhere else. I never went to see any other clubs, and, from thirteen to fifteen, I had an association with the club where I would come to Arsenal in school holidays. At fifteen, when I left school, I joined the Arsenal full time as an apprentice. It was all very exciting because I was a football fanatic, and just to be in touch with and see players I'd only seen on television was wonderful.

Bertie Mee was the manager at the time, and it was he who brought me to Highbury, but I'd say, just like the

divisions. I think anybody leaving any club to come to Arsenal would find a great difference. It's a one-off club as far as I am concerned. It's got an aura about it as you walk through those doors. Everything about it is very traditional, and it's become a big part of my life. It is more demanding for sure. You are expected to win every game, so the pressure that brings is not easy to deal with at first, and a lot of players in the past have become overawed by that. You are in the

Liam Brady joined Arsenal as a youngster from Dublin: "It was all very exciting because I was a football fanatic, and just to be in touch with and see players I'd only seen on television was wonderful."

what I call the black hole when the only players I remember are Terry Mancini and Alex Cropley. Terry Mancini was a lovely bloke, but I shall never know how he came to wear an Arsenal shirt. Then came Terry Neill's side with Liam Brady, and I still think he's the greatest player I've ever seen, and the greatest game he ever played was a game we lost. It was the League Cup semi-final against Swindon Town, 1979-80. We were 2-0 down, came back to 3-3 and lost 4-3 after extra-time.

Brian Talbot, now head coach of Rushden and Diamonds in the Vauxhall Conference, was a team-mate and admirer of Liam Brady and of another Irishman, Pat Rice. As he has already admitted, Bob Wilson was one of those who believed that Rice did not have the ability to become a professional footballer. Brian Talbot recognises that Rice had qualities different from the skills shown by Brady, and that those qualities were of immense value to the team.

I played with Liam Brady, and I think Liam was a world-class player. I'm not knocking Liam, but sometimes when you're away and under the cosh you're saying "Where's Liam?" But then Liam could produce a flash of brilliance which could turn the game. It takes all sorts to make a team. I used to love to watch Glenn Hoddle play, but there were times he could infuriate managers. But I think you've got to be able to accommodate players like him.

We had Rix and Brady in the same team, which would be a luxury today because pace and power have come more into the game, but they both had ability. They didn't have much power, but Brady had tremendous pace over a few yards. I still think Brady would be in anyone's side today – no problem.

The strength of the Arsenal side in which I played was the skill of Rix and Brady, but mostly it was the will to win. I never forget when I joined them, they were determined to get to Wembley. They felt they'd really let themselves down against Ipswich. Pat Rice was not the best player in the

position I'm in today where Arsène doesn't really know who I'm bringing in at the age of thirteen and fourteen, at that particular time Gordon Clark was the chief scout, and it was Gordon who was responsible for bringing me here.

I got a chance in the first team when I was seventeen and then, sporadically until I was eighteen and a half and then I held my place regularly.

Liam Brady was a "natural", a footballer of flair with outstanding ball skills and creative vision. Don Howe also considers that he was "a great leader". Supporter Andy Charalambous believes that Brady brought Arsenal out of one of their darkest periods.

A few years after the Double came

world, and he'd be the first to admit that, but he was a tremendous captain, and his will to win and his willingness to get everybody together, do or die, was tremendous. It's proven now. He's got back to the top as coach. He's everything that's Arsenal. He was so determined to become a top player, and top coach, and he's made it. Nobody thought he was going to make it as a player, but he is such a determined guy.

Pat Rice's former manager Bertie Mee endorses Brian Talbot's opinion.

Pat Rice was already there when I became manager. Pat was tremendous. In terms of skill and technique, he was very limited, but he would graft away. You'd say to Pat, "Look, Pat, that left foot of yours isn't as good as it should be." He'd come in every afternoon to practise with it. "Pat, another couple of yards, and you'll be outstanding. You'd be able to catch any winger." He'd be back sprinting. Lovely lad.

Few men can have shown such dedication and determination as Pat Rice. He is totally honest as to the limitations of his own abilities, but here is a man who played a major part in the winning of two Doubles. Arsenal has been in his blood for more than 40 years.

I joined Arsenal in 1964 when Billy Wright was manager. At that time,

they used to have the old PE teachers going round the schools, and they would pick out the two best players in the area in which you were going to school. I was picked out with another chap, and we had trials against Tottenham because they were having trials almost every night, and, quite rightly, Mr Bailey, who was in charge, said that I wasn't good enough to get in the side, but if I wanted to come and train with the Arsenal on Monday and Thursday nights, then I could do so. I said yes that I would do that because I only lived down the road, and that's how I got started here.

I started off as a Manchester United supporter because, basically, all the kids in Northern Ireland supported either Manchester United, Celtic or Rangers. When we moved over here I saw Manchester United beat Arsenal 5-4 just before the Munich disaster, and ever since then I've supported Arsenal.

Nobody gave me a hope of making a professional because I'm really a man-made player. It's not just about your capabilities, but whenever I played I used to try to win the ball and give it to those who were more talented than me – people like Alan Hudson, Frank McLintock, Jonnie

Arsenal in 1964-65. Back row (left to right): Geoff Strong, Gordon Ferry, Alan Skirton, Don Howe, Bob Wilson, Jim Furnell, John Snedden, Ian Ure, Peter Simpson and Terry Neill. Front row: Jim Magill, Terry Anderson, Freddie Clarke, Joe Baker, George Eastham, David Court, Billy McCullough, George Armstrong and John Sammels.

Like Pat Rice, George Armstrong played a significant role in two Double-winning sides. In 1970-71, he played in every one of Arsenal's 64 League, Cup and European games. In 1997-98, he was reserve-team manager. He was signed by George Swindin, so his Arsenal pedigree goes back a long way.

Sammels, George Graham or George Armstrong, and especially Radford and Kennedy, brilliant players. You've got to listen to people with the experience and knowledge of Bertie Mee who wouldn't tell you something just for the sake of telling you. You've got to take it on board and do something about it, otherwise you'd be out on your ear. The best advice that I ever got was that if they were going to say to me, "I'm sorry, it's not going to work here for you", then at least I could have walked out of those doors knowing that I'd given it everything I could, but I just wasn't good enough. I was very, very fortunate in that I was in the first Arsenal FA Youth Cup-winning side, and Sammy Nelson was in that side, too.

The club had good coaches, good young players. They also had a good first team that was on the verge of winning something, as they did when they won the Fairs Cup. From there it just took off. I was very fortunate in that the Double-winning side wasn't actually formulated because what used to happen was that when we played Everton they used to put Peter Storey in midfield to mark Alan Ball and bring me in at right-back. As it happened, in the Double-winning side, the first game was against Everton, and we drew 2-2 up there, and I think Charlie broke his leg. And in the second match, I was sub, and that was West Ham away, and, if my memory serves me correctly, we drew that 0-0, but after that I just got a run in the side, and it just took off from there. I missed that second game, but I did about 145 on the trot at one time.

Like Pat Rice, George Armstrong was to play a most significant role in two Double-winning sides. In 1970-71, he played in every one of Arsenal's 64 League, Cup and European games; in 1997-98, he was reserve-team manager and helped mightily in the development of such players as Anelka and Wreh. His arrival at Highbury was very different from that of his friend and colleague Pat Rice.

I was signed by George Swindin. I was with Hawthorne Leslie, and I'd been with the county of Durham, as it was then, in Germany with the National Association of Boys' Clubs. When I came back the local scout, a man named Ernie Fuller from South Shields, had been up to see my brother and told him he'd got a group of lads coming down to the Arsenal, and he wanted me to be one of them. I'll be honest with you, I said no I wasn't interested because I was just serving my time as an electrician, and I was only in my first year, and I was enjoying it. But my brother said, "Look, go down there for a weekend, all expenses paid, and it's a trip to London for you." So it was only through him that I came down here because I wasn't that bothered.

When I came down and played in that period it was a red hot Saturday afternoon, and Arsenal used to have lots of players then, and there were a couple of trials. We virtually played a team from the south who all knew each other whereas our team was, "What position do you play, son? No, we've got too many of them." They said to me, "Where do you play?" I said, "Inside-forward." Inside-left in the old days. A lad named John Pearce said, "Can you play anywhere else?" So I said, "You play me where you want to play me." He said, "Can you play on the right wing?" I said, "I'll play anywhere. I'm not bothered." I didn't have it in my mind that I was going to stay there.

As it was, we went out there, and I'd just come back from Germany with the county team, and I was fit. I'd trained with my brother who was a good semi-pro, and I just waltzed through the practice game. George Male invited me back, and I came back and stayed, I suppose, another ten days of intense training and had trials against the first team. In those days, they used to have trials at Highbury, The Probables against The Possibles. I played in the game, and by half-time, I was very, very tired because I'd not been used to training at that level, and big Alf Fields came to me and said, "George, come on. Get yourself a shower. The boss wants to see you."

I didn't know whether it was premature to be a footballer or what to do, but he said to me, "No, we want you to sign as a full-time professional." I said to him, "Well, look, I want to be an electrician as well." He said that we could get round that, and what I used to do was train in the mornings and go back to Southgate where Len Goodman had a sports shop, and he used to do all the club supplies. He got me a job at Mason's, a little electrical shop opposite his own, and I used to work there in the afternoons, and I enjoyed it.

I ended up at Highbury with Ron Franklin, and they were good to me because when I was eventually granted my testimonial I didn't have any problem for all the ground staff knew me. I was like one of them. I was accepted. I had no problem.

Liam Brady looks upon George Armstrong as one of the finest of footballers with whom he played, and certainly no man ever worked harder for any club. Brady himself left Arsenal to join Juventus in 1980, and he played in Italy for seven years. Rarely has a departure been more mourned as Arsenal supporters grieved openly. Brady followed a path that others had trod before him, Jimmy Greaves, Joe Baker, Denis Law, John Charles and Gerry Hitchens among others. Not all adapted to Italian football so well as Brady, nor met with as much success.

In the years immediately after World War Two, football outside England was treated with scepticism, even contempt. In contemplating the game she had given the rest of the world, England remained insular and arrogant. We were initially disdainful of the World Cup and the European Cup, but defeat by the United States of America in the World Cup in Brazil in 1950, two humiliations at the hands of the Hungarians, and a glimpse at the quality of football played by the Brazilians and by Real Madrid caused even hardened attitudes to soften. The Treaty of Rome, unnoticed by all but the shrewdest of football managers at the time, was to provide the opportunity for English football to gain an extra dimension, but that opportunity was not fully grasped until the Nineties. Top quality players like Liam Brady went to Italy to develop their full potential, to pit themselves against the best in the world. Two decades later, a move abroad is no longer necessary. Vieira, Petit, Overmars and the like are playing in England, which Brady accepts.

When I broke into the team I'd say the best players were Alan Ball and "Geordie" Armstrong. I regret that I didn't play with Charlie George enough, but at that time he wanted to leave. It was a sharp contrast when I went to Italy, but I'd say now there is little difference. We've raised our standards to reach their level, but it was a huge culture shock when I went there. I liked it. I liked it from day one, and I got on well with people, and thankfully it went well for me.

Now, British football is importing rather than exporting, and we have been privileged to see top quality players like Dennis Bergkamp grace the Premier League and settle in England as easily as Brady settled in Italy nearly twenty years ago.

I wanted to come to England, and Arsenal were one of the teams who wanted me. As soon as I heard the name "Arsenal", I started to think of their European success and of the players who were there. England is different from Italy, and Arsenal is different from Inter Milan. It was a great change for me. You are still playing football, of course, but the main difference is that it is much more relaxed in England than in Italy. The demands on you at a club like Arsenal are very great because of the traditions that surround the club, but I have been playing professional football since I was seventeen, and you know that there is always pressure, but it doesn't seem like pressure with a team like Arsenal because all the players are there for you. The manager is there for you. The club is there for you, and they don't really put pressure on you. They just want you to enjoy yourself and be part of Arsenal. I was made to feel at home very much. The English players are very friendly in that way. They talk to you and teach you a lot of things about English football. We are very happy in England. Amsterdam is a very beautiful place. I was born there, and I lived there 23 years, and I still go back there, but my wife and I have settled here very happily. It has been good.

John Jensen remains equally enthusiastic about Arsenal and his time in England. A tough, ball-winner in the Danish national side, Jensen had tremendous energy. His work-rate was phenomenal, and, in 1992, he scored a spectacular goal in the Final of the Europe Championships when Denmark beat Germany 2-0. He was brought to Arsenal by George Graham, but Alan Smith is not quite sure if

Graham ever really knew what he wanted of Jensen.

He was the type of player who could win the ball and give it, but I don't know what George expected him to be. I don't think he did himself justice, but he was a really nice bloke, a really good lad. I think if he'd been playing really well, people wouldn't have made so much of him not scoring goals. He was a hundred per center.

Jensen was immensely popular with the crowd at Highbury, but, arriving, as he did, on the back of a wonderful goal in the European Final, it was believed that he would score goals. In fact, he scored just one – another spectacular effort against Queen's Park Rangers at Highbury. He was in the left-wing position and curled the ball at considerable pace into the far corner of the net. Arsenal lost 3-1. His failure to score more has become a humourous part of Arsenal folklore, but scoring goals was not Jensen's principal job, and those with no sense of history or with short memories did not recall that Wilf Copping played 203 competitive matches for Arsenal and did not score once. Signed from Hamburg, Jensen remembers his time at Arsenal only with utmost joy, pride and pleasure.

It was a great honour to be asked to join Arsenal. The major difference to other clubs was the total professionalism, and the feeling that everybody from the cleaners, secretaries and youth players to the team itself was part of one family with a common goal.

I wanted badly to make the Danish side for the 1996 European Championships, and the Danish manager would only pick players playing first-team football. I was in and out of the Arsenal side and spoke to Rioch about the situation. He understood fully the position I was in and suggested a free transfer if I could find a club that was interested in me and that I would like to join. This, for me, underlined the greatness of the club.

I will always say what a wonderful time I had at Arsenal, and this was due in no small way to the magnificent staff at Highbury. I have never known such a positive attitude all through a club.

When I left Hamburg I was told that there were three teams in England – Liverpool, Manchester United and Arsenal. For me, there is only one!

Jensen returned to his first club, Brøndby in Copenhagen. After a period of resettling, he took on a new lease of life. He was appointed club captain, and, in 1997-98, he emulated Tony Adams by leading Brøndby to the Danish League and Cup double.

John Jensen is something of an exception to Bob Wilson's rule that players who leave Arsenal find it difficult to settle elsewhere.

The only people I've ever known to have any real satisfaction when they've left Arsenal and gone to another club are those who didn't have much success at Arsenal, like John Hartson. I think he's a big fish in a small pond, with due respect to West Ham. I think it's perfect for him, but I'm not sure that alongside Bergkamp and every-one, even now, it would be right. I think that 98 per cent of the players I know who have left Arsenal and gone to other clubs say, "It's never the same when you've left." Unless you go to Manchester United like George Graham.

I don't regret that I retired when I did, not now I don't. There are so many people who say you should play until you can't play any more. Well, there are two things that happened to me. First and foremost, my education came to the front when the BBC asked me to do some work for them, and I started seeing television in terms of analysis. Nobody had done any analysis of play, and when we went to the 1970 World Cup, and I was on the panel, the BBC had so many people that I said suddenly, "Look, you don't need me on your panel, but could I go into the video tape area and put together pieces on players and teams tactically?" And I really was the first one to do that. It used to take all day to do a two and a half/three minute piece. Nowadays, it takes about half an

hour to an hour. That was the start. So I always had in my mind that I quite liked doing that, but I only ever really wanted to present football. I never really wanted to present boxing or Formula One.

I would definitely have played on until I was 36, 38, 40, had I not had the injury I had in the 1972 semi-final. It was an injury to my natural take-off leg. It was cartilage, ligaments and tendon. I've had five operations on that knee now. It's a mess. Although I got to play for two seasons more, it was the beginning of the end, and what really did me was that I was an Arsenal man through and through by then, and I could not see myself wanting to play for anyone else in this country or elsewhere. I didn't want to go and play anywhere else you'd wish to mention. I was just lucky that I was given the alternative.

The BBC at some time had said to me, "Look, if you get to the point where you've got a problem or anything, let us know because we want to take you on board." I had that in mind, and what happened was that Bertie changed the coaching staff. Steve Burtenshaw went, and then Bobby Campbell came, and on the very first day he came, we became aware that he wanted to sign three players – the Queen's Park Rangers goalkeeper Phil Parkes, a full-back and a centre-half. Basically, it affected me, Bob McNab and Frank McLintock. It happened on the very first day that he arrived, and we rebelled.

We had finished first or second in a major competition for six seasons. We still had a lot to offer, but he thought that the secret lay in the likes of Eddie Kelly, Charlie George and people. They couldn't see the strength of Bob McNab's character, the strength of Frank McLintock's character. They were putting their trust in youth. You've got to have the mixture, experience and youth. It's the perfect blend. So they made an error. I will always say they made an error – they won't agree to it. I stayed in the side for another year and a bit, but the writing was on the wall. They were looking.

Bobby Campbell was a Scouser. Obviously, he was the Liverpool way. He was an incredible enthusiast, a very good coach, but he got off to a bad start. He put us all in a room, and he started to pull us apart. It was in the first two days he was with us, and it was an error because these were the guys who'd done the Double, which everyone remembers, but we also went to Wembley – we failed; we went to Wembley – we failed; we won the Fairs Cup – we succeeded; we won the Double – we succeeded; we went back to Wembley – we failed; and we were second in the First Division the following year. For six seasons, we finished first or second in a major competition. These were guys who still had a lot to give. So they made an error. The Double side broke up too soon.

Decisions on how and when to leave are not always in the hands of the player. For Alan Smith, as for many others, the end came because of injury.

My last three years were a disappointment, being in and out of the team. I wasn't playing well, and I wasn't enjoying it. I was sad to leave the Arsenal because it's very special there. You have an attachment to the club if you've played there, and you never lose it.

Alan Smith celebrates a goal against Manchester City in December 1994. "I was sad to leave the Arsenal because it's very special there. You have an attachment to the club if you've played there, and you never lose it."

It was all right for us. There was the great side of the Thirties, and the Double side, but we were making history. We were winning everything. It must have been difficult for the side in the Eighties because they all had history behind them, and they weren't winning, but for us it wasn't too bad. I can imagine it would be hard if you weren't winning because everyone would be telling you about the Double side and the rest.

You know inside yourself, when you go out, whether you are confident or not. I had to make sure I did the job for the team even if I wasn't scoring, but, in front of goal, I ceased to feel confident.

As the years have passed, I've missed the game more. The decision was made for me by the surgeon, and I accepted it because I wasn't playing well, and I wasn't enjoying myself, but it has hit me quite hard in the years that have followed.

For Laurie Scott, the injury that brought an end to his career was sustained while playing for England.

I was injured against Wales at Villa Park, I remember, a chap named Clarke. It was a pure accident. I was running back with him along the touchline, and suddenly my studs must have stuck in, and I turned over. It wasn't his fault, just an accident, but the cartilage had gone. I was in terrible pain, and they brought me back to London. We used to have a special wing in the Whittington Hospital – everybody used to go there – St David's wing, I think it was. They put me in there for the night, and I was in agony. Then it turned out that I got back in the England side, but it wasn't working, and I had to have another operation. I tried again and went with the England side to the World Cup, 1950, but I couldn't play, and that was virtually the end.

I came back and struggled for a bit, and then the job as manager at Crystal Palace came up, and I took it. The contrast when I went to Crystal Palace was so great. You just can't compare it to Arsenal. In the first place, you haven't got the players. I don't just mean players as players, but players as gentlemen. It was difficult at Crystal Palace to try and change things. You've got to have the good players around you.

A few years later, it was terrible, our daughter, just ten years old, we lost her, and I was glad to get out of it. I didn't want anything more to do with it. I'd been chasing all over the world, and I couldn't see any point in it. I just wanted to spend a bit of time with my wife so I finished. The chairman at Crystal Palace asked me if I'd like to go and work for him. So I did, and that's how it ended. To keep me in football, I went to Hitchin and coached them, and there wasn't too much pressure on you there.

Laurie Scott was troubled by injury and left Arsenal to move into management. Others have gone because they have become conscious of changing patterns within the club and have wondered whether their time at Arsenal had run its course. Offers to move on can be tempting, however happy one is at Highbury, and decisions are not always easy to make, as Brian Talbot remembers.

Don Howe was manager when I left Arsenal. It was strange really. Don was there, and in those days – thirteen years ago – people had the impression that once you had turned 30, you were coming to the end of your career. Nowadays, people accept 35 or a little bit older. The situation was that Don took over, and he brought Steve Williams in, but I'd had a good season and was still playing. I might even have been top goalscorer with twelve goals. Then, in the summer, Graham Taylor, with permission from Arsenal, got in contact with me and said, "Will you come to Watford?" To be honest, I didn't want to leave Arsenal, but he made it sound so attractive to me – being the captain, giving me a three-year contract. The financial package was good as well – Elton John was backing the club at the time – and it

would have been difficult to turn it down, for I only had one year left at Arsenal.

In those days, we weren't on the wages they're on today. I had a young family, and we'd just bought a big house in Brookman's Park, so, to be honest, I went for the finances as much as anything else, and I did feel my days at Arsenal were coming to an end. I thought they were looking to replace me.

Maybe, if I'd have stood my ground and stayed there as David O'Leary did, I could have been a squad player for twenty years. I thought I was well liked within the club, and I always gave my best. In hindsight, if I am honest, I wish I hadn't left. Something always turns up in life. I was enjoying my football at the time and playing well. I know I was 32, but I was quite fit. I think as you get older it's easier to play at the top than in the lower divisions.

There may have been some worries by those in charge at the Arsenal that I was the Professional Footballers' Association Chairman, but I like to think that I went a long way to establishing good relations between the PFA and the clubs. When the PFA asked me to take over I said on one condition, I don't actually like unions, but what I want to see is fair play. If the club is right, the club is right. If we don't make any waves, it is because it is the right thing.

I went to West Brom eventually and finished my career there. What amazed me there, without disrespect to the lads, is that they can't find the easy passes whereas the good players do it so easily, passing and moving the ball around the pitch. At Arsenal and Manchester United, you see it all the time, but in the First Division, they can't do it. The ball is changing hands so many times, and when you're on the ball they don't make options so well for you. They don't think as quickly, and sometimes you're caught in possession, and the crowd think, "Look at that old bastard." But you haven't been given any options. They don't move for you.

I'm nearly 45, and I play with my lads at Rushden, and obviously they are much quicker than me, but I still think more quickly.

I look back on my career, and maybe I was a better player than I realised. I used to be able to keep possession of the ball. You can say he couldn't do this, he couldn't do that, but when I look at players today you need someone who can keep possession of the ball to link things together.

Arsenal is unique among football clubs in the hold that it has on those who have once been part of it. They are tied to Highbury by an umbilical cord which can never be severed. There is ever the desire to return "home". George Armstrong believes that it was right for Charlie George to leave Arsenal for Derby County when he did, that the move helped him to become a better player, yet part of Charlie remained ever in the region of Gillespie Road. There was a café in the area bearing his name, and when his playing days were over he returned to North London and acts as host to visiting groups on match days. Armstrong himself left Arsenal in what he would describe as a less happy period in his life, but his love of the club was never weakened, and his career has come full circle.

When Terry Neill came it wasn't the happiest time for me. I was 30, 31, and I felt it was time to move on. I went to Leicester, and I'll be the first to admit that things didn't work for me at Leicester, and Leicester fans will say that I didn't do the business for Leicester, but it's a two-way thing. The mistake that I made is what I warn players here about – if you're going to leave, you go to a club that's on the up. I went to a club with Frank, Frank McLintock, who were on the way down. There were a lot of cliques in the club, and I thought, "Oh dear".

Given my time over again, I wouldn't have rushed into it. Strangely, I was probably playing my best football at that time, carefree and performing well. There's many factors that were involved, but I just think

that I shouldn't have gone to Leicester. I'm not knocking Leicester. They're a good club.

The difference is that this club is great not just because of the facilities, but because of the tradition, and that's why I hope we never lose those values of discipline, the old-fashioned standards. I don't think that you should accept that life has changed and allow those standards to be tarnished. You still have to have rules, and if you step out of line, you get punished. I remember Eddie Clamp getting transferred because he made a bad tackle. Money has become so important today that it can affect judgements. I'm not criticising Arsenal. I'm talking about society itself, and I hope Arsenal can remain aloof from all this.

George Graham brought me back to Arsenal. I was in Kuwait, and I'd done very well. I'd begun with a club side – Dave Mackay helped me initially – and I ended up with the national side and spent five years with them. The Kuwaiti people were great. I had a few, little problems, but I got help. I enjoyed it there, but I needed a change. I was offered other jobs in the Middle East, but I rang Bertie Mee one day, and he told me to get in touch with George Graham. He'd heard that Theo Foley was leaving. So I phoned George, and he asked me when I was coming back, and I told him the first of June. He said, "OK, I will do nothing until then. I've got a lot of applicants for the job, but I'll do nothing until you come back."

When I came back we talked about a few things, and then he said, "All right, I'm going to tell the board I want you." I'll always be grateful to him.

Like George Armstrong, Pat Rice is a double-Double man whose career has come full circle. He was in Arsenal's first FA Youth Cup-winning side, and then he returned to have two youth sides of his own that won the trophy. Arsenal has always been in his blood.

I left in 1980 because I felt I'd run

my course at Arsenal. John Devine was in the side, and I felt to myself that I might as well move on, and I went to Watford. I had four terrific years under Graham Taylor and Elton John. I really learned a lot from them, and it was Graham Taylor who started me on the coaching. I learned the way that he thought about things. I was involved in the staff meetings and in the coaching and in the whole running of the club, but you love Arsenal. The club is in your blood, and you always think to yourself, "Well, maybe one day…" You never think it's going to happen, but you're always hoping.

So when the opportunity arose, when Don Howe gave me the chance to come back here, there was no thinking twice about it. I was very lucky, lucky enough to be involved with a number of very good players. In my association with them, we won the Youth Cup twice, the Southern Junior Cup, and we won the League, but that means nothing unless you get a player through, and so many players never do come through. In fairness, it would be wrong of me to take all of the glory, but I had people like David Rocastle, Michael Thomas – Niall Quinn started with me – Andrew Cole, Alan Miller, Andrew Marriott, Paul Merson. I was pretty lucky.

I came up through the ranks, and the only thing I have bypassed is the reserve team, but I have been very fortunate, and, in fairness, if it hadn't been for Bruce Rioch, I wouldn't have been in this position of first-team coach.

I came back under Don Howe. Don was moving people up. Tommy Coleman was moving to the reserves, and Terry Burton was moving to the first team, and Don phoned up Graham Taylor. I was at a pre-season staff meeting, and Graham said to me, "I want to have a word with you on your own." And he told me he'd had an approach from Don Howe, so I asked him what it was about. He said, "Well, he wants to offer you the youth

team job at the Arsenal. Personally, I don't want you to go. It's entirely up to you." Once that happened, I knew that if I didn't take it, I would never have another chance of coming back, and, you know, your love of the club draws you in.

For Armstrong, Rice and others, all has turned out well. They are back where they belong, an integral part of the success of another generation of Arsenal footballers. There are others to whom life was not so kind. Arthur Milton remembers the last days of the great Jimmy Logie.

Expectancy was high at Highbury. They prided themselves on their record and their behaviour, which was what I liked. They didn't stand any nonsense on the field or anywhere else. They'd leave you out. That's what happened to Jimmy Logie. The trouble was he was 90 per cent of the side. I don't think they realised what they were doing when they let him go.

Pat Rice: "Nobody gave me a hope of making a professional …I'm really a man-made player …whenever I played I used to try to win the ball and give it to those who were more talented than me." For all that, he managed over 500 senior appearances and a host of honours.

It was the saddest thing the way he went. He lost faith. We played Spartak of Moscow, and there was a Russian referee, and Jim was captain that night. We lost 2-1. About five minutes to go, I got past the full-back and went to the near post, and the centre-half has got to come to me. Jimmy was in the middle there. The centre-half was done, but he took me out with his body, and the referee gave an indirect free-kick. I was only about three yards from the byline by the near post, and he gave a free-kick instead of a penalty.

It was close to full-time, and when he blew the whistle the referee went over to Jim to shake hands, and Jim turned away from him, and Arsenal never forgave him. He was gone a few weeks later.

He went to Gillingham. He played there for a few years, and he got married to a young girl, and it all went wrong for him. It ruined his life. He kept a pub for a while, and then he sold papers in Piccadilly.

For me, I got out and went to Bristol City for half a season before giving up to concentrate on cricket while I still had two good legs. I was prepared for the difference when I left Arsenal. I knew I'd miss the people and the game, but the facilities on other First Division grounds in those days were nothing like those at Arsenal. They were always at the head of the game right from before the war.

The days of your youth you think are never going to end. You remember mainly the good times, the people. I miss the people I played with.

Money, Marketing and The Supporter

IN THE years immediately after World War Two, the official Arsenal Handbook cost sixpence, which would be 2½p in today's currency. It was pocket-size and was 160 pages in length. The printing was small, and there were no pictures. It was far more literary biased than it is today and contained a review of the season, a history of the club and the laws of the game as well as the complete statistical record that it retains today. It was, in effect, the only official merchandise that was sold by the club. It doubled in price in 1949-50, but it did include pictures for the first time, seven black and white photographs of good quality. Remarkably, it was to retain its price of one shilling (5p) for eighteen years when it again doubled and then spiralled after decimalisation. Its format changed. It became bigger in size and the literary content was gradually eroded as the photographic content increased, but by the Nineties it was vying with a host of publications, official and unofficial.

When the championship was won in 1948 a souvenir brochure was produced on behalf of the players. It was compiled, in the main, by Fleet Street journalists, was 26 pages long and had one tinted team photograph and several black and white pictures. At two shillings and sixpence, three times the price of the Underground fare from Wood Green to the centre of London, it was not cheap for 1948, but the players were attempting to supplement an income that was pegged at £9 a week. This, in spite of the fact that, the following year, the Football League's aggregate attendance was a record 41.2 million, and Derby County established a transfer record when they paid Manchester United £24,500 for Johnny Morris.

Transfer fees rose annually, but players' wages rose more slowly and a ceiling was maintained. By 1960, the maximum wage was set at £20 in winter and £17 in summer, and players were restricted by contracts which denied them the opportunity of moving to clubs of their choosing when those contracts expired. The whole matter came to a head as leading footballers were tempted abroad by large salaries offered them and huge transfer fees paid to their clubs. The Professional Footballers' Association, led by its chairman, Jimmy Hill, threatened strike action, and, in January 1961, the maximum wage was abolished. Johnny Haynes, the Fulham and England inside-forward, became the first £100 a week footballer.

The League was more reluctant to end the "slave contracts", as Hill described them, and it took a long meeting at the Ministry of Labour and a volte face by the League to resolve the problem.

Arsenal were closely involved in the events. George Eastham wanted to move from Newcastle to Arsenal and challenged his contract in the court, declaring that it was a restraint of trade. The High Court ruled in his favour, and Eastham became an Arsenal player. He cost £47,500. A delightful ball player with a creative genius, he scored twice on his debut against Bolton Wanderers at Highbury and became a great favourite with the crowd, but his six years at Arsenal covered a period when the club seemed to have lost direction and when the urgency of expectation so long associated with Arsenal appeared to be waning. There were many good players who came and went, but the order and balance had been lost. It coincided with the time when Tottenham did the Double and enjoyed, arguably, the best period in their history, and, for the first and only time in the half-century since the war, Arsenal supporters felt inferior in North London. It was not a pleasant feeling.

The rise in salaries brought about by the abolition of the maximum wage had to be met by money that came from gate receipts, for these were the days before sponsorship and large incomes paid for television rights. Older players, like Laurie Scott, whose careers ended before the abolition of the maximum wage, find it hard to accept today's structures.

> I think it isn't right that one player gets £20,000 a week, and another gets £2,000 a week. It doesn't make sense to me. When we were playing it was a flat wage all the way through. You all got the same wage and did the same job. I was paid a manager's salary at Crystal Palace. It's a different sport altogether, completely different.

George Armstrong sees outside dangers in the advances of technology and business.

> We were hungry for it, and there were fewer outside interests. Technology is changing. You've got mobile phones and you've got agents, which we never had. To be fair, we used to be criticised for playing snooker, but we used to play snooker in the afternoon at Burns in Southgate, five or six of us, but it was team spirit. We were together. We worked hard.

Bertie Mee, highly respected as an outstanding manager and a man of dignity and intelligence, is acutely aware of how much things have changed in financial matters since he masterminded Arsenal's success in the Seventies.

> You can only keep a squad together providing you've made life contractually comfortable for them. They're alert to so much now. They're put up to things by their agents, and contracts can be drawn in such a way as to make it possible for players to be upgraded if others are signed whose contracts are better than theirs. They're alive to every trick in the book. But Arsenal have kept their players happy.

> These changes, of course, have coincided with millions coming into the game – TV money, marketing, sponsorship – and it's been passed on to the players. It's going to rebound, make no mistake about that. The backroom staff has shot up to something like twelve – and I'm talking purely in terms of dressing room staff.

> In my day, players had ticket touts rather than agents. The ticket tout then was Stan Flashman, and Stan, every Friday, was outside the ground taking tickets from players. It was a bit embarrassing because the locals, when we were sold out, were turning up to buy tickets and couldn't, but they saw the players selling tickets.

> I had a word with the players about it, but I didn't get anywhere with that approach so I said, "Get Flashman in! I'll have a word with him." So I got him in and dressed him down and said, "I'll kill your business. I'll deprive the players of tickets, and if I can't stop you dealing, get around the corner and out of sight of the ground."

> He was Jack the Lad was Flashman. And I said, "All right, clear off! I don't want to see you again." He got to the door and turned round and said, "You couldn't let me have two together for tomorrow, could you?" You couldn't win with Flashman.

> Agents were just starting to come in, but they were not as prevalent as they are now. Of course, they're trying to control them. They're having to put up a bond of about £150,000 and have to be FIFA recognised.

> Money is so important today. This is a problem Tottenham have had. They've been perpetuating mediocrity. They've not been getting the players that would take them right to the top, world-class players, the Bergkamps of this world. There is big competition, and then wages. You're

competing with very, very big wages – £300,000 to £400,000 a year.

That must be terribly difficult for a manager, but that is why I think managers are now quite happy to allow somebody on the board to look after the financial side. They're happy now on the managerial side, quite happy for two reasons. One, they don't want the responsibility of handling that sort of money; and two, even more important, if the players are being paid half a million, then the manager has to be paid that as well. That obtains. It is not a frivolous remark. I was born twenty years too soon.

Bob Wilson echoes Mee's worries on the financial future of the game because of the dependence on television money, and he questions, too, whether loyalties can be as strong today as in the Seventies because of the freedom of contract. At the age of 24, a player can realise that he is soon to become a free agent and will go to whoever is willing to pay him the most money.

Attitudes are totally different today. When I say totally, I mean the nitty gritty of it is that when they go out to play they don't think about the money. They don't think about other things. The lads who won the championship in '89 and '91, who did everything this year, when they go out there, they are playing for themselves and they are playing for the team. They are wanting to win. At Arsenal, you have to be a winner otherwise they don't dwell on you. That remains the same. What is different is loyalty. There was tremendous loyalty in our period. You lived, ate, drank, slept Arsenal Football Club.

The pay was beginning to improve in our time, but today it doesn't even bear comparison to our day. In the Double year, when we also got to the semi-final of a European competition again, the best paid player got £17,500. In real terms now, I guess that's about a quarter of a million, £250,000, but these guys are on threequarters of a million, £750,000.

So there is no comparison in the question of loyalty – can't possibly be. But I have to say, if put on the spot and asked, "How would you approach it?" I'd have to say that I can't blame the guys. They've got families, and they've got the chance to secure their families and the rest of their lives. If I were playing today, I would finish my career, and I would not have to worry about working again for the rest of my life. These guys are millionaires. In our day, we thought that Kevin Keegan must be *nearly* a millionaire, Johann Cruyff must be *nearly* a millionaire. People were astonished when Johnny Haynes became the first £100 a week footballer.

There were agents, but nothing like today. Certainly no foreign agents. I had an agent called Reg Hayter, a lovely man, one of the great characters of Fleet Street. He said, "Look, I'm in the Fleet Street business," and he was very good. I got a little autobiography out, and he got me a column in *The Sun* newspaper on a regular basis, which was at the time when *The Sun* was far more respectable than it is today. I used to love to do the column, but when I moved to television it was hopeless. Reg didn't understand the television world so I moved to another agent who is very famous in the football world, but that didn't really work out, and, ultimately, my wife became my agent.

It wasn't as it is now where some of the agents even take a percentage of a player's wage, which I think is outrageous. If they negotiate a new contract, ok, I think they should be paid a flat fee for negotiating that contract. If they are getting all the outside work like adverts, then they get their ten, fifteen, twenty per cent. I don't have any argument with that, but to take anything out of a player's salary is dreadful.

Support is different. Much of it is on television. You've got to realise the pulling power of the game of football. There were two satellite television companies, Sky and BSB, and BSB went under, and they became the same company. They were losing money like it was going out of favour. They were on an absolute downward spiral. Their news channel and everything else could not make ends meet. Suddenly, they put this enormous sum of money, whatever it was, £354,000,000, for the total rights of the Premier League, for live football. In a short period, in real terms, Sky Television has made an incredible profit until this year when it has suddenly levelled out. They have 5,000,000 regular subscribers, and they pay either £32 a month if you have all the channels, or, like us with just the sport, £18 or £19. If you average that out at £24, £25 a month and you multiply it by 5,000,000, you don't have to be a great mathematician to realise the money you are talking about. But suddenly, it's levelling out, and they are not getting as many subscribers. A lot of people are getting anti because they are being faced with so many extra charges. A lot of our friends have stopped subscribing. But Sky have made giant profits which shows the pulling power of football.

Channel Five has come on the air with millions of losses in the first quarter, so what are they doing to turn it round? Football, football, football! We know the pulling power at ITV. Sky television has only once had an audience of more than three million – the England-Italy game. Now we've never been below 10,000,000 for any Manchester United game, often twelve to thirteen million on terrestrial television. It shows the pulling power of the game.

It also shows two other things. Firstly, there are those who are happy just watching football on television, which, ultimately, will be bad for the game, although, at the moment, Arsenal have never been less than 38,000 over the past couple of years. But what really worries me is that the guys who used to stand on the terraces

are getting priced out. They're getting priced out first because it is costing so much to get to the ground, and they're getting priced out from watching it on television apart from the highlights on terrestrial television, *Match of the Day,* because Sky are upping the cost all the time.

What worries me more than anything else is that we have this explosion at the moment with players earning these incredible fees, and the television people are paying all this money, but if Sky suddenly say, "Wait a minute. We want the Champions League. We know that the bigger audiences are there. It's heading towards a European League." If they suddenly pull out from supporting the Premiership, then we are in big trouble. Heaven help us if they change their option.

The influence of television on football has become a strong debating point among fans, and Ian Botham's solicitor is not alone in surrendering his season ticket because fixture lists were juggled to accommodate Sky coverage. To book holiday dates which would allow you to see Arsenal and Spurs at Highbury before you set off and then to find, just a fortnight before you are due to leave, that the game has been put back until the Monday is a frustrating experience. It does not make for good public relations. Supporters still feel that they are the club, that they are the fabric of its history. They are well aware that the money they pay to come through the turnstiles no longer generates the income that the club needs to survive and prosper, but they remain keen that their voices should be heard and their opinions respected. As Arthur Milton has said, "When you play in front of a big crowd you imagine what it would be like if they weren't there."

At Highbury, in the years immediately after the war, crowds in excess of 60,000 were not uncommon, but attendances began to be eroded when a wider range of entertainments and leisure activities became available. Where once there was soccer in the winter and cricket in the summer, there was now the opportunity to play squash, badminton, tennis and golf, and for some years, speedway and ice hockey had immense followings. After years of austerity, there was, too, the lure of shopping. The biggest influence on attendances, however, was to come after the Hillsborough tragedy in 1989. In its wake came the Taylor Report and the all-seater stadium, and, in the opinion of many, football has never been the same since. Laura Levy, a passionate Arsenal fan who rarely misses a match, home or away, has no doubts as to the influence that all-seater stadiums have had on the game.

My father first started taking me around 1970. He used to go with my grandad. They would go to Arsenal one week, and Spurs the next. Then I think my mum probably said to my dad, "If you're going out Saturdays, you take her with you. So I started going with my dad, just to the home games, for two or three seasons. Then he realised that it wasn't just the fact that I was out with him that I liked; I was actually enjoying it. Then we used to go all over the country. I must have been about thirteen then, and we used to go everywhere, but not when there were schooldays, except, perhaps, for the odd Cup game.

My dad stopped going to away games when my mum had my sister, and he was needed at home, and, about ten years ago, after he had his heart by-pass, he stopped going altogether.

I wouldn't go to Spurs now unless Arsenal were playing. I think it was an older generation that did that. I had my passion for the Arsenal from my very first game. I think it was going with my dad that did it. We were living in Totteridge at that time.

I used to stand with my dad in the North Bank. There was a wonderful community feeling. I prefer to stand than to sit, and it seems a natural impulse for some people. When I was watching Arsenal at Barnsley I had a seat in Row E, and Rows A, B, C and D stood the moment the game started. There was no need. They could see perfectly well. And look at the Clock End at Highbury, there's no one sitting there at all. There's no need for the first five rows to stand up, but people want to stand behind the goal at football. Again, I think it's the community feeling.

I think the atmosphere is not what it used to be at Highbury since they've put the seats in; it just isn't the same. It's a hundred and fifty per cent better at away games because of the atmosphere. George Graham always used to say that the atmosphere in northern clubs was worth a goal.

Years ago, people used to stand together at every match. It was a special camaraderie, but, unless you apply for your season tickets together, you can't choose who you're next to today.

When you go to every away game, and bear in mind there's only about 1,500 that go to every away game and about 2,000 that go to more than half, you're not spread out. Even if you don't know each other's names, you recognise each other and say, "Hello, how are you?" And everyone sings. The atmosphere is a hundred times better, and there's something good about going into a service station on the way home and seeing a couple of hundred other Arsenal supporters wearing red and white. You're all in a good mood. It's togetherness.

A lot of people go on the Supporters' Club coach, but I prefer to be able to stop when and where I want to, and to have a meal when I want one. When you go by coach you're driven into a car park and herded about, and I don't want to be treated like cattle. We always meet up at a certain bar or restaurant. When we go to Southampton we always go to the same restaurant – it's good fun.

When we went to Villa Park for the semi-final I was struck by how lacking the facilities are there compared to those at Highbury, but I still think the atmosphere has gone. When our large screen tells you to shout, "Come on you Reds," you don't take any notice. There is a constant buzz, but nobody sings, "We are the West Stand." The spontaneity has gone. When we stood we always knew where the rest of us were, but you have to sit where you are when you have a seat. When we stood we couldn't see half the game, but we cheered. I think the report that came out after Hillsborough was necessary, but it went too far. It didn't need to do what it did.

I think another thing that's wrong is the different prices you have to pay. When West Ham supporters come to Highbury it costs them £14, and they have an uninterrupted view. We pay £24 to go there, and Chelsea was £22, and it was pot luck whether you saw anything. The cheapest game was Barnsley, £15, and Southampton at least make clear whether or not you have a restricted view.

Andy Charalambous lived in Caledonian Road and was first taken to Highbury by his father when he was six or seven. It was the time, in the late Sixties, when nearly everyone supported his or her local team, and to go to school on Monday and say that you had been taken to the Arsenal was a very prestigious thing. Like most of us, Andy was sold on Arsenal from the moment he walked into the Lower East Stand, went up the steps and saw the pitch and the stadium and thought it was the most amazing place, but, like Bob Wilson, he fears the game is in danger of losing a generation of young supporters.

I used to stand at the Clock End. Personally, I prefer to sit and watch a match in comfort, but I think people should be allowed to stand. I think something of the atmosphere has been lost with everyone sitting unless it's a very big game, like those against Sampdoria and Paris St Germain, but if you are watching on a cold afternoon, and Arsenal are playing, say Barnsley, much of the atmosphere gets lost. You used to have the North Bank and the Clock End and the away supporters with everyone standing up. When you were standing in the crowd, and there was community singing, you got a real buzz.

We never had fences at Highbury, but people didn't run on the pitch. The only time I can remember it

happening is when Spurs played Wolves in the semi-final, and Spurs' fans ran on the pitch; and, in 1981, last game of the season, against Aston Villa who won the championship. There were 57,000 people there, biggest crowd we'd had for years, and Pele was the guest of honour. When he came out everyone started singing, "Sign him up!" There were hundreds of balloons in the centre circle which were going to be let off before the kick-off, and this idiot came running out from the North Bank and just dived on them. They all went off. Villa won the League, but we beat them that day and qualified for Europe.

The biggest changes that have taken place since I first went to Arsenal is what it costs now to watch football. The influence of television on the game, which has got out of control; all-seater stadiums – these are negative things; on the positive side, there are the foreign players – there are some magnificent players we now have a chance to see – and you genuinely do feel safer than you did. The trouble element has gone out of the game, the roughs who wanted to fight. Some of it still goes on. A couple of years ago, the League Cup semi-final against Aston Villa, trouble broke out, and those fighting were in their thirties or early forties. They were the same yobs who had just got older. It was the same with some Chelsea supporters this year. They were walking up the street fighting, but they weren't youngsters. They were grown men with children.

I think the average age of the crowd has probably risen by ten to fifteen years. If you sit in the West Stand where we sit, there are one or two kids now and again with their fathers, but there are no youngsters on their own. I used to go and stand in the Schoolboy Enclosure and pay 30p to get in, and I remember standing at the Clock End when it was £2.10, and that was a lot of money then. Now a good ticket is £17 at least. My mum and dad couldn't afford that.

I think that there are a lot of genuine people being forced out of the game. You have to wonder now if you can afford it. In the old days, you never had that thought. Your Saturday was going to cost you ten bob, and that was it. Work it out now, if you go to the Arsenal and you're a casual supporter – not a season ticket holder – the first thing you have to do is get a ticket. That isn't easy now because first you've got the ticket registration scheme, which means that you've got be a registered member, and that costs you £10. So, once you've done that, you decide you want to sit in the North Bank, and three tickets are going to cost you £15 apiece, that's £45. Then you've got to get there, and you want to drive, but you can't drive because the parking restrictions round the ground are so heavy, and you're likely to be towed away. So you get the train, and that will cost you at least a tenner. You've spent over £70 already, and the programmes are £2, and the kids want one each. You'll end up spending at least £80 to sit in the cheapest seats at the Arsenal. Are you honestly telling me that the majority of people in this country can afford to do that, often twice a week? There's a danger that we're going to lose a generation of people.

When my little girl gets to the age of fifteen or sixteen she would have been to the Arsenal a couple of times with her dad as a treat, but it won't be in her blood. It might even be anathema to her. In fifteen years time, when all these little people have grown up and some of us are too old or dead, there'll be a danger that they won't want to go. They won't be in the habit of going. There is a generation who will only ever support Arsenal from what they see on television and will never see them in the flesh, and that's sad.

Laura Levy agrees with Andy Charalambous that the violence that once plagued football subsided and that going to a match is no longer attended by the fear that prevailed in the mid-Eighties. Her views about internationals are those shared by a majority of fans who often see them as an intrusion into the League programme, which, as we have noted, was not the case 50 years ago.

There are more girls go to football now than ever before. It's so much safer than it was. Ten years ago, we would never have stopped at the Watford Gap Service Station when there were Leeds supporters there, but today we stop and meet and chat and wish each other luck. We always drive, and we always stop on the motorway. The only time we take a train is if Arsenal are at Newcastle, Middlesbrough or Blackburn, places up north where my friend Tracey thinks it's too far to drive.

I'm not passionate about England, nor is David. I support my country, and I always want them to win, but I wouldn't pay £40 to see a friendly international at Wembley although I would play £20 to see Lee Dixon's Benefit Match. I paid the earth to see Arsenal in the San Siro, but I wouldn't do that for England.

The economic structure of the game outlined by Bob Wilson and the cost of watching football and its threat to the future which troubles Andy Charalambous are problems of which clubs are acutely aware, but not all husbandry is as efficient, visionary and realistic as that in operation at Highbury. As in all major sports, gate receipts no longer cover costs. It is necessary to raise income from a variety of sources even if that means facing realities and breaking with traditions. Only in recent years have football clubs developed their commercial potential, and in this area Arsenal, as in so much else, have become leaders. Having spent so many years associated with the club, Don Howe is aware of the developments.

The club has changed in things like marketing, the commercial side. It's now a whole department, and, in our day, it was a little shop that sold a few rosettes.

Fifty years ago, walking from Finsbury Park Station to the ground, one might see two or three street vendors selling rosettes, scarves and rattles. Happily, the rattle has vanished, and the

The Arsenal Museum, situated in the North Bank, provides supporters and public with a series of exhibits based on the history of the club. From the shirts and boots worn by famous players, and cups and medals, right through to a film show on the Arsenal story and inter-active computer games and a database of Arsenal statistics, there is something for supporters of every age.

official merchandise available from World of Sport and other club outlets is legion. It is not fifteen years since Brian Talbot was an Arsenal player, but he is well aware of great changes and applauds them.

I remember Dennis Hill-Wood, the Arsenal chairman, whom I did not know well, saying, "We're not going to have advertising logos on our shirts. That's not our way." Now they market everything, sell shirts, have sponsors and advertising boards. They have to. It's part of the income, and I think David Dein and the rest have done brilliantly with this aspect of the club.

Ever aware of their traditions and responsibilities, Arsenal have followed the pattern established in the Thirties in that success on the field has been reflected by developments in the stadium which have been aimed at giving better facilities for supporters. The stadium has always been palatial, but over the past ten years it has increased in splendour with the installation of the large television screens, the visual display of messages of welcome and emergency, and the refurbishment of lavatories which, thankfully, leave those of the past a faded memory. Andy Charalambous recalls taking his father back to Highbury:

My father was never keen, but he first took me, and I took him to see Arsenal 25 years later when they played Omonia Nicosia. As I say, he didn't really like it, but he sat there and looked around the ground, and he didn't recognise anything. We've got red seats where there used to be wooden seats. Everything had changed.

It is hard now to visualise what the North Bank was like in those years just after World War Two. Initially roofless, it is looked back on by many with the romantic aura of remembered youth, but it had none of the majesty that it has today, with its shop, its toilets, it spacious entrance hall and its museum.

The North Bank had to become an all-seater area to comply with the new regulations, but the facilities that were included in the redevelopment brought the whole project into the 21st century. The idea to provide supporters and public with a museum founded on the history of the club was inspirational. The task of setting up the museum and becoming its curator was entrusted to Iain Cook who had joined Arsenal in 1979 and worked in the box office.

I'd always been an Arsenal fan, and when I was at school I saw a job in the ticket office advertised. I applied and got the job, but to come from school to a place that was so busy was a rude awakening, mind blowing. It was the year we got to two Finals. We got to the Final at Wembley against West Ham, and the Final in Brussels against Valencia. We lost both within the space of four days, which was rather a sad ending to what had been a particularly lively debut season for me.

I'd been in the box office for the best part of twelve years when the new stadium was being planned, building the North Bank, and it was decided to put a museum together. I was offered the possibility of setting up the museum, and, as this was being done from scratch, obviously the opportunity would never come again. I had done a good spell in the box office, and it was time to move on so I was very happy to take up the challenge although I had no background in that type of thing. It was exciting.

I was pretty useful at history and knew a lot about the club. The directors had a choice of getting someone from outside who knew about museums but knew little about the club, or having someone like me who knew very little about museums but was quite well informed about the history of the club.

Having been appointed, I spent about a year touring round, having a look at other museums in the country, seeing what was good and what was bad before deciding what I wanted to do in setting up the Arsenal museum. I chose some designers and other people to work with, and then got it together in the North Bank. It came together very well in the end.

I was given almost a free hand. The basic idea was to tell the story of the club which had been going for 107, 108 years – now it's 112 – in as many varied and interesting ways as we could. There are some very interesting pieces in there. We aimed to make it as exciting as we could for a varied age group. We had to get across the whole divide, and, in the end, we were pleased with the result.

The problem that you have in London is that there are so many counter-attractions. When we first started we opened a lot more than we do now. Some days we were very busy – Friday, in particular, when we had a game coming up or people just happened to be around because it was Friday – whereas midweek it was not particularly lively, so we decided to open on Fridays and match days.

As I have said, there is so much else on offer in London. If you want to go somewhere like the Wimbledon tennis

museum, you make the trip to go there for the day, and it is the same in some regional cities, but at Arsenal you can get on the Underground and you are in the centre of London in twenty minutes. It is a different situation.

Another service we offer is to give tours of the stadium. We take up to about 35 people and show them the dressing rooms, trophy cabinets, board room etc, and we finish by taking the party round the museum, and they see the history film.

There are certain exhibits in the museum which are permanent, but we change others every three months or so. Obviously, older players who aren't with us any more may have their shirts replaced by shirts belonging to more recent players like Bergkamp or Overmars. We keep updating, but then we will bring back shirts from players from previous days – the shirts are always in reserve and can be used again. We've got Ian Wright's shirt in the museum at the moment, but when he comes to the end of his career we may replace it by a shirt worn by Petit or Vieira, but we will still have it to bring back from time to time. Football is a living game, and we like to keep the museum that way, but you must never forget the past.

When you are first confronted by this huge open space, and you know you've got to fill it, it is very daunting, but, in the end, I got everything in there I wanted, and we just about ran out of space. We had to skip over one or two areas, and you are always going to have people saying, "I've got a particular favourite player, and you've only got one picture of him." If you take the Sixties, for example, it was not a particularly successful era, but we cover it although not in as great a detail as other periods.

The most important part of the museum is the history film which was put together for us by Chrysalis, the Football Italia team. Having visited a number of museums with their films and videos, I hit on the idea of having a cinema in our museum which would show either a continuous film or could show the film on request. Our film started at about twenty minutes, and now it's 23 because, obviously, there have been a few additions to it. It's similar to the films you see at art galleries which try to give another dimension to the exhibition only ours is a hugely condensed version of the Arsenal history. It's really crammed, but you can see that the fans get a real buzz when they watch it.

We try to cater for all the fans whatever their particular favourite era is. For the older fans who remember the 1936 Cup Final, we have the ball that was used in that Final; for the fans who remember the Fifties, we have the shirt belonging to Reg Lewis who scored both the goals that beat Liverpool; more recently, for those from the Seventies, Charlie George has some pieces on show. So, right the way through, we cater for all ages.

Children mostly enjoy things like the inter-active games, and there's a data base where they can call up information on all their favourite current players. That's an important item because, obviously, for the people who have been around a long time, all their information about them can be put up on the walls, but for those who are still playing it is best to have the information on a data base so that you can update it all the time.

For the younger children, we've even got part of a bus. When the club wins a trophy they usually do a tour of the streets on an open top bus that's been hired, and we've got cut out figures of people like Wright and Bergkamp, and the children can go up on top and have their pictures taken.

There is a nominal charge for going to the museum, £2 for adults and £1 for under-16s and over 65s, and this entrance money goes towards the upkeep of the museum. I have some part time help, and two others do stadium tours with me. When the

museum is open I have two or three assistants. Stadium tours were in operation before the museum opened, but they were not as frequent as they are now, never more than one or two a week and generally only by very special arrangement.

Everybody wants to see the dressing rooms, but, with the older fans, it's the board room which they like. We can't get in there if a meeting is going on, but it's open most of the time, and, for the older fans, the highlight is to sit in the chairman's chair and have their picture taken. Initially, they are often nervous about it, but when most people have wandered out they sit in the chair and have their photo taken very quickly, and they have that for posterity. There's no doubt that that's one of the most popular parts of the tour.

Working at Arsenal, you see them win, and lose, so much that you get used to it over the years. Those two Cup Final defeats in 1979-80 were very upsetting at the time, and it's always good to see them win, of course, but you become more objective. I don't get around football as much as I did. I used to go all over London to see a good game, but with Arsenal playing as well as they are, it's brilliant.

We haven't got an official statistician, and I try not to get bogged down in stats myself. Fred Ollier did the super record book, but last week I had a chap in who said Fred should have done the opposing sides as well as the Arsenal line-ups! It was hard enough for Fred to find out all the Arsenal line-ups and the amount of research he did was vast. The idea of having the opposing line-ups as well is frightening.

We get a lot of people phoning who think that they've found an item in their attic which is worth a fortune. Sadly, in most cases, it is not. Occasionally, people do come to see me with most interesting things. We don't deal in football programmes or football memorabilia ourselves, but we've often seen things of great interest, and we put the owners in touch with Christie's of Glasgow who have an auction about once a year. Sometimes people do discover something that is worth quite a bit, but it's rare. Certainly, pre-Wembley Cup Final programmes can fetch ridiculous prices. I think one went for £8,000 at Christie's last year.

At Arsenal, we've got bound sets of programmes going back to 1902-03. When you see Arsène Wenger giving his pre-match announcement on the big screen, the red binders behind him are those sets of programmes, and others are held in the managing director's office. They are kept in airtight conditions to preserve them. Before we moved to Highbury some records were lost so we can't always guarantee to answer the many queries we receive.

We are always looking to develop the museum, and this year, of course, we are making history. We have won the Premier League and so have qualified for the Champions League, and that is a major achievement. When we are doing well it brings even greater interest in the museum and the stadium. We have tourists arrive who just ask to look at the pitch.

We have pretty well everything covered in the museum. In one sense, we were lucky that we didn't win anything until 1930 because this means that we have been able to cover all the years of success. They are in living memory. At the end of a tour of the museum or the stadium, the visitors are always anxious to go to the shop to buy mementoes. The museum closes when the match begins, but I stay there for security reasons and watch the game on television. I am right underneath the North Bank so that I always know when anything happens by the noise from above. It's quite a peculiar feeling, rather surreal. In the years I was in the ticket office, I didn't see a game apart from the last twenty minutes, but, after being at

work for about a year, I always knew what was happening from the reaction of the crowd. I think those who work at the Arsenal, like the stewards, know that they have a job to do, and if they get to see the match, it's a bonus.

When the club is doing as well as it is at the moment we get a lot of requests for information. The press are always looking for links with the past. For example, before we met Wolves in the Cup semi-final, there were people who wanted to know what had happened to Alan Sunderland. He had scored against them when we last played them in the semi-final, and he did play for both clubs. We discovered that he was coaching in Malta. Brian Talbot helped us to find that out because he had spent some time managing out there.

Players don't come to the ground very often because they train in Hertfordshire, but they occasionally come to the museum. David Platt and Dennis Bergkamp wanted to be shown around when they first joined, and that often happens.

It is not surprising that players new to the club feel the need to absorb something of its history. The achievements and traditions of Arsenal impose that on players and supporters alike. It is part of the legacy, the expectation, of the Chapman/Allison era which most embrace willingly, but which some, as Lee Dixon has mentioned, find too great a burden. History can offer comfort as well as burden, and when Spurs went 2-0 up in the Cup semi-final at Wembley in 1991 there were those of us who consoled ourselves with remembering that Arsenal had been 2-0 down to both Chelsea and Stoke City in the Cup semi-finals of 1950 and 1971 and had gone on to win the trophy. As all will agonisingly recall, that was not to be the case in 1991.

That sense of the club's history is part of those of us for whom, as Pat Rice says, Arsenal is in the blood, and the museum that Iain Cook has lovingly and fascinatingly created underneath the North Bank can find parallels in many a "shrine" to Arsenal in several parts of the world. Some focus their attention on vast collections of programmes, photographs, posters and scarves; others decorate bedrooms and dens in red and white. Len Bourgaize has transformed his house into a monument to the club which he supports so fervently. He lives in Braye Road on the island of Guernsey. His house is named Highbury Cottage, flies the Union Jack on which the name Arsenal is inscribed and has a red and white blind over the downstairs front room window on which is written "The Gunners". A figure of an Arsenal footballer hangs in the window, and an Arsenal away shirt serves as curtains for the upstairs front room. In the front garden, stand two life-size figures. They are of Ian Wright and Dennis Bergkamp, but, as Iain Cook says of the Highbury museum, exhibits are inter-changeable.

Written records of Arsenal's history have proliferated with the years, and Iain Cook draws attention to Fred Ollier's magnificent *Arsenal: A Complete Record, 1886-1992* which was published by Breedon Books in 1992 and updated in 1995. As well as potted biographies of every player who has made a first-team appearance, the book records the eleven men – plus subs in recent years – who have taken the field for Arsenal in every match, including wartime, over a period of 106 years. It is a mighty piece of research, for the club's official handbook did not list team sheets, scorers etc, as it does today, until the 1937-38 edition. Its character has changed much in the years since the war, and the emphasis has moved from the literary to the statistical.

Programmes, too, have altered in that they now list a complete squad of 30 players rather than record the eleven that will take the field, and the editor tends to sweep more widely and generally over footballing topics than concentrate all on that day's match. There are, too, far more photographs – many in colour – which were far too costly in the immediate post-war years when "technology" was not a word found in everyone's vocabulary.

If programmes have moved with the times and with public taste so, too, have fanzines although the word "fanzine" did not exist when *Gunflash* was launched in 1950. *Gunflash* was, and is, the official magazine of the Arsenal Supporters' Club whose policy was "To help, not hinder". The officials and committee had that sprinkling of show business people who have always seemed to be attracted to Arsenal. Dance band leader Billy Ternent was the

Len Bourgaize has transformed his house in Guernsey into a monument to the Arsenal. "Highbury Cottage" flies the Union Jack on which the name Arsenal is inscribed and has a red and white blind over the downstairs front room window on which is written 'The Gunners'. A figure of an Arsenal footballer hangs in the window, and an Arsenal away shirt serves as curtains for the upstairs front room.

president, and impresario and dance band leader Jack Hylton, holiday camp founder Billy Butlin and comedian Cardew "The Cad" Robinson were among the vice-presidents. The Supporters' Club and the magazine were centred then, as now, at 154 St Thomas's Road.

Initially, *Gunflash* was concerned mainly with giving information on ticket prices and travel arrangements to away matches. It also carried articles which ranged from pieces on those who worked behind the scenes at Highbury to comments on the transfer system by a journalist from a national newspaper and a series on famous football clubs. There was also evidence of links between the Arsenal club and supporters and the first Celebrity XI which played Sunday matches to raise money for charity. Anthony Newley, Pete Murray, Mike and Bernie Winters and Bernard Bresslaw were among the stars of the day to play in these matches which were often refereed by Tommy Docherty. The magazine was published monthly from August to May and was fourteen pages in between covers which carried advertisements and announcements. There was a generous supply of black and white photographs. The magazine was free to members of whom there were nearly 29,000 in 1962.

Competition and rising prices have, inevitably, brought changes, but *Gunflash* is still published monthly during the playing season, has doubled in size and has a good supply of colour photographs. It is still kept alive by voluntary labour under the dynamic editorship of Barry Hatch, easily recognisable on match days from the flamboyant clothes which announce that he is an Arsenal supporter. Eager that more and more fans should know about the magazine, he has seen that it has a page on the internet, and he has investigated why, with such a strong contingent of supporters in Norway, there are only twelve subscribers from that country. He found that there was a problem in currency exchange which meant that the Norwegians were paying an extra £10 on their subscription. He solved the problem by opening a bank account in Norway into which the supporters could pay their subscriptions which would later be transferred to England at no additional cost. In 1998, a subscription for eight issues cost £16 at home and £22 in the rest of Europe, but the magazine is ever striving to be self sufficient, and an increase of £2 is likely to come in the near future.

Today's *Gunflash* includes match reports, comment and news, and there is a firm editorial belief in the club itself that routs those who have moments of doubt. Interestingly, the 444th issue, which was published in March 1998, included a letter from a Norwegian fan, Tony Liavik, and a contribution from D.R. Brown of Leicestershire who is registered as Supporters' Club member no. 70,409, but one doubts if that number remains active. The years pass.

Following a game at White Hart Lane, in which Arsenal had gone a goal down in the first minute and had come back to win 2-1, came another fanzine which, by its name, reflected the events of that match. This publication was joined by *Highbury Hill* and *The Gooner*.

The Gooner published its 84th issue in January 1998, and is noted for its forthright views. Editor Mike Francis maintains good literary standards and is rightly critical of tabloid newspapers who give much time to the invention of transfer rumours and tales of unrest, dissent and the fans' disenchantment with the club. The magazine, which is attractively produced, runs to 44 pages, contains some colour photographs and sells for £1.50. It is not without humour, which is refreshing,

and is particularly severe on Tottenham Hotspur, which some find equally refreshing. Its quality of immediacy is also its greatest liability, and severe and ill-judged criticisms levelled at Arsène Wenger, Nigel Winterburn and Chris Wreh at the start of 1998 must have made highly embarrassing reading for their authors in May. And does one really give credibility to a writer who describes Kevin Campbell, 60 goals for Arsenal's first team and a vital contributor to the winning of the championship in 1991, as "completely devoid of talent" and one of "the imbeciles chosen to wear the red and white shirt"? This is the very stuff of the tabloid press of which editor Mike Francis is so critical. Much has changed for the better since 1946. There have been significant developments in many directions, but no Arsenal player or manager suffered such vitriolic or unjust criticism at the hands of "supporters" in the late Forties and early Fifties. There were favourites, and there were failures, but even those dire days in the mid-Fifties when two very useful centre-forwards, Goring and Holton, were playing at right and left-half, none was written of as an "imbecile... completely devoid of talent". That is the ill-considered use of language of the last years of the century, something that the footballer of today is forced to live with.

The fanzine is, of course, divorced from the club itself although in the Sixties, and for several years afterwards, *Gunflash* advertised the only form of merchandise that was related to Arsenal and was sold by the Supporters' Club. The most expensive item was a car or motor cycle badge which cost 25s (£1.25). You could buy a blazer badge, silk wire and silk embroidered, for 21s (£1.05), and a silk, navy blue tie with gold guns would cost you 17s 6d (87½p). At the lower end of the market was a pennant for your bike at 1s 9d (approximately 9p) and a ball-point pen with "Arsenal" embossed in gold on a red barrel which was priced at 2/6 (12½p) or a red and white pencil for 6d (2½p). In all, there were some thirteen items offered for sale, with, inevitably, scarves and rosettes dominating. It was to be more than a quarter of a century before the full potential of marketing merchandise related to Arsenal Football Club was to be fully realised. In his years with Arsenal, John Jensen was quick to see that the commercial department was a vital and integral part of the financial structure of the club.

Regarding players, the set-up was based on the team as a whole, and not on star players as it is at many other clubs. The wage structure reflected this. There was a continuity between older and younger players, and older players were never discarded. There was a great sense of respect in everything Arsenal did.

The players were also asked to contribute to the school football scheme and to do autograph sessions at the shop. This was all part of being a player and was obviously a part of the massive market that exists off the football pitch. I felt that the commercial department were just as professional as everybody else at Arsenal.

There had been a shop in operation at Arsenal Stadium for some time before World of Sport opened at Finsbury Park in time for the 1990-91 season. Totally aware that it was essential to expand the marketing facilities of the club, David Dein had the vision to earmark the individual railway arcade close to Finsbury Park Station as a flagship retail shop, and it was John Hazell who was chosen to lead in the development of the new commercial department although, as with everything at Highbury, success is ever the result of team work.

John Hazell had always been an Arsenal supporter and arrived at Highbury with the experience that was necessary for the job.

I had a clothing, merchandising, leisure wear type background. I'd always been on that side of the business. Before I came to Arsenal I used to run a jeans company called Lois Jeans. They are Spanish, and I ran their UK subsidiary for seven years. Before that I had worked for Marlboro Leisure Wear, associated with the racing team. I also used to handle Kappa, the famous Italian leisure wear company, who were kit sponsors for Barcelona, so I had a valuable grounding in the marketing and merchandise and business, and I simply applied for the job at Arsenal like anyone else. It was advertised in

Marketing Weekly and *The Sunday Times*, and the post was there because the club wanted to develop the new commercial department. It was also a help that I had had experience of perimeter advertising, and I had played football myself. I played for Watford a little bit when I left school, and then I played senior amateur stuff so that the game has always interested me.

There were great opportunities for commercial development in several areas. As I have said, my background had been the leisure industry, and the target market was the people who were coming here on a Saturday afternoon. I felt they wanted things to be more subtle, a bit more interesting than they had been. Times had changed, and they were perhaps more fashion conscious than in the past. It was our job to respond to what we saw as a demand. We have developed a tremendous amount in what we sell, but we always test things first.

Take a look at our catalogue. There is training gear, rucksacks, shoe bags, baseball caps, T-shirts, swimwear for ladies and men, pyjamas, babygrows, bibs and a host of other clothing as well as lamps, clocks, watches, bath towels, teddy bears, key rings, shampoo, deodorant and, of course, anything and everything to do with the playing side of Arsenal Football Club. If there is a product on the market and that product is as good a quality as any other on the market and not more expensive, then we would probably consider it. All that we ask is a quality product.

We seldom have a sale because there is nothing to reduce. Maybe at the end of a season if the kit is being changed we will sometimes clear out stock of the old kit and offer to the fans at cost price.

Today, it is demand that tells us what to sell. I don't agree with the bad press that you sometimes see given to replica kits. They remain our best sellers, and I would say that I have been at Highbury for nearly nine years, and, in that time, I could count on one or two hands the letters of complaint I have had, but I can show you cabinets full of letters from fans who say, "Why don't you change the kit every year?"

We change the kit every two years, which we think is fair, but we get some mums who write to us and ask, "How do you expect this shirt to last for two years? He's grown out of it." Mums also say that they don't find them expensive because the kids are never out of them. They are good value for money, and we, the retailer, make less profit on a replica shirt than we do on other merchandise, and, at the end of the day, that profit doesn't go the shareholders or anybody else. It is reinvested into the club for better facilities, new players etc.

We are selective in what we endorse. We have been asked, but we have refused to endorse things like cigarettes and tobacco.

We produce a catalogue of merchandise twice a year now. We pioneered that as a club, and we have mailed out more than 200,000 catalogues this year. It is the catalogue which set the mail order business going, and we set up a data base. Mail orders this year have been phenomenal.

All aspects of modern technology are now at our disposal. Sam Hill-Wood, one of the Arsenal family, came down from university and was with us for a while. He got us on the internet, set up the web site, and we've got the best web site in the business now, certainly the best football web site. We are now selling merchandise through the web site.

We are always looking to develop, to do more things. I still keep a very close contact with the fashion business, and I changed from the traditional football wholesalers, souvenir wholesalers, to the type of manufacturer who was active in the fashion trade because the target market is the fifteen to 25 age range,

and they are people who want to be wearing nice, fashionable, competitively priced clothing. So the first thing I did through my connections with the leisure business was to go to people who were making for Next, River Island and other high street stores. I never considered going to football people, and I think that now we've probably got the best innovative range of leisure clothing for the very reason that we go to the people who make for Next etc, and they're only too happy to have Arsenal on their portfolio.

Our suppliers have to be flexible because we don't take any risks at Arsenal. Without the benefit of a crystal ball, I don't know what is going to sell. You never know in the football business, and our suppliers have to be flexible whenever we select a line. They have got to make minimums, and they have got to be able to react immediately to the repeat business. When the catalogue goes out you know, within two or three weeks, that all the minimums will sell, but, with a T-shirt, for example, you never know, and you only ever print a hundred to start with. We had a T-shirt that started with 100 and sold 10,000. We don't build up a huge stock straight away.

The retail alone for Arsenal this year is going to be around five million pounds. It's growing all the time. On the licensing side, I would guess that we are generating fifteen million pounds in addition to our five. That isn't reflected in our figures, but that's a lot of money. The big slice, of course, is from Nike, which is a sponsorship agreement, but they also have a licensing agreement to sell our shirts, replica kit and related training wear. That is the biggest licensing agreement, but there are many other products on the market now. There is even Arsenal milk. We did a deal with Dairy Crest. The milk is less expensive than milk in the supermarkets, it's the same quality and there are advantages in the packaging, so again it is beneficial to our supporters.

There are three club shops – the Gunners Shop, the North Bank Shop and, of course, World of Sport – and they are always packed, especially on match days, which are obviously the best days, when we probably do 40 per cent of our turnover, but we are also very busy in midweek.

There is now an official Arsenal magazine, and this is the result of a new licensing agreement with Northern and Shell. When you consider that the price of the magazine is £2.50, and the circulation is already 40,000 a month that's another million pounds a year turn-over.

In our marketing, we never lose sight of the fact that our greatest asset is the eleven players on the field. In my years, I've been very lucky. I joined in 1989, and we won the League title, and then we won six different trophies under George Graham. In the time I've been here, we've either won a Cup or been in a Final or qualified for Europe. If ever we got on a bad run or, God forbid, if Arsenal were relegated, I don't know how long that would take to reflect income for the club. I would guess even in the worst scenario we would still have a hard core 20,000. You can see with West Ham that, however good or bad they are doing, they always get a crowd of 17,000 to 18,000. The popularity of the club is definitely reflected in our turnover. We are living in an age when people want success.

Replica shirts, as I have said, are our best sellers. They account for 30-35 per cent of our turnover, but books and videos do well. They are licensing agreements. The days of producing match videos are gone, but we do a compilation each quarter – four a season. The video of Ian Wright's record goalscoring achievement sold phenomenally well as, obviously, did the end-of-season video, 1998.

Players are co-operative in helping

us to promote the merchandise catalogue, and I think there are something like twenty players involved in this latest catalogue. It's a fine art now. It's all shot within a two-hour period. There was a time when we used to go to the training ground and do outside shots and move around, but that was too time consuming, and now we set up a studio at London Colney, and they come in, are snapped and out again.

With regard to the hospitality boxes at the Clock End, we have hospitality managers to look after them on match days. Originally, they were sold on ten-year leases, and they are all sold. There are none available for hire. The leases have another year to run, and there's a waiting list a mile long to buy them. It was one of my first jobs to sell the boxes, and, initially, we decided to keep ten back for hiring, but they gradually got sold, and the demand is such that they are increasing in value all the time.

The mail order department is growing all the time. This is reflected in the growth of our data base and sales from the web site, but we want to develop our mail order service even more. Let us look at the Arsenal supporter who lives in Stevenage and can't get to the ground – we want him to buy from our mail order company as opposed to going to the local sports shop. There are Arsenal supporters all round the world, not just in the UK, and they have to have the facility for purchasing.

We are looking for more outlets for selling our merchandise, principally in Central London. We have been looking for some time, but it has to be in the right position – Carnaby Street, Oxford Street, Piccadilly, maybe – somewhere like that. Rents are high, and we have to select carefully.

We don't sanction the street traders who sell T-shirts with unpleasant messages written on them, but they are becoming fewer in number, and we do supply street traders who have licenses from Islington Council. They are not the ones who sell in front gardens behind brick walls. Counterfeiting is a problem for the club, particularly around the ground on match days, but Arsenal do supply "official" street traders with license papers.

A more recent problem and development has been the relaying of important away matches to be screened at Highbury. This mainly comes under the province of Ken Friar, but it involves the stadium manager and permission has to be granted by neighbouring clubs and programmes brought from the "home" club.

I have a commercial page in the programme for each of our home matches, but the programme comes mainly under the control of Claire Tomlinson, a new and important appointment as Head of Communications.

One of our most recent innovations has been the launching of the Arsenal affinity card, a credit card in association with the Bank of Scotland. We waited until we could get the best deal, the best interest rates for our supporters before issuing the card. The funds raised by the card go towards Arsenal's youth development programme. It is our investment in the future.

One feels that the Arsenal credit card will prove to be as successful as all the other recent innovations have been, for they are all based on the principle of providing the supporter with something that is beneficial both to him and to the club. Crowds in excess of 10,000 have come to Highbury to watch Arsenal playing at St James's Park or Old Trafford, with the game being transmitted live on to the big screen. There is a wonderful feeling of togetherness, and "virtual reality" is enhanced by the sale of official programmes for the match.

The vibrant activities of the commercial department have transformed a Saturday afternoon or Tuesday evening at Highbury. Where once you looked out on a crowded mass of grey, you now survey a North Bank which is a sea of red. Where once the clock stood rather bleak and lonely, you now view a compact structure, warm and embracing. The stadium has long a grand place steeped in history. For

some, on first meeting, it had the awe of a cathedral; for others, it had the splendour of a great theatre. Now, it is a place of wonder. The red seats, adorned with a white cannon and the name of the club, the red and white and yellow replica shirts worn by men and women, many no longer in the first flush of youth, have moved history from black and white into technicolour. By 1998, Highbury was a place on which to feast your eyes.

Claire Tomlinson, a graduate experienced in public relations and in working for the Football Association, together with her assistant, Amanda Docherty, is responsible for the arrangement of press conferences and interviews for manager and players and for seeing that true, rather than bogus, information is broadcast by the media. This is not always an easy task, and it often occupies Claire and Amanda late into the evening. The world of sport has ever been a world of false rumour, and the appointment of a competent communications officer who was versed in dealing with intelligent and perceptive journalists was as wise as it was important. The appointments reflect, too, the increasing role that women have come to play in the administration of Arsenal. This was not the case 50 years ago, and the administrative success has been mirrored on the field where Arsenal Ladies, under the stewardship of Vic Akers, have swept all before them in recent years. League champions in 1996-97, they had to be content with two Cups in 1998. The technical quality of their play is outstanding, and they have been a major force in the battle to have women's football taken as seriously in England as it is on the continent.

If Chapman, Allison or Whittaker might have been surprised to see Arsenal Ladies in action at Highbury, they would have been less surprised that the club attracts celebrity support. That has remained constant, but where once there was Cardew Robinson, Jack Hylton and Dai Rees, there is now Clive Anderson, Melvyn Bragg and Frankie Dettori. In other areas, there have been significant changes, none more so than in the development, training and treatment of young players. Since the Bosman ruling, a comprehensive youth policy has become of prime importance to any ambitious football club.

Youth and Care in the Community

BRIAN Talbot is not only senior coach at Rushden and Diamonds where he is working hard to win them a place in the Football League, he also acts for the Football Association in looking a youth schemes that clubs in the London area are developing. He is emphatic in his response to the way in which Arsenal are facing the challenge.

David Dein brought Liam Brady back to produce youngsters for Arsenal. My team is the Arsenal. I support the Arsenal. I don't have a bad weekend if they lose any more. I am disappointed. I think, having been a professional footballer, I have a bad weekend if Rushden and Diamonds lose, but my lad is thirteen, and he plays for Arsenal Under-14s. Arsenal are spending millions on their youth policy. They've got Liam Brady and David Court at the top. They've got great responsibility. I know Brady is working very hard, and he's got a good name. He is a good figurehead with a good, clean image. It's a brilliant appointment for Arsenal.

Arsenal have a school now at Hyam's Park. It costs them £25,000 a kid. They wanted my son, but we turned it down for him because we thought it was best for him to stay with his pals and play for his school and for Hertfordshire and have a normal education. If he's good enough when he's sixteen, he'll still come through.

They train every day as well as doing normal lessons. It's very well organised, but we thought it was better for our lad to be able to play golf when he wants to, to be told off by his mum, to go to the cinema with his mates, to play in the garden and all the rest. If he's good enough when he's sixteen, he'll have another fifteen years of aggravation and pressure, so let him have an ordinary life until then. You've got to enjoy your childhood while you can. It's over too soon.

Liam Brady covers millions of miles in his search for young players who might one day become good enough to wear the red and white. It is a demanding job, but, as he says:

I was delighted eventually to come back to the Arsenal. This is a very time consuming job, and it's a very tough job on my family. I wouldn't do it for anyone else.

I couldn't quantify the number of youngsters I see each year – hundreds of thousands. I go and watch youth tournaments all over the world. I'm going to France next week, probably Scotland after that and then Greece in the summer. Africa is producing good footballers, but I doubt whether they will come here because we have strict employment laws, and, unless they've played so many times for the national team, we can't get them, so we can't really bring in youngsters. If we could, I'd be going to Africa as well. In

Europe we are safe because of the Treaty of Rome. We have a seventeen-year-old boy here who we got from just outside Paris.

What I'm looking for in a youngster is a wide range of things. Principally, you're looking for ability. You want to see that they can play the game, that they've got technique, that they can dribble the ball, that they've got awareness. There are very many others factors, like personality, attitude, whether they want to win hard enough, physical strength; the game has gone that way these days, you've got be physically strong.

There are many ingredients that make up a footballer. You can't give a boy speed, but you can improve it. Courage you can't give to anybody. Attitude is helped when they see the whole set up at the club. We breed good standards. They know very early on that if their attitude is not right, they're not going to have a future here.

I'm in charge of the Youth Development scheme, and David Court is my assistant. Don Howe is in charge of the coaching of the young boys. I don't interfere with that. I bring in the youngsters, and Don Howe, Donal Givens and Neil Banfield do the coaching. There is no better person than Don Howe to be doing this job. He is one of the very best coaches in the world, and to have him working with the youngsters is a tremendous asset to the club. He has lost none of his enthusiasm.

There have been lots of changes since I first joined the club at the age of fifteen. There's much more for the players now with little things like the diet being so much better than it was in my day. We used to have eggs, chips and beans, and all that's gone out of the window. They have pasta and boiled fish – we try to educate them to look after themselves properly. That's what I see as my job here, or a very essential part of it, to make sure they grow up to be good professionals and look after themselves. They do that

right from the start, from the time that I bring them in because that's the best time to get them.

We set standards for them from the beginning. On match days, for example, it's club dress – collar and tie or club track suit if they are travelling.

The YTS system, I think, created finance for clubs and encouraged them to take boys on. Unfortunately, a lot of clubs went for quantity rather than quality, but that didn't happen at Arsenal. I'd like to think that any boy we take on has a chance to make the grade because that's what we believe. A large percentage of them are not going to go on and play in Arsenal's first team, but when we take them on at fifteen or sixteen we believe that they have a chance of doing so.

Another thing that has changed is that we educate the youngsters in ways other than football because we know there is going to be a fall out. We have a GNVQ course in Leisure and Tourism, and they go to study every Monday. It was optional in my day. You could go to school if you wanted to. There wasn't the same obligation on the club to try to give the boy an alternative background should football not work out for him. Today, and I believe rightly so, there is more and more onus on us to do something for the boys, to educate them properly in things like diet that will stand them in good stead for the rest of their lives, regardless of whether they play football or not. We do give them principles here.

In the late Sixties and Seventies, at the time when Liam Brady first arrived at Highbury as a youngster, Bertie Mee, who had first served Arsenal as physiotherapist before becoming the manager who recaptured the glory days, travelled far and wide in an attempt to find young players who might, one day, graduate to the first team.

I drove 40,000 miles a year in search of players, and I saw my youth team every Saturday morning. I knew my youth players better than my first team because they were the ones I concentrated on. One statistic – inevitably, because of the type of background I had, I had to keep statistics in relation to the treatment of injury, recovery periods, how long the recovery period was for a hamstring strain, sprained ankle, or what you will – but even more important statistically was the number of players you saw in order to recruit one first-team player.

Let's go back to the beginning. You have a scouting organisation right throughout the country, looking at young players, schoolboys. That scouting organisation sees 4,000 schoolboy games. Let's make it simple and say there are twenty players on the pitch. Multiply 4,000 by 20, you get 80,000. So, in any one season, you see 80,000 young players. Out of that number you invite 40 down in the school holidays, half-term, to look at and decide whether they are going to be good enough, and out of those 40, you recruit ten, your YTS boys. Of these ten, five make the first team. In other words, you see 16,000 youngsters in order to recruit one Premier League player.

It's a frightening statistic. It's a very hard thing to do, to terminate, to say "cheerio" to a YTS boy who arrived at sixteen with stars in his eyes, who had come in dreaming. Occasionally, one or two slip through the net, but it's very rare. If a lad hasn't got it, he hasn't got it, and that's that. There are certain players who, if they work hard, will improve. Pat Rice is a very good example, but they are few and far between.

Don Howe was coach under Bertie Mee and again, later, under Terry Neill, and he returned to Arsenal for his third spell at the start of the 1997-98 season, his appetite for the game undiminished.

I had been working for the past three years, and coaching youngsters is not really any different from coaching first-team players. You've got to be a little more patient. These boys have to be coached like professional players because that is what they are going to be. The sooner they work like first-team players the better. I don't think I was tough with the first-team players. I said what I felt I had to say now and again. I don't like swearing. I don't like anything negative said to them. I've got two coaches I work with, Donal Givens and Neil Banfield, and I always say you can criticise the kids as long as you are constructive with them. You say, "Son, don't do that, do this!" As long as you do that, you're OK, and that's what we try to do with the young boys. The problem is only there with players when you say, "Don't do that!" and stop there.

At this club, you demand that they play well. You demand that they apply themselves. You demand that they are disciplined. I think that they are better off for that. A lot of people say, "No, you've got to give them a lot of free expression." If you do that, they will just take the easy way of doing things. I think they are better off and appreciate it if you say, "Now, I want to see you doing this." Everybody needs guidance.

The system is that Liam goes all over the place and finds the youngsters, and they start at our centre of excellence, which will be an academy next year. So we have this school where a certain amount of our kids go for their education and, obviously, for football coaching. At the age of sixteen, when they're leaving school, they come here, and it's handed over to us, but they do have an early period of work and coaching at our centre of excellence from the age of nine upwards. The centre of excellence is at Highbury where we have all age groups – eight, nine, ten, eleven, right the way through, and the ones who are good enough become YTS boys and are handed over to us.

I'm enjoying this as much as any job I've done. It's a very enjoyable job. I am very aware of the responsibility of the job because the kids have got to be treated right. We have to give them guidance with their parents because they can be exploited if you want to exploit them. They can't turn round and say, "What are we doing this for?" Kids will do as they're told. They're pretty good in that way. So I do realise, in the circumstances, I've got to get the job done right, and I'm for ever looking at myself rather than at the kids, and I'm saying to myself, "The trust that these parents have given to me and the trust I've got with these kids, am I getting it right? Am I giving them a fair crack of the whip to make the grade?"

We've got 25 youngsters at the moment, and they're not all going to make it. Some kids come at first, not so good, and gradually start to improve; others come who are impressive but somehow it's not registering, and they start to fall away. You can tell after six months, twelve months, two years… You have to make a decision after two years as to whether you are offering them a pro contract or whether you let them go. For instance, this year, we've let six go, and it's a little bit heart-breaking because they are nice kids, and I've got to know them. They're not scallywags. They're nice kids who've been great with me, and I've tried to be great with them as well. I don't like it. That's the hard part, but it's got to be done. It's the professional side of any job.

Happily, they are trained for other things. When the academy started they had to go to school, and further education is going to be an important part of the new academies. They will have to continue their education so, should it be that they don't get pro contracts, they've got something else. They can go off to university perhaps. They can get a qualification for other jobs. They can get "A" Levels. They can do that now, which is a terrific thing.

They are training, too, for a coaching licence, and while working for that, they are doing laws of the game, first aid and other things. This means that if they shouldn't get a pro contract here, these boys could, perhaps, get a scholarship in America with this qualification. It opens things up for them. They're not thrown out on the scrap heap at the end of it.

It's very different from when I started. You spent a lot of your time sweeping the dressing room and cleaning boots. If you weren't given a pro contract, it was, "See you again, son. Cheers." And nobody was really interested in you. Today, I think there are a lot more people with a lot more thought about these young players than there used to be. If they don't get a pro contract here, they are going to be able to say, "That's not the end of things. I've got this, and I've got this, and I've got this."

One of the main reasons for Don Howe working on the youth development side at Arsenal is his conviction that all successful sides have a large percentage of home-grown players. He cites the Double side of 1971 with men like George, Rice, Simpson, Armstrong and Radford; and Neill's side which reached four Cup Finals in three years with Brady, O'Leary and Nelson, all of whom had come to the club as youngsters. The Graham era, too, was founded on Tony Adams, Paul Davis, Michael Thomas, Paul Merson and David Rocastle who had all come through the youth scheme.

When there has been success at this club it has come through the development of youngsters rather than through the cheque book. Even the young players who have been brought in today, like Anelka, are here to develop, and it's wonderful if you can bring in lads who are eighteen or nineteen. You are breeding for the future, and that's good management.

When Nicolas Anelka joined Arsenal from Paris St Germain in February 1997, he was still a month short of his eighteenth birthday, and few would have thought that the shy, introverted youngster would be scoring the deciding goal in the FA Cup Final little more than a year later. He impressed reserve-team manager George Armstrong who, initially sceptical, was genuinely surprised by the talent he witnessed.

Nicolas Anelka, for a kid, has got

YOUTH AND CARE IN THE COMMUNITY

more ability than any one I've ever seen, but that's not everything. Football intelligence, passion, desire, he still has to convince about those qualities because he's a young man in a strange land. Arsène Wenger brought him here, and, to be fair to the gaffer, I couldn't believe it when I first saw Anelka – he's quick, two good feet, good passer, dribbler, and he scored a lot of goals for me. But when he went up a level I think what we hadn't realised is that he's still a baby in the game, and a baby in a strange land. A boy like Michael Owen has been brought up in the nitty-gritty English way which Nicolas is still learning. Owen would be the same if he was in France, but Nicolas has the ability. With regard to technique, he's got it all.

I know how important it is to bring on young players, that's my responsibility with my reserves, but I know their capabilities. I'm not going to put somebody into a key position if he's not up to it. I know that you never know until you try, but I want to help a kid. I don't want him to go into a team and struggle. I want him to go into an environment where he can show what he's good at.

When I first went into the Arsenal first team, Blackpool away, I was nervous, of course I was nervous, but I didn't think, "Oh, we've got to win today." As it was, we won 1-0, and I remember crossing the ball, and Geoff Strong scoring the goal. It was great, but then I went out of the team, and that was right. Let a youngster have three or four games and then take him out. If you leave him in, you can destroy him, or he can become complacent. No one likes to be left out of the team, but it's the way it's done.

I think the main change since I joined the club is that there is more influence from upstairs, but this is understandable because of the sponsorship, the marketing, television and all other financial aspects which are part of the game now. The other

main development is the youth policy, and we've got to go along with that because that's the only way forward, and I think Liam will do well. Give the lad a chance, he loves the club as we all do, and he will get it right.

One of the early Arsenal youth policies was to send some newcomers to the nursery club at Margate, but that was a fate that Laurie Scott avoided.

There were a few players at Arsenal I didn't even get to know because there were fifteen or sixteen down at Margate. When I first went down I was in digs at Southgate, and I was with Mel Griffiths who'd been down at Margate and who did play a couple of games for Wales.

Alex James was still around when I got to Arsenal, and he used to take the youngsters like myself, three or four of us, to do special ball control business, and, of course, he was the right man to do it. He was a wonderful ball control person and could read the game. I couldn't believe what he could do.

He'd have me at full-back, not in a game but in practice, against Cliff Bastin. When an inside-forward hit a ball to the winger you, as a full-back, had to make up your mind whether you can get this ball if it's coming over the top or, if you can't get it, you turn round and go back and try to cover. Not with Alex. You thought you could get this ball, but it went straight through your hair. It was incredible. Things like that were so difficult to understand when you first got to Arsenal. To me, Alex James was the perfect player, but I used to get fed up with him.

We used to train at the college which used to be at the Clock End, and, as I said, he took the youngsters for ball control. He'd have us throw the ball up against the back of the clock. There was a concrete wall there. We had to throw it against the wall and kill it when it rebounded. He'd have us doing it for hours. He could pull it down from anywhere. He was incredible. I've got a lot to thank Alex

ARSENAL IN THE BLOOD

for really. He did me a lot of good in
ball control, and, in top-grade
football, you've got to be the winner of
the ball first. The opposition doesn't
mean anything unless you can control
the ball, so you've got to make sure
that you control the ball, and it's got to
come automatic. It's got to be natural.
You don't have to worry about it.

By the time Arthur Milton had completed
his National Service, Arsenal's youngsters had
been relocated.

We young lads went to Hendon.
When we came back out of the forces
a lot of us used to go up there under
Ernie Collett and George Male, and we
used to play in the Eastern Counties
League, Lowestoft, Yarmouth, King's
Lynn and all up there. I came down
now and again, but I was stationed at
Chilwell, RAOC depot, most of the
time. We used to play in the Notts
Thursday League. We had a profess-
ional side almost.

George Male and Ernie Collett were
right characters when they looked
after us in the Eastern Counties
League. If we lost, they wouldn't buy
us a drink coming home. That's the
time we really needed it.

I think you really have to learn the
game yourself. You watch good players
play and take what you can from them
into your game, what suits you own
temperament and capabilities. I could
really play when I was in the cradle. It
is just something that is in you. We are
all born with a certain amount of
talent but the rest of it depends on
what you've got in your head and
heart. The really greats have got it all,
try all the time, which is difficult when
you're doing something day in day
out. It becomes work.

Arsenal had signed Freddie Cox
from Tottenham, and he kept scoring
the odd goal and was a sort of good
luck charm, but I started in March
1951, against Aston Villa on my 23rd
birthday. We beat them 2-1. They were
struggling at the time. They were
languishing at the bottom, and there
were fears that they would get

relegated, but they got out of it. I
always remember I had a 50-50 ball
with Con Martin, and he went right
over the top and I had six stud marks
on my thigh. I didn't do any damage to
my knee, but it was very sore. I was
fortunate. He played everywhere, even
in goal. They had a couple of brothers,
and Dicky Dorsett, I remember, he
played.

Laurie Scott has spoken of youngsters being
coached by Alex James in an area behind the
Clock End, and, for many years, this part of the
stadium offered a training space before the
move to London Colney in the Fifties. In 1988,
the Clock End was redeveloped, but the seating
and appealing hospitality boxes, which are all
that are on view to the public, conceal another
aspect of a significant addition to life at
Highbury, the club's vital and continuing
contribution to the life of the local community.

Behind the hospitality boxes are administrative offices for the vice-chairman, commercial department and others. Beneath these
is the Arsenal Sports Centre, built at a cost of
£1.5 million and offering the highest quality
facilities to the local community for seven days
a week, fourteen hours a day. The indoor sports
hall is able to provide soccer pitches, tennis
courts, a bowls rink and a hockey pitch and is
used by local schools for sports lessons within
the curriculum and for extra-curricula
activities such as competitions and inter-house
tournaments. There are after-school clubs from
3.45pm to 6.00pm every week day, and two
sessions of bowls a week are enjoyed by the
more senior members of the community.

Friday evening after school is reserved for a
girls-only football session as befits the club
who were the first from the Premier League to
enter a team in the Women's Football Association Premier League, which was the only ladies'
side to have a full-time professional coach. The
development of soccer for women and girls is a
top priority for Arsenal.

The lunchtime seven-a-side adult football
league involves 22 teams from local business,
council offices, colleges and community
projects, and Sunday sees the veterans in action
with 34 teams of over-35s competing in three
divisions.

On Saturday mornings, during the school
holidays and at half-term, the Sports Centre is

one of several venues for Arsenal Soccer Schools where thousands of children learn and improve their soccer skills, but the involvement with the local community is not restricted to events at the Sports Centre itself. Arsenal's local primary schools sports initiative sees members of the sports staff and trainees conduct sports lessons with the older pupils at twelve local primary schools. This scheme has been in operation for more than a decade, and the skills in which the Arsenal staff instruct the youngsters include hockey, cricket and mini-tennis as well as soccer.

From Chapman's time, the club have been wonderfully supportive of what is now the Islington-Camden Schools Football Assoc-iation. Arsenal have given financial aid, kit and equipment and have provided transport, coaching and management support. Highbury has been the venue for important matches staged by the Islington-Camden SFA, and, in 1997, hosted the second leg of the Final of the English Schools Trophy which, sadly, Islington-Camden lost 5-1 after beating Liverpool 2-0 at Goodison Park four days earlier.

The club's support is not restricted to schools in the immediate area of the stadium, for, more recently, Arsenal have launched a programme in Brent secondary schools aimed at encouraging senior pupils to organise five-a-side soccer for juniors and to be given instruction in the administration, coaching, managing and refereeing of the game.

This initiative was launched at Cardinal Hinsley RC school by Remi Garde in 1997, and the French international has also helped to instigate a programme aimed at stimulating youngsters to learn French. Visits to schools by Arsenal's contingent of French players is to act as a focus for the programme.

Back at the centre, there are facilities for meetings, courses and fitness sessions, and, among those who utilise these facilities is the Metro Sports Club, for blind and partially-sighted people, who hold an annual Fun Day with the help of Alan Sefton's staff and trainees. For nearly a decade, the Arsenal Sports Centre has been the focus of an inner city hockey development programme, and youngsters who have attended after-school sessions can graduate to the Loughtonian Gunners who are attached to Old Lough-tonians, one of England's top hockey clubs.

Five players under seventeen have already tasted first-team National Hockey after developing their talents through the programme.

While sport is, inevitably, the core of the centre's activities, it is the social emphasis which is revolutionary. The club has been fervent supporters of the Islington Education Authority anti-truancy drive, a campaign to encourage and reward 100 per cent attendance at school. Every secondary school pupil who attains this target receives a certificate from Arsenal Football Club which is signed by the players. The club has also donated prizes for the project, and Tony Adams was guest of honour at Islington Town Hall when the campaign was launched.

Once a week, the centre hosts a football coaching session for clients who have been referred by the Social Services and other support groups. This project was instigated by Islington Probation Service and Divert. The object of the sessions is to assist in rehabil-itation, and several of those who have participated have been able to gain football coaching qualifications which have enabled them to find work in the community.

The Sports Centre was one of the first to be accredited as a National Vocational Qualific-ation Centre in Leisure and Recreation. The Sports Centre has its own staff trained as verifiers and assessors, and, each year, some 30 young people, both school leavers and unemployed, are trained for a career in leisure management and coaching. They are trained to NVQ Level Three and are given practical working experience in the community.

At every first-team match at Highbury, one can see messages flashed on the electronic notice boards which welcome people who are visiting the stadium for the first time or which simply give birthday wishes or congratulations of some kind. To get such a message screened, one must contact Beverley Nicholas, the lively and cheerful guardian of the Sports Centre and part-administrator of the NVQ project, who will accept the message on payment of a small donation to the Arsenal Charitable Trust.

The Trust was founded in 1992 and has now raised nearly half a million pounds for charity with money distributed each year to local causes and nominated charities. Money has been raised in a variety of ways including from the method mentioned above, from quiz nights, from runners in the London Marathon wearing the red and white of Arsenal and from charity football matches. Foremost among these are the games played by the Arsenal Ex-Professional and Celebrity team. As we said earlier, celebrity teams associated with the club were taking the field in the Fifties, but never on quite the organised basis of today's team under Freddie Hudson. The side plays matches at the request of a charity who will receive 70 per cent of the proceeds; the other 30 per cent will go to the Arsenal Charitable Trust. The club and player input, of course, comes free.

For Arsenal to contribute to charity and to have an involvement in the community is not new. Visits to the children's ward in Whittington Hospital and to other children's wards and hospices by players have long been a part of the club tradition, and darts matches in aid of certain causes and appearances at functions were part of a player's commitment in the late Forties.

In the 1960s, the Metropolitan Police Band played before the kick-off and during the interval at Arsenal home matches, and their programme was famous for the "Singing Policeman", but one doubts, with the change in mood and fashion, whether Constable Alex Morgan's rendering of *Because* would receive a fair hearing today, and when he and the police band were at their height the club were apologising for having to raise the minimum entrance fee to four shillings (20p). Sky Television's attempts to have pop groups performing at half-time at televised matches in the early Nineties met with a somewhat hostile reception.

Arsenal's involvement with the community and efforts on behalf of charity are, then, nothing new, but the last decade has witnessed what amounts to a revolution. What the club is doing and has done for charity, for youngsters, for schools, for those in need of help is rarely reported and passes unnoticed by many supporters, yet it constitutes what is, in effect, a new and realistic meaning to the term "care in the community".

Highs and Lows

THE strange quality about the first post-war season was that, although Arsenal won only four of their first eighteen matches, were bottom of the League for some time and in danger of relegation for rather longer, the expectancy of success never really went away. Perhaps it was founded on an arrogance built on the triumphs of the Thirties. Perhaps that unquestioning self-belief was passed on from an older generation to their younger successors, but nobody really considered that Arsenal could be relegated. In the end, they finished thirteenth, ahead of any other London club – Tottenham were in the Second Division – but there were two low moments. They were both concerned with Aston Villa.

When Arsenal were struggling, with players like Male, Bastin and Joy obviously past their best years, George Allison reportedly made a bid for Harry Parkes, the Villa defender. The press recorded that Parkes had turned down the move, saying he had no desire to join Arsenal. Trivial as this may seem today, for Parkes was an honest but unexceptional footballer who was to spend his whole career at Villa Park, this was taken badly by older supporters who saw it as a slight upon the club, remembering that there was a time "when everybody wanted to join Arsenal". It was the first indication, one feels now, that not all was at it had been in 1938 and 1939.

The second disturbing occurrence was a 2-0 home defeat at the hands of Aston Villa in early January. It ended an unbeaten run of six matches which had coincided with the arrival of Ronnie Rooke, and it reversed the result at Villa Park earlier in the season when Arsenal had won even though they were in dire form at the time. A crowd of 61,000 had come to Highbury to see the Villa match and were obviously expecting a resounding victory, but everything went wrong. Leslie Compton had been moved to right-back, his pre-war position, from his usual and best position of centre-half to cover for injuries, and he had a

torrid time against Les Smith and the Welsh centre-forward Trevor Ford who had just joined Villa. Ford had the ability to unsettle people temperamentally, and Smith, who had succeeded Denis Compton as England's wartime outside-left, could be very tricky. The confrontations ended with Leslie Compton sending the winger sprawling over the touchline. Today, the referee would have instantly flourished a yellow card – some may have even produced red – but, during that period, one can remember seeing only the name of Reg Lewis being written in the referee's note book (there were no cards then) and that for lifting his foot as he went into the tackle. No Arsenal player was sent off until Alec Forbes was dismissed in a Cup-tie against Norwich City in January 1954, and then the referee admitted later that he had made a mistake.

Laurie Scott considers that referees today are often too quick to caution players.

If I mistimed a tackle, which obviously does happen, and I caught the other player, I'd be the first person to go and pick him up and see if he was all right. If the foul had been intentional, I'd have been for the high jump. It wasn't accepted at Highbury. You had to play the game as it should be played.

I think referees have problems. They have to make up their minds whether they've seen a mistimed tackle or an intended foul. Often they choose a yellow card because they want to assert themselves. I disagree with them to be honest, but I think they're trying to prove they're not going to stand for any hard play.

Scott did not play in the game against Villa mentioned above, and it is hard to explain after a lapse of more than 50 years why it seemed, and seems, a low point of that season, but it suggested vulnerability and a fall from grace. It was, of course, soon forgotten with big victories over Manchester United and Preston North End, and, the following season, Arsenal won the championship by a wide margin, and God was back in his heaven and all was right with the world again.

In 1948-49, Arsenal were fifth in the League, and Rooke's brief, masterly career at Highbury came to an end, but, a year later, Lewis's two goals brought victory over Liverpool at Wembley and the pattern of the Thirties appeared to be re-establishing itself. That certainly seemed to be the case in 1951-52 when Arsenal looked set to become the first side this century to complete the League and Cup Double. It was not until April that injuries began to take their toll, and the League challenge began to falter.

They were not helped by needing a replay to beat Chelsea in the semi-final although without the drama of the tie two years earlier, while their opponents in the Final, Newcastle United, were having a more leisurely stroll in the closing weeks of the season. Newcastle dented Arsenal's League hopes by drawing at Highbury over the Easter, and doing it with what was virtually a reserve side. In the end, Arsenal were heavily beaten at Old Trafford in the last game of the season, finished third in the League and went to Wembley with fitness doubts surrounding several players.

For Arthur Milton, this was the low point of his Arsenal career.

> If I had a disappointment, it was not playing in the 1952 Cup Final. I played in one of the ties because Jimmy Logie had got injured, and I played inside. Billy Milne, our masseur, really caused the injury. He gave Jim some pimples that went septic. He came out of hospital to play in the Final, and he ran out of steam eventually because Wally Barnes was injured, and Don Roper went to full-back, and we were down to ten men. That was my disappointment really because I'd liked to have played at Wembley again. We had played Luton and I had scored, and I thought that would keep me in the team for I'd had quite a good game playing inside, but Freddie Cox was on the wing, and they kept him in.

Newcastle United, it must be said, were the

Cup holders. They had beaten Blackpool 2-0 in the 1951 Final and had shown outstanding Cup form in reaching the Final for the second year in succession. They overcame Aston Villa, Tottenham Hotspur, Swansea Town, Portsmouth (one of the best sides in the country in that period) and, after a replay, Blackburn Rovers on their way to Wembley so that their pedigree was undeniable. They were also in sight of a record, for no club in the twentieth century had won the Cup in two successive years.

That 1952 Final was, paradoxically, both a high point and a low point for Arsenal. Milton was unfortunate not to play at Wembley, but Freddie Cox was looked upon as something of a talisman and he had scored three times in the semi-final, once in the first game and twice in the replay when Chelsea were beaten 3-0. George Swindin was still in goal although the following season was to be almost his last, and Wally Barnes, now captain of Wales, had switched to right-back after Laurie Scott's departure. Lionel Smith had been converted from centre-half to left-back where he was a good enough player to win six England caps. He was predominantly left-footed, but he was also very quick, strong in the tackle and good in the air. Forbes and Mercer remained at wing-half, but Ray Daniel had succeeded Leslie Compton at centre-half. A Welsh international and, as we said earlier, a highly talented footballer, Daniel played in the Final with his forearm in a light plaster cast as protection against further damage to an injury which had kept him out of

There's quite a queue for the gents' toilet as crowds arrive at Wembley Stadium for the 1952 Cup Final between Arsenal and Newcastle United. Note the rosette sellers.

the last six League games of the season.

Injury had taken its toll of Reg Lewis, one of the very best and most intelligent forwards never to win a full England cap, although he still managed to score eight goals in nine League games and four in three Cup ties before missing the Final, and Doug Lishman, who had joined Arsenal from Walsall in 1948, was now at inside-left. He was a class player with the great gift of scoring goals, and, for five seasons in succession, he was Arsenal's leading scorer. Until the advent of Ian Wright, Doug Lishman could claim to rank second only to John Radford as the club's most prolific goalscorer in post-war football.

In 1950, Peter Goring had been preferred to Cliff Holton as centre-forward; two years later, the positions were reversed. Holton had scored seventeen times in 28 League games, but he had been out of the side with injury from December to March, and the Final was his only Cup appearance of the season. Logie, the key to any Arsenal success, was not fully fit, as Arthur Milton has said, and took the field heavily bandaged. Cox and Roper were on the wings.

The Final was played on the first Saturday in May and was greeted by rain. The Wembley pitch at the time was notorious for its stamina-sapping turf, and the rain only made the conditions worse. Arsenal started brightly, and if Holton seemed a little subdued, Lishman was prominent and a constant threat to the Newcastle defence. Four minutes into the game, he produced an overhead kick which was inches over the bar with goalkeeper Simpson beaten, and a defender raising a despairing hand.

There was artistry from Jimmy Logie and from Bobby Mitchell, both Scotsman, but the crucial event came in the nineteenth minute. Wally Barnes attempted to change direction as he tackled Jackie Milburn, but his studs held in the porous turf so firmly that his knee ligament gave under the strain. He fell in agony. This was an injury which no magic sponge would cure and none had dreamed of substitutes. Barnes was carried from the field, and Roper went to right-back where, not for the first time, he performed nobly in an emergency. Barnes reappeared with his knee heavily bandaged and took up a position on the wing, but, after eleven brave minutes, it was apparent that this

Joe Mercer watches the ball drop on to the top of the Arsenal net at Wembley in 1952. Goalkeeper George Swindin appears to be attempting a header. The Gunners lost 1-0 after being forced to play with only ten fit men.

was asking too much, and he left the field for the remainder of the match and the whole of the following season, so bad was the injury.

There was further concern when Ray Daniel fell heavily, and it was obvious that he was ill at ease with the light plaster covering on the healing fracture. The Arsenal resources were fully stretched, but Mercer strung his men across the field in a wonderful rearguard action. This was the battle at Rorke's Drift. This was Custer's last stand. Wembley had never seen its like before. A cross from Cox, and a header by Lishman, and the Arsenal fans were on their feet in ecstasy, but it was the side netting in which the ball nestled, not the goal. There were chances at both ends, but the Arsenal defence was heroic, and, in one, last desperate effort, Jimmy Logie tore off his bandages as he foraged in search of a goal.

With six minutes remaining, and Roper lying injured on the turf, Mitchell aimed to shoot, but opted instead to float a cross to the far post where, momentarily, Arsenal defenders were static. George Robledo, the Chilean international, got in behind Lionel Smith and glanced a header which went in the net off the inside of the post. There could be no recovery from this, which was perhaps as well, for to ask Arsenal's ten men to play another 30 minutes would have been cruelty.

As Geoffrey Green was to report regarding

Newcastle United, "It was sad, indeed, that their feat of winning the Cup twice in consecutive years – unmatched in the twentieth century – should have a hollow ring about it at the very moment of achievement. But that was the way of it. Arsenal, beaten 1-0, won all the sympathy of that rain-drenched 1952 Final."

The Arsenal ten received an overwhelming ovation at the end, and, at the Arsenal banquet at the Cafe Royal in the evening, Tom Whittaker gave the perfect epitaph when he said, "I have never been prouder of Arsenal than in defeat this afternoon."

It was, perhaps, a typically British response to turn defeat into a moral victory, but we were proud, we did rejoice. Whether the plaudits would have been quite so great had we known that it was to be nineteen years before we were to appear again in another Wembley Final, one doubts, but, momentarily at least, this was a high, rather than a low, point in Arsenal history and in the minds of the fans.

So the season ended with Arsenal third in the League and runners-up in the Cup. It was the season when floodlit football, something of a novelty, began to take hold at Highbury. Chapman had nurtured the idea of floodlights, but the Football Association had banned their use until 1950, and the first floodlit game to be played at Highbury was the match between Boxers and Jockeys, once an annual charity

match, a year later. In the 1951-52 season on which we have been dwelling, there were four floodlit games played at the stadium. The first was a friendly against Hapoel (Tel Aviv) which was watched by a crowd in excess of 44,000. A London Cup-tie against Hendon was watched by 13,000 people whereas only 5,000 had watched games played in the afternoon. The potential was obvious, but, although we did not know it at the time, the doubt was whether the lights would shine or dim on Arsenal.

For the moment, they continued to shine. In 1952-53, the Football League First Division was won for a record seventh time, but it was a very close thing. Throughout the closing weeks of the season, Arsenal and Preston North End were neck and neck, and when Preston beat their close rivals 2-0 at Deepdale and then won their final match they went top of the table. Arsenal had one remaining game to play, at home to Burnley on the Friday evening (not floodlit) before the Cup Final. If Arsenal won, they would take the title on goal average. This was the period when places were decided on goal average, goals for divided by goals against, rather than by goal difference.

A crowd in excess of 51,000 arrived to see the game on a gentle, balmy spring evening. Burnley were on the brink of becoming one of the best sides in the land. George Armstrong admired them. They were a side who played good football and were Spurs' closest rivals in the early Sixties.

I can remember the Burnleys and the Wolverhamptons. They were top teams at one time. Burnley had great players. You didn't need a programme then. You recognised them all. Now I have to keep looking to see who number two is, who number six is. The lower divisions are even worse. I think that, apart from the top eight or nine teams in the Premier League, the football is very ordinary. The press hype it up in order to try to sell the game, but I worry because people think it's fantastic, and it's not. There's a lot of work to do yet.

Arsenal had played Burnley at Turf Moor in the fifth round of the Cup and won a superb victory 2-0. Holton had scored a magnificent goal from a long accurate pass from Forbes of the right. The Double had again looked possible, but Blackpool won a crunching sixth-

Left: Arsenal's Welsh international full-back Wally Barnes (right) injured knee ligaments in the 19th minute of the 1952 Cup Final and Arsenal were left with an uphill task. They performed heroically but, alas, in van.

Right: Joe Mercer, wearing unfamiliar stripes because of the clash of colours, is challenged by a Blackpool player during the FA Cup sixth-round game at Highbury which was watched by over 69,000 spectators in February 1953. Arsenal lost 2-1 and the Seasiders went on to win the Cup in the famous "Matthews Final".

Arsenal's Cliff Holton has just scored in the 2-2 draw at Highbury on 21 March, 1953 as West Brom take a point off that season's eventual League champions. The Albion players (left to right) are Jimmy Dugdale (5), Len Millard (3), goalkeeper Norman Heath and right-back Stan Rickaby on the goal-line.

round tie at Highbury 2-1 and went on to win the Cup, the "Matthews Final". In spite of that setback, the League remained Arsenal's for the taking, but they began the match against Burnley very nervously, and Mercer was fiercely competitive in trying to stir his men. They suffered the worst possible start when a shot was deflected past Swindin in the eighth minute, but this proved to be the shock Arsenal needed to jolt them into action. A blistering shot by Forbes from the edge of the area levelled the scores almost immediately.

Arsenal now took control and surged forward in fine style. The game was still only thirteen minutes old when Roper crossed from the right, and Lishman, with that instinctive knack that is the quality of the great goalscorer, moved swiftly into space to drive the ball past Thompson, the Burnley 'keeper. Thirteen minutes later, Logie put the ball into the net to end a flowing move and put Arsenal 3-1 up.

The title now seemed assured, but, with sixteen minutes to go, Elliott scored for Burnley, and the last fifteen minutes of the match saw Swindin and his defence hold out against some determined attacks. So Arsenal won the title on goal average, 1.516 against Preston's 1.417, a difference of .099 of a goal. Rarely has it been closer. There was jubilation. In the space of six seasons there had been two

championships, one FA Cup triumph and one heroic runners-up spot in the Cup. It seemed that the old order prevailed, but the lights began to go out on Arsenal. In a move virtually unprecedented, Ray Daniel asked to leave and was transferred to Sunderland. Arthur Milton and Jimmy Logie went. Milton always loved the matches against Tottenham, for the "60,000 in the ground, all of them Cockneys, and never any trouble". He also had a habit of roasting the Spurs, and the September day in 1952 when he and Jimmy Logie tore them to shreds at White Hart Lane burns bright in the memory as one of the highs before a period of lows.

The careers of George Swindin and Lionel Smith drew to a close, and one of the saddest aspects was that Don Roper, a good and faithful servant if ever there was one, became a butt of the crowd in his closing days with the club. He was forced into a number of roles, one of them being that of withdrawn centre-forward after the fashion of Hidegkuti in the great Hungarian side and of Don Revie for Manchester City. He played his part well, but the Highbury faithful were becoming disaffected. The anticipation, the expectation of success had disappeared. It was to be eighteen years between championships, and some of those years were to be troubled ones.

Within three months of winning the

Bill Dodgin heads clear from Aston Villa centre-forward Don Walsh in the third round of the FA Cup at Highbury in January 1954. Arsenal won 5-1 but went out at home to Norwich in the next round.

Cliff Holton gets in a header against Spurs at Highbury in February 1954. The other Arsenal player is Doug Lishman. Arsenal lost 3-0.

League, Arsenal began the 1953-54 season with six defeats and two draws in their first eight matches, and they languished at the foot of the table. They recovered to finish twelfth, but they were no longer a force in the land. In the memories of most, they were "the team of the Thirties".

There were voids which were never adequately filled. Bill Dodgin, lacking confidence, found it hard to step into the shoes of Ray Daniel, while some of those who wore the red and white were not of the calibre of their

In August 1954, Everton marked their return to the First Division with a visit from Arsenal at Goodison Park and over 69,000 fans saw the Merseysiders triumph 1-0 with this goal from Tommy Eglington. Jack Kelsey is the Arsenal goalkeeper.

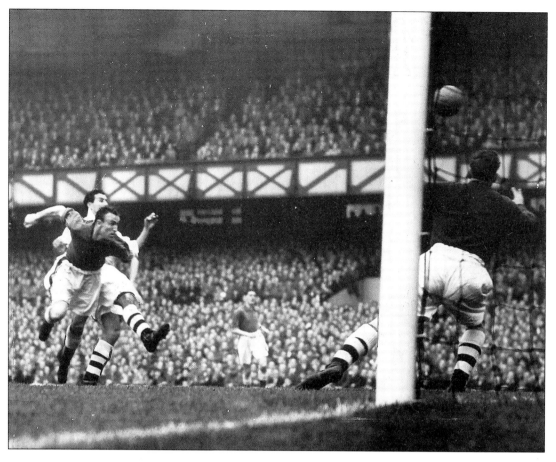

Derek Tapscott gets in his shot despite the close attention of Spurs goalkeeper Ted Ditchburn at White Hart Lane in September 1955. That season the Gunners finished fifth in the First Division and again reached the quarter-finals of the FA Cup before going out to Birmingham.

predecessors. There were, of course, the occasional high points to savour, and one of them came at White Hart Lane on the evening of Wednesday, 13 March 1957.

A good Cup run had ended in defeat at home by West Bromwich Albion, and that was followed by another home defeat when Luton won 3-1, so that the match away to Tottenham was not anticipated with any relish. Dave Bowen, successor to Joe Mercer and captain of Wales, picked up a loose ball on the halfway line and ran unopposed to the edge of the Spurs penalty area from where he struck a beautiful shot into the top left-hand corner of the net. A Tottenham fan turned and said, "Well, he'll never do that again if he plays for a hundred years." He was wrong. Bowen did the same thing again ten minutes later. Tapscott, who always played as if possessed, added a third, and Arsenal won 3-1. A double over the Spurs has always provided some comfort even in the darkest days.

Incidentally, Dave Bowen played 146 League games and sixteen Cup-ties for Arsenal, and they were the only two goals he ever scored.

There was a ray of hope in George Swindin's first season as manager, third place in the First Division, with David Herd and Vic Groves scoring freely, and Groves, Danny Clapton an Jimmy Bloomfield appearing together in an England Under-23 forward line. Clapton went on to win a full England cap, but a potential, which had seemed so great, was never fully realised and he faded into insignificance. It was in this season that Peter Goy played his two games for Arsenal. His second chance came after Jack Kelsey had broken his arm in the Cup replay at Bramall Lane. Jim Standen had taken over, but he was on cricket duty with Worcestershire when Arsenal met Birmingham in the last game of the season, a game Arsenal had to win to clinch third place and prize money. It was Goy's great moment. He was on National Service and had made his debut against Leeds United in the February.

I was told to report to the camp commandant, and I went there in fear and trembling, wondering what I'd done wrong, but he was smiling all over his face. He shook me by the hand and told me that I'd brought honour and distinction to the company by being selected to keep goal for Arsenal against Leeds United the next day. It went well, and we won 1-0.

I'd joined the Arsenal ground staff when I was seventeen. We used to train twice a week, sweep the terraces and do other odd jobs. I had my own brush for sweeping.

The only one who never did any work was John Barnwell. He came down from Bishop Auckland and said that he'd come to play football. He hadn't got time for sweeping. He was a character.

The maximum wage at this time was £20, but there was a bonus of £80 at the end of the year if Arsenal beat Birmingham and finished third, so that there was considerable pressure on Peter Goy when he was called up for that last game of the season.

I was sitting in the dressing room, very nervous, and Jack Kelsey, whom I'd never had much to do with, came up to me and said, "I've got eighty quid riding on this. So don't let me down."

I played an absolute blinder. It was one of those nights when everything went right. I felt marvellous, but I knew it had come at the wrong time for me. If you do well, you can expect a decent run in the side, at least three or four games, but this was the last match of the season, and, in September, you start all over again, and Jack and Jim would be fit.

The lads were delighted. We had won 2-1 and finished third, and they'd earned their bonus money. I wouldn't get that, but I would get a £4 match-winning bonus on top of my £20.

Next morning, in *The Daily Express*, Desmond Hackett gave me a tremendous write up. His report was headed "Great Goy". I was on top of the world, but even more important to me was that straight after the game, as I was changing, Ron Greenwood, who was Arsenal's coach at the time, came into the dressing room and walked straight over to me. He shook hands with me and said, "Well done, son, you've played yourself on to the summer tour." I was so excited because they were off to Italy and were going to play teams like Juventus.

When I saw George Swindin, the manager, he said nothing to me except, "Don't let it go to your head."

The next week I got my pay packet, and I was £2 short so I went to see the boss and said, "Sorry, boss, but there's been a mistake in my pay packet. I'm £2 light. I've only got £22."

He said, "It's no mistake. I think £24 is too much for a young player so I cut you down."

David Herd scores Arsenal's first goal in the memorable game against Manchester United at Arsenal in February 1958. It was United's last League game before the Munich air disaster. The Gunners went down 5-4.

I didn't know what to say at first, but I went back to him and kept on about it, and, in the end, he gave it to me.

He said nothing about the summer tour, but I thought I would be told the details soon enough; and then I heard that they had borrowed Nigel Sims from Aston Villa to take on tour. Evidently, he thought I was too young and inexperienced. George Swindin never said a word to me, and neither did Ron Greenwood. I think Ron was too embarrassed. He left shortly afterwards to go to West Ham, and I don't think he and George Swindin had ever really hit it off.

Swindin had been a wonderful goalkeeper and should have played for England, but he was not a good manager of men. If we laughed at training, he got annoyed and told us to shut up because football was a serious business. Ron always said there was no point in playing or training if you didn't enjoy it.

I think George Swindin was probably right in thinking that I was too young and inexperienced to go on that tour, but he said nothing to me, and that's what hurt. I never forgave him for that.

I stayed with Arsenal another fifteen months, but I never played for the first team again. Southend asked for me, and I moved there and had three happy years. In 1964, Bill McGarry, who was manager of Watford at that time, offered Southend £2,500 for me, and they accepted. Bill had just sold Pat Jennings to Spurs for £30,000, and I was signed as Pat's replacement. It was a good move because Watford had missed promotion by two points the year before I joined them, and we did well in the year that I was there.

At the end of the season, Bill McGarry left, and Ken Furphy became manager. New managers have new ideas, and he cleared out a few players, including me. I went to Huddersfield.

John Barnwell is just to late to prevent Preston North End's 16-year-old goalkeeper John Barton collect the ball at Highbury in December 1958. Barton was making his League debut after playing mostly for Preston's fourth team that season and he helped his side to a 2-1 win. Arsenal, though, had a good season and finished third in the table.

It wasn't until I left Arsenal that I realised how good a club it was. Everything they did there was first-class. It was all done properly. There was under-floor heating, and the dressing rooms were palatial. Your kit was always set out neatly for you, and you didn't see your boots until Saturday when they were left in your place, clean and in perfect condition. And all the teams were treated like that. Not just the first team. It wasn't until I went elsewhere that I realised how good it had been, but I never got over the way I was treated after that Birmingham game. I was at Highbury at the wrong time.

Some good players flowed in and out of Highbury in the Sixties; Eastham, Baker, Snedden, Brown, McLeod and Ure, all came and went, but nothing seemed to gell. As one weakness was healed, another appeared. The momentary rays of hope and expectancy became less frequent.

One evening in October 1963, Tottenham came to Highbury, and, had Arsenal won, they would have gone top of the League. Eastham had a marvellous game and scored twice himself, but the match was drawn 4-4, and

Arsenal finished eighth in the League. They reached the fifth round of the Cup but lost 0-1 to Liverpool and had Joe Baker sent off. A crowd of 67,986 watched the game against Tottenham, and more than 61,000 saw the Cup-tie against Liverpool, but the season drifted to its close, and the last home game, against Blackburn Rovers, attracted just over 26,000. It was a desultory 0 0 draw. Going to Highbury had become a matter of habit rather than a journey of eagerness and anticipation.

It was in the second year of the Bertie Mee/Don Howe regime that things began to change. Arsenal returned to Wembley and lost to Leeds United in the Final of the Football League Cup. They went back a year later, and this time lost to Swindon Town. The defeat by a side from a lower division was a terrible blow, but the match was played on a Wembley surface that was like treacle and that eradicated the difference in class between the two sides. For Frank McLintock and his side, it was agonising. It was McLintock's fourth Wembley Final, and his fourth time on the losing side. Bob Wilson remembers:

If you don't score, anything can happen. All that anybody remembers is that in extra-time they played great stuff and scored two goals. What they

George Eastham sees his penalty saved by Sheffield Wednesday goalkeeper Dave McLaren at Highbury in March 1964 in front of only 18,000 spectators. Arsenal drew 1-1 that night but six days later won 4-0 at Hillsborough.

Goalkeeper Tony Burns, a former Arsenal junior, punches the ball away against Wolves at Highbury in January 1965, despite the "help" which centre-half Ian Ure is trying to offer.

forget is that we hit the woodwork six times, and the Man of the Match was Peter Downsborough, Swindon goalkeeper. That was football at its most amazing. In extra-time, I hold up my hands and say, OK, we were knackered. We had a sort of 'flu bug. The pitch was an absolute disgrace, and good luck to Swindon. They did really, really well to hold out for 90 minutes, but in that 90 minutes we absolutely murdered them.

For Don Howe, the defeat by Swindon was, in many ways, the making of Arsenal. It was a catalyst that brought into being a great Arsenal side.

The biggest success I had when I came here was when we did the Double in the 1970-71 season, and there's lots of reasons why we did it, but the main reason was we got success after failure, and I think that failure is a test of character. For instance, in 1968, we got to the League Cup Final, and we lost 1-0 to Leeds. Losing to Leeds in those days wasn't a disgrace; and we lost to Swindon, and I wouldn't say it was a disgrace, but it wasn't far from a disgrace. The pitch was diabolical. We'd lost two games, two Finals, and that could have destroyed a lot of teams, a lot of clubs, a lot of players. Failure can have that affect, but, with us, it kind of strengthened things.

It was the year after losing to Swindon that Arsenal won what was then called the European Fairs Cup and is now known as the UEFA Cup. For many of the players of that period it remains the high point of their careers. For Arsenal, as manager Bertie Mee insists, it was a watershed.

I think winning the European Fairs Cup in 1970 was vitally important because the club had never won a European competition before, and it was a long time since staunch Arsenal supporters had seen a trophy at Highbury. Even now, I remember supporters coming to me with tears in their eyes after that success. It was the end of a bad period for Arsenal when they had had players who were not good enough. Mediocrity was being perpetuated. That was painfully obvious to me, and that's why I went into management because I thought I could change it. The standard needed raising 30 to 40 per cent.

George Armstrong, associated with two Double triumphs, the first as a player, the second as reserve-team manager, still sees that European victory as the best moment of his career:

Winning the Fairs Cup was my best moment as a player. I remember Jimmy Robertson who joined us from Tottenham and with whom I had a friendly rivalry because we were both wingers saying to me – he was a very intelligent man – "You know, Geordie,

Terry Neill (hidden) tucks away a penalty in the 4-0 win over Spurs at Highbury in September 1967. Nearly 64,000 fans saw the game.

Arsenal in the 1969 Football League Cup Final at Wembley. The Gunners lost 3-1 to the Third Division side. A year earlier they had gone down 1-0 to Leeds in the Final. Here, Bob Wilson gathers a high ball despite the attentions of Swindon's Peter Noble. Ian Ure and Bob McNab look on.

John Radford rushes past the post after scoring Arsenal's second goal in the 1970 Fairs Cup Final second leg. Charlie George (10) and George Armstrong also look quite pleased. The Gunners won 3-0, giving them a 4-3 aggregate victory and their first major trophy for 17 years.

April 1970 and
Anderlecht
goalkeeper
Trappeniers
punches the ball
clear during an
Arsenal raid in
the second leg of
the European
Fairs Cup Final at
Highbury.

April 1970 and Anderlecht goalkeeper Trappeniers punches the ball clear during an Arsenal raid in the second leg of the European Fairs Cup Final at Highbury.

the trouble with our team is that we'll never believe we're a good side until we win something." And I think winning the Fairs Cup, we thought, "Here we go, we're a good side".

I think that the Fairs Cup is as difficult to win as the European Cup because all the teams you meet are on the way up. They are on their way to the top. In one way, I suppose we were lucky because, in Anderlecht, they murdered us. They could have got six, but Ray Kennedy got the goal to make it 3-1, and over two legs we had nothing to lose. If I remember, at Highbury, we did the business correctly. There was plenty of water on the pitch, and the crowd was phenomenal. We believed it was going to be our night.

Arsenal's route to the Final was impressive although losing to Glentoran in Ireland after beating them 3-0 at Highbury in the first round gave no indication of the glory that was come. The second and third rounds followed the same pattern, goalless draws in Portugal and Rouen respectively and victories at home. The fourth round gave Europe warning that the English giant had awakened from its slumbers, a 2-0 win against Dinamo Bachu in Romania was

followed by a 7-1 win at Highbury with John Radford, Jon Sammels and Charlie George hitting two each and George Graham one.

The Arsenal fans warmed to the competition slowly. Seventeen years in the wilderness had been a long time, and it was not until the first leg semi-final against Ajax that the attendance topped 40,000. Arsenal turned on a fine display with Charlie George scoring twice in the 3-0 win. The second leg was lost 1-0, but Arsenal were in a European Final for the first time. Bob Wilson did not play in the earlier rounds through injury, but he was fit from the third-round tie Rouen onwards.

The championship night was the biggest night in real terms. The most memorable and exciting, though, was most definitely the Fairs Cup win against Anderlecht. There'd never been a night like that at Highbury, and there never will be again. There were 60,000 people there, and we were 3-1 down from the first leg, and we won 3-0.

What we had at Arsenal was the perfect jigsaw throughout the side. We had balance down the left side, extraordinary, McNab, Graham, Armstrong. We had two at the front who were not only brilliant together on the field in their understanding of how each other played. They loved each other off the field. We had a captain who, together with another Scot, Billy Bremner, was the inspirational captain of the time. Frank's strength was that he was the most impulsive character I've ever met. He'd look at your tie or shirt and say, "I like that. I must have one of those." And ten minutes later, he'd forgotten about it. But that's what brought us back in the Anderlecht game. We'd lost 3-1, and he was almost crying in the dressing room, but he was the first one to lift up his head and say, "We'll come back!" The jigsaw was perfect.

Ray Kennedy was an unknown quantity to most supporters in 1969-70. In the League, he started a game only twice and twice came on as substitute. In the Fairs Cup, he was brought on for Charlie George near the end of the game in Belgium and headed a goal in the dying minutes. It was that goal which gave Arsenal some hope. He did not play in the second leg at Highbury, but the following season, he appeared in every game bar the opening one at Everton and forged his wonderful striking partnership with John Radford.

The match against RSC Anderlecht at Highbury on 28 April 1970, was every bit as memorable as Bob Wilson suggests it was. There were 60,000 in the ground. The anticipation and expectancy had returned.

Lifted by the vibrancy of the crowd, Arsenal were soon dominating the midfield and put considerable pressure on the Anderlecht goal. The Belgians looked unsettled, but they were dangerous on the break. Perhaps "patience" has always been a motto of successful Arsenal managers, and the Gunners never followed the path of desperation which so often leads to disaster. They remained calm, were intelligently and forcefully constructive and waited patiently for an opening. It came after 26 minutes. The ball broke loose on the edge of the Anderlecht penalty area, and Eddie Kelly took possession. Bringing the ball swiftly under control, he drove it past Trappeniers and into the far corner of the net before a defender could get in a tackle. The goal broke what tension may have lurked in the Arsenal side. They were now just one goal away from a European trophy.

More and more pressure was mounted on the Anderlecht goal at the start of the second half. As ever, George Armstrong was everywhere, sometimes seemingly skipping down both wings at one and the same time, and John Radford's height, strength and power in the air was an ever-increasing problem for the Belgian defence. Twenty-four minutes into the second half that power and strength paid dividends. Overlapping down the left, Bob McNab crossed for Radford to outjump the defenders and head Arsenal into a 2-0 lead. The sides were now level on aggregate, but Arsenal had the advantage of Kennedy's goal in Belgium. If the score stayed as it was, Arsenal were the trophy winners, but they were rampant now, unwilling to settle for victory by technicality.

Within three minutes, they had scored again. Charlie George, on the left, drifted a pass towards the inside-right position where Jon Sammels suddenly appeared to drive home a third goal. Anderlecht were a beaten side. Arsenal were in total control, and when the final whistle blew crowds of people swarmed on to the pitch in celebration. The Cup was presented, but few could see it among the shouting and dancing mass on the pitch, but, joyful and confident as people were, none could have anticipated the glories that were to come the following season, except, perhaps, Bertie Mee.

In one sense, nothing really surprised me. It didn't surprise me that we did the Double because we had a team who were never beaten. We had won the Fairs Cup, and there was a lot of skill in the side, but, even more important, they married their skill with the will to win. People like "Willow" in goal, McNab, George Armstrong, John Radford, Frank McLintock, they wanted to win. They never gave in.

I think the Arsenal of my time were conscious of the legacy of the Thirties, but I don't think they were burdened by it. I would have said early on, when I first joined the club, I think they were burdened by it then, but the main reason was that they were not as good as those players had been. But once the Seventies side had proved themselves in European competition and in

Charlie George gives John Radford a hug after Radford scored the only goal of the game against Manchester City at Highbury in February 1971.

Ray Kennedy and Ipswich Town's Mick Mills chase the ball at Highbury in February 1971. Arsenal won 3-2.

winning the Double, there was no longer any burden. No one talked about the Thirties team. I suppose now, after what was done under George Graham, and the second Double side, they've forgotten about the Seventies side.

George Armstrong, Bob Wilson and Pat Rice have been associated with both Double sides and, inevitably, there are always comparisons. George Armstrong dismisses them.

We were fortunate in that we had a good group of kids, and Frank was a great captain, smashing guy. He had everyone's respect. The spirit was phenomenal, and Bertie must take credit for that. Don did his piece, and my only disappointment was that the team broke up too early. I think there was pressure from above for more flair, but that was a load of rubbish created by the press. We had players in the team – all right some were better than others – but they could all play. They talked about comparing us with the team that won the Cup in 1950. I

think that we were better than they were, but you can't compare. You can only be the best of your time, and we proved we were.

The Double maybe I was not quite as excited as people thought I might have been. It all happened so quickly. It was a one-week job in the end. We won at Tottenham, and then we won at Wembley on the Saturday. I think that because it was all so quick, it worked for us, and with a bit more patience we could have done it again.

Armstrong and Wilson are among those cited by Bertie Mee as having the determination never to be beaten. Bob Wilson believes that that determination ran through the whole team.

The championship for me personally was the biggest memory, that night at Tottenham. The most glamorous is obviously the FA Cup, and it was bizarre to win it and do the Double in a five-day spell. In a way, you're spoilt. For me, at 30, and there was only Frank McLintock, our captain, older than me, I could cope with it because it had been a long and strange roundabout route into the game. For Frank, whose fifth Final and first win it was, it was a big day, but, if you're a professional footballer, the real test of whether you're a real player is week in, week out, day in and day out, month in and month out, and there's only one way to measure that, and that's the championship.

From the personal point of view, the biggest honour I ever had was getting the Arsenal Player of the Year in the Double season because, to be honest, all seventeen squad members should have had a communal one, but I got it. That was my season. I remember that Les Shannon, the Blackpool manager, was the only manager in the League who gave us a chance of winning the Double. Most of them had said, "Not this season, nor any other season." But I had a scorcher against Blackpool at home when we won 1-0, and he said, "With that bloke in goal, they could win everything."

Peter Storey (far right, grounded) looks up to see his header enter the Blackpool net despite Adcock's effort to head it out. It was the only goal of the game at Highbury in March 1971.

Eddie Kelly scores a hugely important goal against Stoke at Highbury on 1 May 1971. It proved to be the winner and took Arsenal to within touching distance of the League championship.

In the game against Tottenham, we were fine as long as it was 0-0, but when we scored all hell broke loose because they did not want us to emulate what they had done in 1961. From a corner, the ball dropped down in the box, and, as was my wont, I went in head first, and Alan Mullery went right through on me and cut me open. I had six stitches in my ear. The Tottenham fans that night were brilliant, and so were the management and staff. They really were excellent. We didn't have it easy. It was the most amazing night.

The strength of that Double side

was its togetherness. I still say that, had I been a manager, I would have known that you will never win anything with eleven Charlie Georges in your side or eleven Bobby Moores or eleven Bobby Charltons. The winning team is a jigsaw. It has smooth bits and rough bits just like the England 1966 side. The rough bit was Nobby Stiles, but he was a diamond rough bit. And there was Bally – the naivety of youth. He ran all day. The yardage he covered was exceptional. Like that side, we had the perfect jigsaw.

The management was near perfect for us as a group, but what it boiled down to was the simple philosophy of football, and, if I ran a business, I'd run it on exactly the same philosophy. I was born in Chesterfield in a beautiful house. We never wanted for anything although we were never rich, but I was a lucky lad. My world of university and the way I spoke and had been educated was totally different to that of John Radford, say, but big John Radford thought I was the best goalie in England, and I thought he was the best centre-forward in England. There was the basic philosophy that it didn't matter how well you spoke, how well educated you were, all that mattered was "Can you play" or "Can't you play". I thought Nabbers was the best full-back. It was a complete belief that we had the best of everything.

You can be as talented as you like, but you are nothing unless you have the understanding in football and footballers of what is real and what is unreal. It's the great thing about football and footballers that if you try to be anything you're not, woe betide you. If you put on airs and graces and try to be something that isn't natural to you, you are in trouble. They'd accept me with my college scarf and duffel coat because I'd been to Loughborough University, and I took all the ribbing and teasing on the chin, but at the end of it was "Can he play? Is

he a good enough goalie or isn't he?" That is the wonderful, simple philosophy of football, and that should be carried into every walk of life.

We never knew when we were beaten. If we scored a goal, we thought that's it, they'll never score. It was team work throughout. The best example of that was in the semi-final against Stoke. We were 2-0 down, and it could have been more than that. I had a very important one-to-one save with John Mahoney when I had one of my head-on dives. If he'd scored when he was clean through then, the game was dead.

At half-time, we went in 2-0 down. We were stunned. The goals were a bit freaky. One was like a cannonball that flew in from a corner and went in at great speed, and then Charlie made a cock-up and presented the ball to, I think it was John Ritchie. Then all hell broke loose in the dressing room, and there was this transformation. "How can we be 2-0 down? Come on! What are we doing?"

The need was to score within a reasonable period of time. As long as we got back in the game, it didn't matter if it went up to the last minute, which it did. We got a goal from the edge of the box, Peter Storey, 2-1, and they were hanging on. Everything was at their end of the field. I was a spectator. Then suddenly – should it have been a corner or shouldn't it? Poor old Stoke argue to this day that it shouldn't have been. Banksie is certain. And from the corner we get a penalty. Peter miscued it. Banks threw all his weight on to his right foot, and the ball is only half a yard from his leg, and that's against the greatest goalie in the world. So we really never knew when we were beaten.

Thank goodness from my point of view in the Final. Within two minutes of letting in a bad goal, I made a very important save from Brian Hall. It could have been 2-0, and within another two minutes we scored a freak equaliser. And I have to say that even

Charlie George leads the celebrations for Kelly's vital goal against the Potters. Gordon Banks, the Stoke goalkeeper, looks back in despair.

though I remember Peter Simpson and Frank McLintock giving me a glare after I'd let the goal in, I only gave it a fleeting thought, "Oh, I've cost Arsenal the Double." I was lucky. I had this very important save to make that was good for me and the team. George Armstrong had missed an open goal. Ray Kennedy had missed an open goal. We hit the woodwork twice.

But, in the end, Arsenal won 2-1 and completed an astonishing double. The first leg had come at White Hart Lane on the Monday before the Final. At Christmas, none gave them a hope of winning the League. They played Southampton at home on Boxing Day. The weather was dreadful with snow swirling, and the crowd down to 34,000 because of the cold. Elsewhere, games were cancelled. Arsenal played very well and bombarded the Southampton goal, but it ended 0-0. Leeds United were ten points ahead in the League, and with, at that time, only two points for a win, they appeared to be out of distance of any challengers. Only Bertie Mee believed, on the evidence of his team's performance against Southampton, that Leeds could be caught. His

optimism appeared to have little substance when there were League defeats at Liverpool and Huddersfield in January. Then, at the end of March, there was a 3-0 victory over Wolves at Molineux. This was the first of nine wins in succession. These were followed by a draw at West Bromwich and, dramatically, by a 1-0 defeat at Leeds. The goal came in the closing moments as the Arsenal defence hesitated expecting an offside decision. This defeat tilted the balance in favour of Leeds United who had stumbled in the closing weeks of the season, losing controversially at home to West Bromwich Albion and drawing matches they should have won.

At home to Stoke on what had been scheduled the last day of the League season, Arsenal won by a single goal, which meant that Leeds, having completed their fixtures, had 64 points and Arsenal had 63. Leeds' goal average was 2.40, 72 goals for, 30 against; Arsenal's goal average was 2.41, 70 goals for, 29 goals against. If Arsenal could win or draw 0-0 against Tottenham on the Monday evening, they would take the title. Defeat or a score draw would give the title to Leeds.

At lunchtime on that memorable Monday, crowds were already gathered in Tottenham,

Jubilant Arsenal players at the final whistle against Spurs at White Hart Lane on 3 May 1971. Their 1-0 victory gave them the League championship and left them on the brink of the Double.

and by three, there were long queues all around the ground. While Bob Wilson praises the Tottenham crowd, players and officials, those of us who queued for several hours are more stinting in our praise of the organisation. To arrive at the turnstiles and find only two gates in operation was not the happiest of experiences and must have been considerably more frustrating for the vast number of people, estimated in some quarters as 100,000, who were left outside when the gates were closed well before the start of the match.

From this distance of time, it is hard to remember whether the tension was greater inside or outside the ground. Inside the ground, there were close to 52,000 people, and there was the constant buzz of excitement as kick-off time approached. The roar throughout the match was unrelenting. Arsenal's dream was nearly realised in the opening minutes when Pat Jennings saved splendidly from Charlie George. Frank McLintock had a shot charged down, and, as they had been all season, Radford and Kennedy were a consistent threat to the opposing goal, but Phil Beal was outstanding at the heart of the Spurs defence.

Frank McLintock organised his back four as solidly as he had done all season although Peters and Gilzean went close, but there were few clear-cut chances. As the final whistle drew near, the tension mounted. A goalless draw and the championship to Arsenal looked more and more likely. Then, with less than three minutes to go, Jennings parried an effort

from Radford. The ball was swept out to the left of the Spurs goal where Armstrong collected it and crossed for Kennedy to head in just under the bar.

There was a tumultuous reception for the goal, but almost immediately there was an air of anxiety in the ground as it was realised, in a sense, that one goal was not enough. If Tottenham equalised, the title was gone. Arsenal now played the longest two minutes football in their history as Spurs threw everything forward. The defence was firm, and Wilson was magnificent. The lasting image is of a Tottenham corner in the dying seconds. The ball came over from the right with, seemingly, everybody bar Jennings in the Arsenal area, and there, soaring above of them all, was Bob Wilson catching the ball cleanly and commandingly. A moment later, Mr Howley, who was officiating in his final League match before retirement and who had handled the game in exemplary fashion, blew his whistle and Arsenal were champions.

The crowd swarmed on to the pitch before many of the players could reach the sanctuary the dressing room. Bob Wilson was discernible being carried shoulder-high. Not only had Arsenal taken the title, they had conquered Tottenham and their supporters had seized White Hart Lane.

They bounced joyously to Wembley six days later, armoured now by a feeling of invincibility. Bertie Mee made one change for the Final from the side that had won at Tottenham.

Liverpool's Steve Heighway puts his side into the lead in the 1971 FA Cup Final against Arsenal.

Eddie Kelly equalises for Arsenal.

Peter Storey had been injured in the game against Stoke, but he was declared fit for the Final and replaced Eddie Kelly. In effect, Storey did not last the match, and Kelly came on as substitute midway through the second half. Arsenal should have won the game over 90 minutes. They had chances. Armstrong and Kennedy scorned opportunities they had been taking all season. Graham hit the bar and one shot was cleared off the line. Wilson saved well from Lindsay, but Arsenal certainly had the edge over Liverpool. Nevertheless, there was no score after 90 minutes.

It was two minutes into extra-time that Bob Wilson had the nightmare of which he has already spoken. Steve Heighway broke down the left. There seemed little danger, and Wilson, on the near post, began to move out anticipating the cross. Instead, Heighway shot low and beat the Arsenal goalkeeper's right hand by the post.

If Arsenal supporters were stunned, the players themselves showed the resilience they had shown throughout 63 previous matches during the season, for, on top of their Double success, they played five games in the League Cup and reached the fourth round of the European Fairs Cup where they lost to IFC Köln of West Germany on the away goals rule. Four minutes before the break in extra-time,

Charlie George is embraced by his team-mates after scoring the Cup Final winner and giving Arsenal only the second League and Cup Double achieved in modern times.

Radford hooked the ball over his shoulder into the Liverpool penalty area where Kelly touched the ball forward. Graham followed it up as Clemence advanced, and, somehow, the ball eluded the goalkeeper and rolled into the net. All believed that Graham had touched it in, and he seemed to be one of that belief, but later evidence showed that no one had put a foot to the ball since Eddie Kelly. No one debated it at the time. The score was 1-1.

It was a hot, demanding day, and a replay looked likely. With nine minutes remaining, Radford moved down the left in a rather leisurely manner. Approaching the Liverpool penalty area, he pushed the ball inside to Charlie George who struck a ferocious right-foot shot past a despairing, diving Clemence high inside the right-hand post. It sealed the Double and remains one of the most famous goals in the history of the club.

Andy Charalambous was not at Wembley that day, but he shared the excitement with millions of others.

I remember the Double year, ab-

solutely riveting. If you go down Caledonian Road, there's a pub halfway down the road near the public toilets, and we were watching the Cup Final there when Charlie George scored the goal. I went outside – I was a kid of about eight or nine – and there were hundreds of people outside this pub going mad, in the Caledonian Road. We'd done the Double by beating Liverpool, and I watched it in black and white. It was in the days before we had colour television.

John Radford was my favourite player, and Charlie George because he scored that goal in the Final. There was the great evening at Tottenham when we won the League. My dad took me there at three in the afternoon so that we could get in, and it was a good job he did for there were at least 50,000 locked outside the ground that night. The crowd swarmed on the pitch after the match,

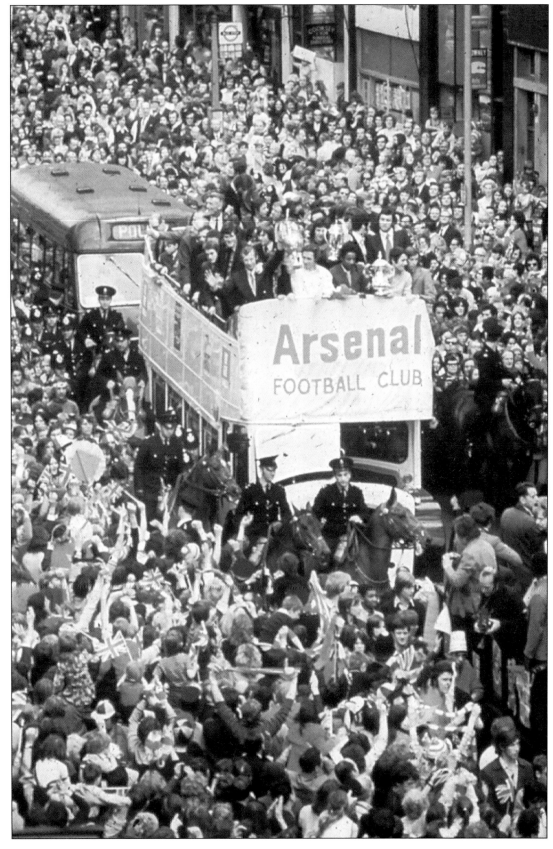

Arsenal celebrate their 1971 League and Cup Double in the streets around Highbury.

and it was a sea of Arsenal supporters. It's the only time I've ever seen that at White Hart Lane.

It is not often possible to live at the heights all the time. The following season was one of bitter disappointments. The side finished fifth in the League, were beaten in the Cup Final, 1-0 by Leeds, and lost Bob Wilson when he was so badly injured in the semi-final against Stoke City at Villa Park that he did not play again until the following November. John Radford went in goal and performed with an heroic lack

The 1971 Double winners. Back row (left to right): Bob McNab, Ray Kennedy, Bob Wilson, John Roberts, Geoff Barnett, Peter Simpson, Peter Marinello. Front row: Sammy Nelson, Peter Storey, John Radford, Eddie Kelly, Frank McLintock, Pat Rice, George Graham, George Armstrong.

of the orthodox, and the match was drawn. Arsenal won the replay 2-1, and Stoke must have been sick of them.

The major disappointment came in the European Cup. In the first round, Strømgodset IF were beaten 3-1 in Norway and 4-0 at Highbury. Then Arsenal overcame Grasshopper Zürich 2-0 in Switzerland and 3-0 at home, which took them to a third-round tie against Ajax. The Dutch side won 2-1 in Amsterdam, which was a fine result for Arsenal, who brought a vital away goal back to Highbury for the second leg. Even though Radford was unavailable, expectations were so high. Bob Wilson remembers the disappointment.

> We'd beaten Ajax in the semi-final of the Fairs Cup, and we'd gone on to win that in real style against Anderlecht. And, in 1972, we'd hung on really well in Amsterdam – I had one of my better games – and we had a real chance. Peter Marinello missed an open goal in the first minute, and then George Graham headed the ball past me. I shouted and everything, but he says he never heard the call.

Bertie Mee still remembers the incident ruefully.

> I never forgave George for putting through his own goal against Ajax in the European Cup, a header from the edge of the area, but that was George.

In fact, Graham headed the ball past Bob Wilson, but it was an Ajax forward who ran it into the net. That goal silenced Highbury. It took the heart out of the place, and one could feel the sense of loss for the rest of the evening. A place in the European Cup, now better known as the Champions League, is hard earned, and what is hard earned is more mourned when lost.

Ray Kennedy rises high over a Stromgodset defender at Highbury during the 4-0 first-round second-leg European Cup game in September 1971. Kennedy scored and the Gunners went through 7-1 on aggregate.

There was more disappointment in 1972-73. Late-season failure meant second place in the League, and there was a Cup semi-final defeat at Hillsborough, 2-1 against Second Division Sunderland who went on to gain a sensational victory over Leeds United in the Final. Pat Rice recalls those days:

The best game for me was when we won the championship at Tottenham, without a doubt. We'd been chasing Leeds all the while, and when you're 21, 22, you don't realise the significance of what you've actually achieved. It's when you try and do it again, that's when you've got the problem. I wasn't really involved with the Fairs Cup. I was one of the subs in Belgium when Ray came on and headed the goal, but I think I wasn't involved after that.

My biggest disappointment as a player was when we got beaten in the Final by Leeds. It was coming back on the Sunday after losing the match, and you're going round Highbury and Islington, and there's all the scarves in the windows and the banners and everything, and you can't help but feel that you've let the people down. We were really bitterly disappointed. Another disappointment was when Sunderland beat us in the semi-final, that was a hell of a disappointment because everyone expected us to win. Damn that game…

Mee's achievements at Highbury are legendary, but even he feels that there were times when he erred, when he made a mistake although many would feel that is being unjust to himself.

Obviously I made mistakes. We all make mistakes. Marinello was a mistake on two counts. He had outstanding ability – there was no doubt about that – and I thought that in our environment at the club he would be disciplined by the rest of the players, and that was the first mistake I made. But there was a more fundamental mistake I made with Marinello. Immediately he'd signed, he came to me the next day and said, "Look, boss, my uncle is a feature writer of the *Express,* and I'm committed to write articles for him." I said, "Don't let that happen again. If you're committed and you've given your word, then OK, but you will not commit yourself to anything again outside this club without my permission." So I think I made a mistake there. It was a learning experience. He had a lot of ability, but he didn't have the necessary get up and go. He got better, tougher, but not enough.

Bob Wilson believes that his old manager is being harsh on himself.

Peter Marinello disappointed, but it wasn't really a mistake. Too much was put upon him. He came down with the glamour boy image at a time when George Best was the hero. He had a brilliant opening game at Manchester United when he went up there, scored a goal and had a great debut. He really did not reproduce what was expected of him after that. There were mistakes. If you are buying players, you are always going to make mistakes. Players will have a great time, and you think,

Left: John Radford and Grasshopper Zurich's Citherlet are airborne as Arsenal skipper Frank McLintock looks on. Arsenal won this game at Highbury in November 1982 3-0 to move through 5-0 on aggregate to the European Cup quarter-finals.

Right: Peter Storey fights his way through against the Swiss champions. Kennedy, George and Radford scored the goals in front of 31,000 spectators. That was as far as the Gunners went, however. Ajax of Amsterdam beat them in the last eight.

Peter Marinello takes the ball away from Liverpool's Steve Heighway at Highbury in September 1972. The result was a goalless draw and Arsenal finished runners-up, three points behind champions Liverpool that season.

Alan Ball loses the ball as Derby's Bruce Rioch – later to manage Arsenal – gets a foot in the way at Highbury in April 1974. Only 26,000 saw the Gunners win 2-0 and at the end of the season they finished tenth and had gone out of both the FA and League Cups early on.

"We'll get hold of him". Jeff Blockley never played as well for us as he played for Coventry. He was brilliant at Coventry.

Marinello was to move to Portsmouth, and Blockley, having played centre-half for England went to Leicester City. Of the Double side, only Pat Rice provided a link with the side that, managed by Terry Neill, reached three Cup Finals in consecutive seasons. Rice was captain in each of those Finals.

Terry Neill made me captain when he came. Alan Ball left and went, I think, to Southampton, and I took over as captain. I saw myself as a liaison officer between the first team and the management and vice versa. If they were thinking of doing something, and I thought it may cause problems within the dressing room

area, then I would certainly tell them. Likewise, if I thought there were any problems coming out of the dressing room area, I would also liaise with the coach or manager and say, "Listen, if you do this, then there is every possibility that this may happen." At least I would give them food for thought.

I was captain in 1979 when we won the Cup, and that was a great moment for me, indeed. We'd been there in 1978 and we'd lost to Ipswich by 1-0, and it could have been more to be truthful because we had players that weren't right and it showed.

When we got to the semi-final against Wolves the following year Liam said, "I wasn't fit in the Final last year. I'm not playing in the semi-final this year. I'm not fit." And, in fairness, Steve Gatting came in and did brilliantly. He was absolutely brilliant.

We weren't at our best against Ipswich and should have been beaten by more, and I remember going round the players in the dressing room and saying, "Remember how you feel now, because when it comes round this time next year we want to be in here as winners."

We won the one that people didn't expect us to and lost the other two, but we were always confident of beating Manchester United because we knew that we had the people for them. Likewise, we knew that in the semi-final we could beat Liverpool because we had the answers at that time to all their terrific players, but they didn't have the answer to Liam Brady.

Liam Brady was a wonderfully creative footballer, and, earlier in the season in which Arsenal beat Manchester United 3-2 at Wembley, he gave a devastating display against Tottenham at White Hart Lane. It was the Saturday before Christmas, and Arsenal gave their supporters the best of all presents, a 5-0 victory at the home of the old enemy. Alan Sunderland scored a hat-trick, and Stapleton and Brady added the other goals. It was breathtaking stuff, but the match of the season from the Arsenal point of view was the Cup

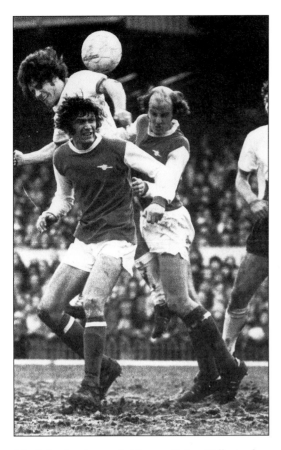

Far left: **Liverpool's Kevin Keegan climbs above Peter Simpson and Terry Mancini at Highbury in February 1975. By now the Gunners were slipping still further down the table to finish 16th.**

Top right: **Manchester United's Stewart Houston – another opponent who one would day manage Arsenal – gets the better of Liam Brady at Highbury in November 1975. Arsenal finished 17th and although 40,000 saw this game, some of the less attractive visitors to Highbury saw less than 20,000 through the gates.**

Bottom right: **This was certainly a low spot for Arsenal, beaten 1-0 at home on the opening day of the 1976-77 season by newly-promoted Bristol City. Here, City's Paul Cheesley heads the only goal of the game.**

Final. In the Arsenal side was Brian Talbot who, the previous year, had played for Ipswich against them.

I got the first goal in the Final against Manchester United, and the year before I'd played in the Final for Ipswich against Arsenal. I didn't think it was strange because I'd always wanted to play for Arsenal. I thought they were the biggest club in the country, and, fortunately, they wanted me as well. When I played for Ipswich against them in the Final, I did know they were interested, and I thought the Cup Final would be my last game. I'm not a very sentimental person in that respect. If I'm working for a club, I give it all my energy. So playing for Ipswich was brilliant, playing for Arsenal was even better.

Whenever I pulled a red shirt on I gave it my best, not least because I wanted to keep in the team. I think my best moment at Arsenal was my first game, I did well. I'd always wanted to play for Arsenal, as I've said, so it was a dream come true. The only other clubs I ever wanted to play for were Ipswich and Manchester United. I was

denied the third although Ron Atkinson wanted to get me there, but he finally got me at West Brom.

To play at Arsenal, in front of a big crowd, big stadium, you run out on to the pitch, and you've played big games, played for your country, but you felt it was a privilege to play there. We beat Nottingham Forest 2-1 on an icy pitch. I couldn't believe it. It was a big day for me.

If I had a disappointment, it was that we never won the championship. I thought we would when I came to Arsenal. I thought we had a good side at the time, a good eleven. I'm not criticising Terry Neill because I'll always be grateful he took me to the club, but I always felt he was one player short – on the right side. He signed Petrovic who'd been the Yugo-slav captain, but he wasn't good enough. At Liverpool, if they had somebody injured, they could replace him with someone who was as good, but we didn't have quite that squad. I think at the time we wished we had a couple more players.

We had a good record against

119

A better day: Pat Rice is congratulated by Liam Brady and Malcolm Macdonald after scoring against QPR at Highbury in October 1976. The Gunners went on to win 3-2 and finished the season in eighth place.

Malcolm Macdonald turns away in delight after scoring against Manchester United at Highbury in April 1978. Macdonald hit two in Arsenal's 3-1 win. The Gunners finished the season in fifth place.

Liam Brady in full flight against Leeds United at Highbury on the opening day of the 1978-79 season, pursued by Brian Flynn and Tony Currie. Brady scored both Arsenal goals in the 2-2 draw.

Liverpool. We beat them in that semi-final which went on for ever, and I got the winning goal in the match at Coventry.

Brian Talbot was that most coveted of players, a tenacious midfielder who could score goals. He and Sunderland arrived at Price's cross together in the twelfth minute of the Final against Manchester United, but it was Talbot who knocked it past Bailey. Arsenal went two up before half-time when Brady jinked his way down the right and crossed for Stapleton to head in. Arsenal were in total control, but, with five minutes remaining, they failed to clear a centre from the right. Willie Young succeeded only in diverting the ball away from the goal to McQueen who drove it into the net. Two minutes later, Manchester United were level. McIlroy came in from the right, had a fortunate bounce off a defender and slid the ball past Jennings. The dejection among Arsenal players and supporters must have been felt in Gillespie Road. Psycho-logically, Arsenal should have been beaten. A comfortable lead had been swept away in the last five minutes of the match, but now three players, in particular, produced a moment of inspiration that, like any thing of beauty, will remain a joy for ever. Brady took the ball deep into the United half and set Rix free down the

left with a precisely-judged pass. Rix took the ball his stride, measured his cross perfectly and swung the ball over the grasping fingers of Bailey. Sunderland, racing in at the far post, slid the ball into the net. He turned and ran

Former Spurs and Aberdeen cent re-half Willie Young goes up for a high ball against Manchester United and Lou Macari appears to be lending an involuntary supporting role. Young made almost 250 senior appearances for Arsenal between March 1977 and December 1981.

Brian Talbot looks determined as he scores Arsenal's first goal of the 1979 FA Cup Final against Manchester United, getting between Martin Buchan and Steve Coppell and past Jimmy Nichol (2). The other Arsenal player is Alan Sunderland.

Frank Stapleton heads Arsenal's second goal. just before half-time and the game looked as good as won. But United fought back to 2-2 in the closing stages, only for Alan Sunderland to score a remarkable last-minute winner as extra-time seemed certain.

back to the halfway line like a man possessed. Within seconds the final whistle went.

Next season, Arsenal were back at Wembley again, but they had to endure an energy-sapping battle with Liverpool to get there. The semi-final was decided at the fourth attempt. There were no penalty shoot outs in this period, and, after a draw at Hillsborough and two draws at Villa Park, Brian Talbot settled the issue with an early goal at Highfield Road, Coventry. Perhaps those four games took their toll of Arsenal who were beaten by West Ham in the Final, a headed goal by Trevor Brooking being enough to win the match. For Laura

Levy, it was the start of a terrible four days, and she was not alone in her misery.

The biggest disappointment was when I was very young, and we lost to West Ham in the Cup Final when Trevor Brooking scored the only header of his career. Then four days later we lost in Brussels. I didn't go to Brussels, but that was the worst week I remember. It was disappointing because we thought we'd win both or at least one. We went down to West Ham, and there was always the excuse that perhaps we didn't play so well because we were holding ourselves back for the big one, because it was a big one. It didn't cross my mind at all before the West Ham game that we'd lose it. I burst into tears, and I remember going home and my mum saying, "That's it. You're not taking her again. She gets all upset."

Andy Charalambous was at both games.

Liam Brady (wearing a United shirt and inside-out) holds aloft the FA Cup after Arsenal's win in a sensational Final which only came to life late in the second half.

Arsenal players celebrate their 1979 FA Cup Final win.

In May 1980 Arsenal appeared in a second successive FA Cup Final but this time finished on the losing side as West Ham lifted the trophy with a rare headed goal from Trevor Brooking. Here, Liam Brady and Brian Talbot close in on Paul Allen, at 17 years and 256 days the youngest player ever to appear in an FA Cup Final.

David O'Leary hammers the ball clear, watched by Willie Young and West Ham's David Cross.

My first disappointment with the Arsenal was the late Seventies, the team that Terry Neill built. We reached three Cup Finals – we got to four if you add the Cup-winners' Cup Final – and we won only one of them. I remember the year we lost to West Ham and then we lost to Valencia four days later, and I was at both those games. That was the worst time ever. There had been other disappointments. It had been difficult to keep the interest going, and then we beat Leeds 7-0 in the League Cup, and to see them beat a side like Leeds by that score lifted everyone, and you were keen not to miss a match again.

The road to the Cup-winners' Cup Final against Valencia in Brussels had been a difficult

one. The semi-final was against Juventus, and there seemed little hope of success when the Italian side drew 1-1 at Highbury. Arsenal's equaliser came late when Bettega headed the ball in his own net from a corner. The return match remained 0-0 until the closing minutes when substitute Vaessen scored and gave Arsenal the tie. One remembers listening to the commentary on the radio, and the excitement and surprise of the commentator at Arsenal's goal contrasting with the funereal silence of the crowd.

In the Final, it was Arsenal fans who were silenced. The Gunners outplayed Valencia for 90 minutes, only to lose 5-4 in a penalty shoot out which had been introduced in European competitions. Brady, the regular penalty-taker, and Rix were the Arsenal culprits. For Brady, it was agony.

My best moment was the 1979 Cup Final, winning against Manchester United. The worst came the following year, losing two Cup Finals in four days, against West Ham and Valencia. The Valencia game was the penalty shoot out, and it still goes through my mind whether I should have put it in the other corner. The goalkeeper saved mine. We didn't miss. Graham and I both hit to the same side, and he saved both times, and they weren't bad penalties.

It is a cruel system, because I thought we were the better side throughout the match, but we were very jaded after a long, hard season. I read nowadays about playing so many games, and players are tired, but I was telling the manager a few weeks ago that we played something like 70 games that season. The West Ham game was played on a boiling hot day, and they got an early goal and just sat back, and we found it very difficult to break them down.

Liam Brady left to play in Italy, returning in the twilight of his career to spend some time with West Ham; Brian Talbot moved to West Bromwich Albion, first as player then as manager; and both Terry Neill and Don Howe departed to be succeeded by George Graham. There was immediate joy when Liverpool were beaten 2-1 in the League Cup Final. Ian Rush scored first for Liverpool, and, at that time, Liverpool had never lost a match in which he had scored, but Charlie Nicholas scored twice for Arsenal. The second goal was a huge deflection, but it gave Arsenal the Cup. It was Charlie's last big gesture for Arsenal. Early the following season, he returned to Scotland and joined Aberdeen.

If the Cup win over Liverpool was the first "high" of George Graham's reign, the League Cup Final the next year, was the first "low", a most bizarre defeat by Luton Town. Like the rest of us who saw it, Andy Charalambous looks back on it with incredulity.

> Then there was the Final against Luton. What a wonderful game if you were a Luton supporter. We were one down, went two-one up, Winterburn missed a penalty, and we were murdering them. I'd flown back from America, and a pal picked me up at Heathrow and took me straight to the game. Then Gus Caesar decided to do his "I'm a comedian" bit. Dear old Gus. Luton got two goals in the last couple of minutes. He was not a bad player, Gus, but everyone will remember that performance.

Indeed, they will. To return home from Wembley and watch a recording of the game on video was a surreal experience. Arsenal began slowly and went one down, and then, at the beginning of the second half, they tore Luton apart. Hayes came on as substitute. and he and Smith scored. Hayes tapped the ball against a post when the goal beckoned. Rocastle was tripped, and Winterburn hit the ball lamely to the goalkeeper's left. Smith missed a chance. So dominant were Arsenal that it seemed, on video, that they must have won, that one had awoken from a nightmare and that the last-minute aberrations had never happened. But they had.

There were to be ample compensations, but there were also disappointments. Bob Wilson and Alan Smith are in agreement as to one of the greatest.

> With George Graham, we won everything. The only disappointment was against Benfica. How they lost to Benfica, I'll never know. They were the better side, and Smithy missed a vital chance. It was like us with Ajax.

Alan Smith was in the game.

> There were disappointments. The Benfica game was one. Over the 90 minutes at Highbury, we could have won 3-0. I had a goal chance, not too difficult. Tony Adams hit the post from about three yards out. It was only in extra-time when we were pushing forward that they hit us. That was a big disappointment. That game was a big influence on George's tactics for the Cup-winners' Cup some years after. He was a bit more cautious in his approach.
>
> I think losing against Tottenham in the semi-final of the Cup was the biggest disappointment for the players. Their players were so gloating afterwards that to lose to them was a sickener. The Double had been on.
>
> Wrexham had been another disappointment, but Jimmy Carter scored a goal which was disallowed for no reason we could see. And you're always disappointed when things are not going right for yourself. You go home, and you're miserable.

Graham Rix leaves Leicester City's Peter Walsh in his wake at Highbury in October 1980, when Frank Stapleton scored the only goal of the game. Rix played in over 450 first-team games for Arsenal. Brian Talbot says that Rix and Brady in the same team would be a luxury today when power and pace are more in demand than outright skill, which both of those players possessed in abundance.

Paul Gascoigne's stunning free-kick beats David Seaman during the 1991 FA Cup semi-final against Spurs which was played at Wembley before a crowd of nearly 78,000. It saw Spurs on their way to a 3-1 win but for Arsenal, a major success was just around the corner.

The 3-1 defeat by Tottenham in the semi-final at Wembley in 1991 was a chastening experience, any defeat by Tottenham is, but this one was especially so because it was one of only three defeats suffered in the entire season. Arsenal were caught cold in the first ten minutes and fell behind to a cross from the right and to a Gascoigne free-kick which had been needlessly conceded by Limpar. Alan Smith pulled one back, and those of us steeped in the history of the club anticipated another recovery from two down to go alongside those famous semi-final transformations against Chelsea and Stoke City in years gone by. Lineker shattered those dreams early in the second half as David Seaman, enjoying a marvellous season, had what was probably his least impressive game for Arsenal. For Lee Dixon, it was one of the few lows he has endured at Arsenal.

I didn't enjoy losing to Tottenham in the semi-final, but that was a one-off day, and we soon got over that. I was very disappointed when I didn't get in Terry Venables's first squad. He came in as a new manager after Graham Taylor, and I hadn't let England down as far as I was concerned. I was quite happy with 21 caps and quite optimistic that I'd be in Venables's first squad. I was playing quite well for Arsenal, but when his first squad came out I wasn't even in it. It didn't even enter my head that I wouldn't be in it. I took it for granted that he'd keep the same players who Graham finished with and have a look at us all, but I didn't get a phone call or anything. That was a disappointment, and it hurt for a bit. Then the second squad came out, and I wasn't in that. By the time the third and fourth came out, I'd resigned myself to the fact that

I didn't figure in his plans so I don't look at the squads any more.

I've had lots of ups and downs at Arsenal, not so many downs, that's been the nice thing about it. I think the highlight came the season after I joined when we won the League at Anfield. We've had a lot of trophies we've won since then, but that one stands out more than any of them, just because of the way we did it.

Copenhagen was big, too. That was a different type of atmosphere altogether. We were total underdogs although we had been underdogs at Anfield, but we should have won the League that year two months before we did. We had it sewn up, and we nearly threw it away, so to bounce back and win it with what was practically the last kick of the game was something special. But Copenhagen, the fans were the biggest influence on that game. There were so many of them there that, although we were the underdogs, we didn't want to let them down.

The debate continues as to what was the high point of George Graham's reign at Arsenal – Anfield 1989 or Copenhagen 1994? Anfield 1989, could not have been scripted better had it been the last act of a great drama. The Liverpool ground was the setting for the last game of the season, and the home side led the table by two points from Arsenal who had not won at Anfield for fourteen years. Arsenal could only only claim the championship if they beat Liverpool by at least 2-0. To add to the drama, the kick-off was delayed by more than ten minutes to give Arsenal fans the chance of getting into the ground after road works had caused traffic congestion.

The first half was goalless although Arsenal had the better of the play, but, seven minutes into the second half, obstruction by Whelan brought an indirect free-kick which was taken by Winterburn. Alan Smith nudged the ball home for what he considers the most important and pleasing goal he ever scored for Arsenal. In the dying minutes of the match, Lee Dixon cleared from deep in his own half to Smith who, tightly marked, executed a reverse pass which sent Michael Thomas free. Smith's

pass caught the Liverpool defence unawares, and Thomas surged past two men into the penalty area and stabbed the ball into the bottom left-hand corner of the net as Grobbelaar committed himself. Seconds later, Thomas was back in the Arsenal penalty area breaking up a Liverpool attack, and seconds after that, the final whistle blew, and Arsenal were champions in the most dramatic of circumstances. For Alan Smith, it was the greatest of nights even though he scored the goal which beat Parma in the European Cup-winners' Cup Final five years later.

There was great togetherness in those days. It wasn't the same in '94. We weren't playing well in the League, and our championship challenge was over after about four weeks. You could see we weren't going to win the League, and George started picking teams with an eye to the future. It was great for me against Parma to get the winning goal, but I didn't think the side as a whole was as good as it had been in '89 and '91 either as a team or in team spirit. It was a decent team spirit, but it was different. In the

earlier days, everybody was fresh to it, and it was all new. None of us had really won anything. A few years down the line, it's very much the same. It was for me, anyway.

I think George was worried about the Final in Copenhagen because we had injuries and suspensions. Our midfield was Ian Selley, Steve Morrow and Paul Davis, which left us a bit short there so I think he was worried. In the approach to that game, you could sense that he was concerned, but he had a very experienced bunch of lads apart from Selley and Morrow, and we were confident we could do the job. But he sent us out there all knowing what to do, what our jobs were. At the end of it, he sent us out there in a confident frame of mind. In his team talk before the match, he didn't betray any worry, and he tried to send us out confident in ourselves.

Bob Wilson's opinion differs to that of Alan Smith and, indeed, to that of some others, but many of those who were in Copenhagen that balmy evening in 1994 would not argue with Bob.

Alan Smith heads a 52nd-minute goal at Anfield in the last match of the 1988-89 season. Michael Thomas a second with almost the last kick of the match and Arsenal were champions after probably the most exciting end to a season in the Football League's history.

Alan Smith has just scored one of his four goals in the 6-1 drubbing of FK Austria Memphis in the European Cup first-round first-leg match at Highbury in September 1991.

The greatest night of George Graham as a manager in my view was when they played Parma in Copenhagen. They had five reserves playing because of injury and suspension. I was part of the group that was in on the team talk. I listened to what he said. He said, "We've got to play it this

Nigel Winterburn challenges Chelsea's Kerry Dixon at Highbury in October 1991. Arsenal won 3-2 and at the end of the season were champions again.

way tonight or we'll get murdered. We've got injury problems. So, Ian Selley – you do this..." And these young kids went out there, withstood early pressure, and Smithy scores a goal from a throw-in. That breaks it, and from then on, George's tactics are always going to win. I thought that the Parma coach who came out and said, "What he did tonight was brilliant," was right.

They won the Cup and the League Cup in the same season. They won the championship twice, and I still say they won both championships with great flourish. If you actually look at some of the goals they scored in 1991, they were dazzling. They lost only one game, and it is one of the great disgraces of football that they were not given the praise or credit they deserved. They were Arsenal and George Graham, and it wasn't fashionable to say, "Hang on a minute, they've lost only one game, at Chelsea. The goalkeeper has let in only eighteen goals. He came as close as dammit to beating Ray Clemence's record of sixteen at Liverpool. He's had a blinding season. They've all had blinding seasons." They scored fantastic goals, and had it been any other team, they would have had praise heaped upon them. They didn't win Team of the Year on Sports Review – that went to somebody else. They only lost three games in the entire season. They lost to Tottenham in the Cup semi-final so they came close to doing the Double. I think that team won with great style.

Perhaps the '89 side was not so stylish, but that first championship was a great achievement, particularly in the way it was won, of course. But again I say Parma was the great night. George Graham would probably always say to go to Liverpool and to have to win 2-0, and to do it was an amazing achievement.

Alan Smith adds a postscript in support of Bob Wilson's view of the 1991 side.

The side of 1991 never got the

Paul Merson leaves two Benfica players grounded in the second-leg match against Benfica at Highbury in November 1991, but the Portuguese champions won the tie 4-2 on aggregate.

credit it deserved. We only lost one game when we won the championship, but people talked about boring Arsenal. In both championship years, we played really good football, and we were top scorers on both occasions – and people tend to overlook that. It wasn't fashionable to praise us. Maybe in 50 years time…?

It's funny as a player, but the cups don't mean half as much to me as the League. I didn't play in the first Cup Final against Sheffield Wednesday. I started the second one, but I wasn't an automatic choice.

In the main, supporters would side with Alan Smith in saying that the victory at Anfield in 1989 was the "night to remember". Laura Levy's experiences have remained firmly in her mind. Her partner, Dave, did not accompany Laura to Liverpool, but he has equally clear memories of the evening, but we should hear Laura's story first.

Tracey and I left Finchley 12.00 to go to Anfield for a 7.45 kick off, which was ample time, but we'd forgotten it

was a Bank Holiday and that there were road works on the M6. At 7.20, we'd just come off the M62, and this big car, we think it was a BMW, pulled up alongside us and got our attention somehow. They wound their window down and said, "Are you going to the match?" Which was a stupid question because our car was all decked out in Arsenal colours. I was just going to make a rude reply when he said,

A black day in the history of Arsenal Football Club as Wrexham's Steve Watkins scores the winner to produce a memorable FA Cup shock at the Racecourse Ground in January 1992.

"You'll never get there. The traffic's not moving. Follow us!"

Thinking we were likely to be mugged or raped, we went off into this side road. He pulled up, told us to park the car and gave a lad £3 to look after it. All we remembered was that we parked it opposite a pub called 'The … ?' We didn't see what.

We got into the car with them, and the chap in front who was driving had flown in from Hong Kong that morning to watch the match. The guy in the other front seat was Australian and owned three restaurants in Chelsea, and his son was in the back seat. We drove into Liverpool where, at the ground, the guard said, "Good day, Mr So and So" and pointed him to a director's car parking space.

We go to our seat. We win. And an hour afterwards, after we'd celebrated, Tracey suddenly said, "They won't have waited for us. Where's the car?" All we knew was that it was opposite a pub called "The … ?" in a street in Liverpool.

They had waited for us. They took us back to our car, showed us how to get back on the motorway, and to this day, I don't know who it was. We'd have never have got there otherwise.

They actually delayed the kick-off. Dave takes up his part of the story:

She promised faithfully before going to the game that when she got in she'd be quiet. She said she wouldn't wake me when she got in because I'd had a busy week, and we were going sailing early the next morning. I watched it on television, and I was pleased they won and went to bed.

At half past two, I'm asleep. The front door slams, and before she's even mounted the first step, she's shouting, "We won. We won – Champions!" She comes up the stairs shouting. There's no way I can stay asleep. And instead of getting undressed and coming to bed, she talks me through the game I've watched on television. Then she goes down to the lounge to watch it on video because she reckons she didn't see Micky Thomas's goal hit the back of the net.

Andy Charalambous's evening followed a slightly different pattern:

The best time with Arsenal – there's only one – winning the League at Anfield. I was there. The atmosphere was unbelievable. We got up there late because there'd been hold-ups, and when we finally got into the ground we found Arsenal had made many

Previous page: Paul Merson and Ian Wright celebrate one of Merson's hat-trick goals against Crystal Palace at Highbury in April 1992. The Gunners won 4-1.

Ian Wright and Alan Smith congratulate Tony Adams after his goal against Newcastle United at Highbury in September 1994. Alas, by the end of the afternoon Arsenal had gone down 3-2.

friends there because they'd come out and given away flowers. All the way through the ground the tension was so high. Then we scored through Alan Smith, but what made it really special was that, towards the end of the game, we thought we'd lost. We'd played really well. We were fantastic. We were winning, but not by enough. It got to the closing minutes of the game, and we were thinking, "Good try, we've done really well, but there you are, we're not going to do it." And then Michael Thomas went through into the penalty area, and I can remember him putting the ball into the net. After that, to be honest, it's a complete blank until I got the papers the following morning. I was with my brother, and I went absolutely ape. I don't remember them getting the trophy. I was doing a jig, singing and dancing. Some of the Liverpool supporters were very fair and clapped us; others were particularly offensive. We were near the barrier which separated us from the Liverpool supporters, and I'll never forget the look on a guy's face near us. He was in a state of shock. He sat there in utter disbelief as if somebody had just shot his grannie. He couldn't believe it because if Thomas hadn't scored, Liverpool would have won the League.

We came back to Highbury that night in the coaches, and we got back to the stadium at about three in the morning, and there were 20,000 to 30,000 people outside the ground. It was like joining a street party. I ended up in the Arsenal Tavern on the corner of Monsel Road. I don't know if he had a license to stay open after 11.00pm, but he didn't shut. People wouldn't go home.

From those at the ground and the millions watching on television, the reaction was phenomenal. It had been eighteen years since Arsenal had last won the title, and then they had taken it in the closing minutes of the last match of the season. Supporters rushed to buy the newspapers the following morning to see written confirmation of what they had wit-

nessed. Barry Lemmon was one who, frustrated by the restrained language of *The Guardian* and *The Daily Telegraph*, added *The Sun* and *The Mirror* because they came closer to the ecstasy with their banner headlines.

Victory over Parma in Copenhagen was different. The emotion was generated by a wonderful defensive performance, a masterly tactical plan which left the Italian side impotent. If Bould was beaten, the forward still had to contend with Adams; if Adams was passed, there was Dixon or Bould again. Brolin hit a post seconds after Campbell had missed a good chance, but once Smith's shot had gone in off the post, the iron curtain descended, and the Arsenal goal was rarely threatened save once, close to half-time, when Seaman, playing with cracked ribs, sucked in a powerful drive and winced with pain.

It is customary to heap praise on flowing, attacking football, but the supreme quality of Arsenal's defensive organisation presented a beauty of its own, and the crowd responded to it with intelligent appreciation; so, for once, did the press who were generally unstinting in their praise.

There were other factors attendant on the

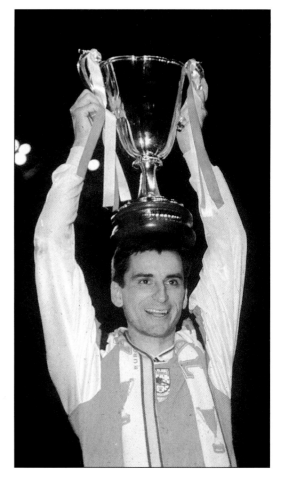

Alan Smith, scorer of the only goal of the game, with the European Cup-winner's Cup after Arsenal's victory over Parma in the 1994 Final in Copenhagen.

match which added to the occasion in both happiness and poignancy. Copenhagen is one of the most beautiful cities in the world. It is spacious and welcoming. Its people are hospitable, and Parken, the refurbished national stadium, was a perfect venue for the Final. By mid-afternoon, the centre of Copenhagen was full of Arsenal and Parma fans. They exchanged scarves, had an improvised game of football and were photographed with their arms around each other.

Many found their way into Tivoli, that magical leisure garden for all ages in the middle of the city, where they ate and drank together and tasted the variety of delights on offer. The Danes are not very fond of Danny Kaye's Hollywood version of Hans Christian Andersen, but "wonderful, wonderful Copenhagen" was the perfect backdrop to Arsenal v Parma.

The poignancy was that two players, in particular, were missing from the Arsenal line up who had done much to help the side to the Final. Ian Wright, victim of his own enthusiasm or impetuosity, had been punished with a yellow card for a rash challenge in the semi-final. It was his second of the competition and brought an automatic suspension from the next match, the Final.

If Wright could be accused of bringing his problems on himself, the same accusation could not be levelled at John Jensen. The Danish midfielder had been playing the best football of his Arsenal career and had been a dynamic force on the path to the Cup-winners' Final. Playing for his country in a friendly international, he was viciously fouled, and his dream of playing in a European Final for the club he loved in his home city was shattered. He was on crutches instead of being on the field, yet the game has happy memories for him.

There were many good moments for me at Arsenal, but the highlights were probably the FA Cup and League Cup Finals against Sheffield Wednesday. We made history by being the first club to win both Cups in the same season, and being part of an Arsenal side that made history was very special. I think the FA Cup Final was the longest ever, and the thrill of winning at the end was unbelievable.

The other highlight was both a marvellous moment, and, at the same time, my biggest disappointment, the Cup-winners' Cup Final in Copenhagen. I will never forget that day, coming to my home town, and unable to play due to injury, yet being every bit as excited as those playing and receiving a fantastic reception from the Arsenal fans. Copenhagen was red and white for a day. It was amazing.

I knew for a long time that my injury would keep me out of the Final and that was obviously a major disappointment, but, again, being part of that great club I was made to feel one of the team that night by players and staff alike. The manager allowed me to stay in Copenhagen after the match, and going into the city with friends to savour the atmosphere was marvellous. The fans were brilliant.

I had a wonderful time at Arsenal, and this was due in no small way to the magnificent staff at Highbury. I had never experienced such a positive attitude all through a club.

Winning a place in a European competition has become the major priority for any club, and Pat Rice was acutely aware of what seemed to be a traumatic result at the beginning of the 1997-98 season.

Everybody wants to win the League and everybody wants to win the Cups, but there's only one team can win the League, and only two teams can win the Cups. We're fighting, but there was disappointment for us all when we were put out by Salonika. It was a difficult tie for us, and we didn't do ourselves justice when we went over there. Europe is very important to the players without a doubt. You always want to test yourself against the best, and there's nothing better than going to play against Milan, Juventus, Porto, Real Madrid and teams like that.

Dennis Bergkamp wondered at the end of the 1998 season whether that defeat by Salonika was not something of a blessing in disguise.

My biggest disappointment has probably been my suspensions, especially in the first half of the season because I was playing well, and then I had to miss three games through suspension. That's what stopped my form, and that was a big disappointment.

Being knocked out of the European competition by the Greek team was a great disappointment at the time, but when you look at it now it might have helped us going out so soon because it meant that we were able to concentrate on the other competitions.

Even at the lowest points there can be glimmers of hope, and highs can come in the most unexpected circumstances and not always on the field or at a match, as Laura Levy discovered.

I was dissatisfied with the job I was in, and I wanted more money. The firm I was working for were doing mortgage repossession, and the interest rates had gone up, and I was generally discontented. I actually applied to Lord's. I thought it would be good to do something sporting, and they were looking for a secretary. I also applied to the FA. I didn't even get a reply from the FA, and Lord's – the money was appalling!

I saw the job I am in now advertised in the *Evening Standard*, and I applied and was interviewed by the office manager. They had had 30 applicants, but they brought it down to myself and another girl, and the two of us had to go back for a second interview with the guy who is now my boss. We'd had to write down hobbies, interests etc, and I'd just written down "season ticket holder football; season ticket holder cricket".

At the interview, he said, "There isn't much to choose between you and the other girl. Which football team do you support? Depending on what your answer is, will depend on whether you get the job."

I said, "Arsenal." And he got up out of his chair, shook my hand and said, "See you Monday." And that was it. He never even got as far as asking me if I could type. I had no speed test. No spelling test. Nothing. We had a general chat

about music, about sport – "Did you see this game? Did you see that game? See you Monday." And that was it.

I started on the Monday, and on the Wednesday, Arsenal were playing at home. He was sitting three rows in front of me. He was a season ticket holder, and I must have been sitting behind him for the past ten years.

I actually got Dave to change my season ticket because I thought that I couldn't be this nice, efficient person at work and this screaming loony at football. I think if I'd have said, "Spurs", he would have said goodbye.

I never lie to him. I can't say I'm having a tooth out, and I don't abuse his trust and kindness. It doesn't matter what time I get back, like from Denmark, I'm in at 9.30 next morning. I think he sent me home at four because he thought I was still drunk and might fall asleep.

There was a time when there was an important midweek game, and I needed to have the day off, or at least half a day off. I walked into the office and he looked up and said, "Don't even think about it." He was going, and one of us had to be in the office.

A half-century of highs and lows – thankfully, not too many lows. There was the fading of Whittaker's side in the Fifties, and the day that David Herd was transferred to Manchester United. Sadly, history was to be repeated twenty years later when Frank Stapleton took the same route. Among the older supporters, he has never been forgiven for that move. It seemed a form of treachery.

There was frustration in the injury that ended "Super Mac's" career at Highbury, a career which flourished all too briefly, and there was frustration that Glenn Helder, George Graham's last signing, never quite fulfilled the immense promise that he showed on his debut. That debut came on the day that Graham left Highbury, and Arsenal beat Nottingham Forest 1-0. It was a highly emotional evening. It had been a highly emotional and disturbing season, and none of us could have guessed in August that we would have been ecstatic about a narrow win over a moderate Forest side in February.

Above: Ian Wright scores for Arsenal against Sampdoria during the European Cup-winners' Cup semi-final second-leg game in Italy in April 1995.

Left: Sampdoria's Roberto Mancini lobs David Seaman, but Seaman's heroics in the penalty shoot out ensured that the Gunners went through to another Final.

Three months later, we all had a nightmare in Paris. Arsenal qualified for the European Cup-winners' Cup Final for the second year in succession. In contrast to the rest of Arsenal's year, which had been one of rumour and despair, the path to the Final had been studded with glory. Wright had scored a sensational goal in Auxerre to snatch victory in the quarter-final after a draw at Highbury, and, in the semi-final, with the score 5-5 on aggregate, Arsenal won a dramatic penalty shoot out 3-2, thanks to the brilliance of David Seaman.

The Final saw Arsenal opposed to the Spanish side Real Zaragoza, who took a one-goal lead. John Hartson equalised for Arsenal,

and the game seemed destined for a penalty shoot out when, in the dying seconds, Nayim, once of Tottenham, hit an up-and-under from somewhere near the halfway line. Seaman was off his line, and although he scampered back, he could not prevent the ball from going in just under the bar. Nayim! A pet hate for Arsenal supporters when he was at White Hart Lane. This was the unkindest cut of all.

There have been other lows – defeat at home by Bradford Park Avenue in the FA Cup in 1948 springs to mind. Arsenal were sweeping all before them in the League, and they went out to a Second Division side in the third round. Arsenal trotted out wearing white,

The hero! David Seaman has just put Arsenal through to the 1995 European Cup-winners' Cup Final with a magnificent display in the shoot out.

looking like the Spurs, and we knew it would be a bad day from the start, but Nayim's goal put even that in the shade.

The "highs" far outweigh the "lows" – from White Hart Lane, 1971, to Old Trafford, 1998 – but they don't take away the pain totally. There are still times when you look back on that League Cup Final against Luton Town and can't believe it really happened, but there have been more than enough compensations since. As George Armstrong maintains, winning tends to make things easier.

I think it's the same story in any part of life, when you're winning you're happy to play every day. The only sad thing about the game is that you still can't play it when you're 60, because you don't lose the ability to think, and even on the coaching side you are always improving your all-round technique. You've got to because you're showing the kids the picture.

Laurie Scott is now in his 80s, his last game for Arsenal 47 years behind him. Was there a particular high point for him during his distinguished career?

I don't think I've got a best moment from my time with Arsenal to be honest. We won the League and we won the Cup, but it was all one great episode to me. Every time I put on the red shirt it sent a thrill through me.

Managers, Coaches and Trainers

FOOTBALL teams have coaches and physiotherapists today; in the years after the war they had trainers. It was Bertie Mee who brought about the revolution. In 1960, he succeeded Billy Milne who was the last of Arsenal's "bucket and sponge" men, and the job was upgraded to physiotherapist.

Tom Whittaker had conducted his own revolution in the Thirties. He introduced sun-ray lamps and other electrical equipment to the treatment room, devised a shooting box and was responsible for the development of head tennis, yet he tended to leave preparation very much in the hands of players themselves. Wilf Copping recalled:

> He just used to say to us, "Go on! Go out there and do your running. I shall know on Saturday whether you've done it or not."

Arthur Milton supports Wilf Copping's assertion. His experience was similar when he trained with Arsenal shortly before beginning his National Service at the end of the summer 1946.

> I went with Don Oakes. We went together, and I did all the pre-season training, and I've never been so fit in all my life. I could have run for a fortnight. I think I was never actually as fit as that ever again, because I was only eighteen.

> Tom Whittaker used to leave it to you what you did. Some blokes liked to do a lot. Others did the minimum. I think we're all different. I don't see how you can do bulk training with

people. Different blokes need different things, and if you know yourself, you'll know what to do. I didn't want much. Once I'd played two or three matches and got match fit, I only needed to stretch my legs once or twice.

In 1947, George Allison retired, and Tom Whittaker succeeded him as manager, but Whittaker still kept an eye on players' fitness as Laurie Scott discovered.

> George Allison was a very good businessman, and he ran the club very well, but Tom Whittaker looked after most things. So when Tom Whittaker became manager it didn't really make much difference.

> I remember on one occasion that I'd had a knock playing for England, and I walked up Avenell Road from the Underground. I got into the dressing room, and there was a message saying that Tom Whittaker wanted to see me upstairs. He was in charge then. I thought, "What the devil have I done wrong?"

> I went upstairs into his room, and he says, "What are you limping for?" I said, "I wasn't limping." He says, "Come here!" From his office upstairs there was a connecting door that led into the board room, and there was another connecting door from there which led to the gymnasium. Wonderful place!

> I went in there, and there was a whacking big mirror on the wall

George Allison at his desk at Highbury. Allison retired in 1947 and Tom Whittaker took over as manager, although according to Laurie Scott, little changed because Allison was a businessman and left most of the football to Whittaker anyway.

George Allison at his desk at Highbury. Allison retired in 1947 and Tom Whittaker took over as manager, although according to Laurie Scott, little changed because Allison was a businessman and left most of the football to Whittaker anyway.

where we did our exercises and everything. He took me down to the bottom, and he said, "Now walk up there." I walked up the gym, and I was rolling all over the place. Things like that used to crop up. It was incredible. They knew exactly what you were up to.

It's a strange feeling, I think, being at Highbury. They treated you like men. They didn't mollycoddle you, and you had your say. When we had a players' meeting – you'd be surprised – you'd go into the room, and Tom Whittaker, and George Allison before him, was in charge, and you had your say at the meeting. If you wanted to criticise somebody else opposite you, you did it, and you wouldn't dream of that happening in other places. You walked out of the room, and it was forgotten. Nobody ever moaned about it or resented it. We were all trying to help the performance of the team, and it was taken that way.

There are lots of things about the Arsenal that I can't think would happen in any other club. We won the Cup. We won the League. But I was fortunate to get everything else, being an international and the rest. It is all part of a great remembrance, and when you come back to it, talk about it, it was incredible – so good.

The initial success that Tom Whittaker had as a manager did not endure. The old guard were never adequately replaced, and fortune and fame faded. Where once, as today, top players jostled each other to come to Highbury, Whittaker now found it difficult to lure the very best footballers to Arsenal. Crowds which, in 1948, had hovered between 55,000 and 60,000, came down to an average 42,000 by the year of Whittaker's death, 1956. The decision to give him help by appointing Alec Stock as assistant manager was not a success, and the image of the great Arsenal began to disappear. Tom Whittaker, who had devoted his life to the club, died of a heart attack at the age of 57. The legendary Alex James had died three years earlier at the age of 51. The deaths of these two great Arsenal men so closely associated with the triumphs of the Thirties seemed to symbolise that the first golden age was finally over. Whittaker was succeeded by Jack Crayston, a stylish right-half of the pre-war era, but his reign was very

Tom Whittaker with Arthur Milton. According to Milton, Whittaker was not a good "reader" of a footballer. "He liked players who could kick the length of the field.

short. A decade which had begun with such promise was to end in decline, as Arthur Milton notes.

The problem was that I don't think Tom Whittaker could read a player. He wanted people who could kick the length of the field. He bought Nutt and Tiddy because he wanted a left-winger, and they were both right-wingers. He had a lad named Walsh, who went to Cardiff in exchange, and he was a better player than either of

them. They went downhill after that, and I think that's what put Tom in an early grave. I could see how it was going with the players he was bringing in. You only had to look at them to see they couldn't play. Players are the best judges of each other. You know what a bloke is like if you play with him.

I have always been a bad watcher. I'd rather be doing something, playing something. In those days, they didn't have substitutes. If you were on the

139

team sheet, you had to be there, and, there was this Saturday, when Con Sullivan, the goalkeeper, another Bristol lad and a keen punter, and I were on the team sheet. But I had a dog at Hackney Wick, and we weren't in the eleven, and once they were on the pitch we were all right. We waited until they'd gone out on to the field, and then my bitch was running at Hackney Wick so we went over there. She was a wonderful dog. Don Oakes and I shared her. We had a lot of good punters at Highbury like Jimmy Logie and Arthur Shaw.

Jack Crayston took over when Tom died, "Gentleman Jack", but it could never have been his job. He was a real gentleman, always looked after us, too nice to be a manager.

This is not to say that kind and pleasant men do not make good managers, but perhaps Crayston, like Billy Wright, did not possess that edge of steel which had been tempered in the

George Swindin's appointment as Arsenal manager was widely welcomed because he had been a favourite when he kept goal for the Gunners after the war. "I thought he was a great guy," says George Armstrong.

wider world and which is so necessary in the harsh world of football management. George Swindin was certainly well-versed in the demands of football management when he was put in charge of Arsenal in 1958. He had fought hard to establish himself as first-team goalkeeper at Highbury, had been a vital part of three championship sides and had played in two Cup Finals. He had played until he was 40, and, more importantly, he had served his apprenticeship as a manager with Peterborough United. It was he who laid the foundations for the phenomenal success that was to attend the "Posh" in the Sixties.

George Swindin's return to Arsenal was welcomed. He had been a favourite with the fans, had played a major role in the club's revival and salvation in 1946-47 and was very much one of the family. He spent a considerable amount of money in bringing players like George Eastham, Tommy Docherty and Johnny McLeod to Highbury, and he was never afraid to drop a star who wasn't performing well. He also brought George Armstrong to the club.

I thought George Swindin was a great guy. He was superb. When I first came down my digs were with Vic Groves, and, to be honest, Vic was frightening. I had to be in bed by ten o'clock, and if I went to the cinema, I used to run like hell to get home so that I wasn't late, but Vic was great, and so were his wife Jo and the kids. And George Swindin was brilliant. To me, he was father figure, and I had great respect for him, but if you were a minute late, God help you.

I came in late one morning with Vic Groves. The offices on the ground floor, where Gary Lewin is now, used to be the manager's office, and Vic was going past the door when it opened, and George grabbed him by the ear. And I was trying to slink by, and George said to me, "Where have you been?" So I said, "Boss, I was waiting for Vic."

I was in digs with Vic, and he was my landlord, but George said, "Don't ever wait for him. You get on the bus!"

It was the discipline that made this club great. Bertie Mee saw the

discipline was kept: collar and tie; no jeans in the club; respect for people; time-keeping; everything else. It lapsed a little after his time.

I don't go along with the view that they work harder today. We trained just as long, and we competed when we ran. Today, they've brought science into the game, but you can bring in all the terms and words, and there's nothing new. I can believe in some of the diets and some of the important stretching exercises which maybe we didn't do, but, on the whole, I think we've turned full circle. We've come back to pre-match meals the same as we had 30 years ago. People went in for bananas, Mars Bars, scrambled eggs. All out of the window now. We've gone back to the steaks, the chicken, the fish – as long as you've got four hours to digest.

To be fair to Arsène, he's refreshing. He's brought some of the old ideas back again, and there's been more thought going into it.

The training facilities at London Colney were in use when I arrived in 1961, but, in those days, if I was playing table tennis with another youngster and a first-team pro walked in, you put the bat down.

There was an incident I remember when George Swindin was sacked. It was the day we played Everton at home, and I think we lost 3-2, and I scored my first goal. It was a volley, and I thought a great goal. But Everton were a good side then.

It was after the game when Vic Groves said to me, "Geordie, come here!" Vic was a great club captain, strong character, good player, but he was coming to the end of his career when I joined Arsenal. He'd already had a long amateur career. He called me over and said, "The gaffer has been sacked."

We went in the little office near the dressing room, and there were three of us crying – me, Vic and the tea lady. It was the first experience like that that I had had, and he'd done a lot for me.

I invited him to my testimonial

Arsenal, 1961-62. Standing (left to right): Ted Magill, Mel Charles, Laurie Brown, Jack Kelsey, John McClelland, Alan Skirton, Allan Young, Terry Neill. Seated: George Swindon (manager), Danny Clapton, John Snedden, Jackie Henderson, George Eastham, Vic Groves, Billy McCulloch, Geoff Strong, Dave Bacuzzi, Bertie Mee (physiotherapist). On ground: John McLeod, Gerry Ward, Len Wills, John Petts.

dinner when I had one, but he reluctantly refused. I don't think at that time he wanted to come back to Arsenal, and I understood that. I know that people say you shouldn't be bitter, but if you think you've had a bad time and been wrongly treated, how are you going to go around with a smile on your face? Sometimes you have a right to be bitter, and you should be allowed to get over things in your own good time. I've always worn my heart on my sleeve.'

The departure of George Swindin was not unexpected. For several months the press had been conducting a campaign which championed Billy Wright as the man who could and would restore fame and glory to Arsenal. How great an influence the press had and whether they were simply reporting news which had been leaked from above, we shall never know, but Swindin was under enormous pressure. The match against Everton which George Armstrong refers to above was watched by a crowd of just over 20,000; the previous home game, against Sheffield United had been seen by 18,000. To make matters worse, these were Tottenham's "Glory, Glory" days. They had done the Double in 1961 and were riding high in Europe. Swindin's position was as unenviable as it was untenable, but Billy Wight

Billy Wright had been a great player for Wolves and England, one of the most famous names in world football after the war, but he failed as a manager. "You couldn't have wished to meet a nicer man," says George Armstrong, "but he just wasn't cut out to be a manager."

proved not to be the messiah that the press had predicted. Among those who knew him, however, there is unanimity in the opinion that Wright was a man of gentleness and charm. George Armstrong certainly holds that view.

'You couldn't meet a nicer person, but he was just not made out to be a manager. I've got great memories of Billy because he was good to me, even after I'd finished. I was in touch with him until a couple of years before he died – Billy, the Beverleys, they were all great – but I just think he needed some experience before he came here, because it was a monster of a club, and I think the expectations were too high for him. George Swindin went because he hadn't won anything, but to be fair to Billy, he brought in people like Joe Baker who was a great player.

'Billy Wright didn't last very long as manager, and I don't want it to be interpreted the wrong way, but I think that Billy's health would have suffered eventually. He was too nice, and I think he felt a failure because he'd been so successful as a player. The old chairman, Denis Hill-Wood, a lovely man, read the situation, I think, and he believed Billy's health would be affected and that Billy himself wanted to be out. He was too nice to be a manager.'

Bob Wilson endorses George Armstrong's opinion and talks about the reaction that was caused by the appointment of Bertie Mee.

'Billy Wright was a lovely guy. If I took my family or relations or some kids to the ground, and he was 30 yards away and saw you, he would go out of his way to come over and say, "Hello, everybody, I'm Billy Wright." He was brilliant like that, but, as a manager, without being too cruel, he just did not come up to it. It was not enough to have had 105 caps for England, and that has been proved along the way. The same could be said of Bobby Moore whom I loved and adored and will love and adore to my dying day. I'm not sure Bobby was cut out to be a manager.

'There are those who still argue

The new manager of Arsenal and two man who would become managers of the club. Arsenal on the eve of the 1962-63 season. Back row (left to right): Ted Magill, Eddie Clamp, Vic Groves, Jack Kelsey, Billy McCulloch, John Snedden, Laurie Brown and Terry Neill. Middle row: Bertie Mee (physiotherapist), John Barnwell, Geoff Strong, George Eastham, Billy Wight (manager), John McLeod, John Petts, Alan Skirton and Dave Bacuzzi. On ground: Joe Baker, Arfon Griffiths and Gerry Ward.

about Don Howe. He's one of the greatest of coaches. He's top of my list. He's still there now with his enthusiasm with the young lads. He's had a triple by-pass, and he's out there with the kids, and he's in charge of the coaching of the Arsenal youth system. He's like a 22-year-old, but he's not a manager. So when Bertie Mee came in it wasn't really a shock.

Billy either couldn't handle the fact that we had tremendous young players coming through or he couldn't see it. What happened was that, if we lost a game, it was never the young home-grown lads like myself – I was virtually home-grown really – that were left in. Always he would leave the big signing in. With great respect to big Ian Ure, he hardly ever got dropped because Billy had paid £110,000 for him. He probably didn't repay that money although he went on to Manchester United, and he didn't have a bad career. He was a lovely guy, but he was prone to mistakes.

To be fair to Billy, we had this real clutch of players coming through, and they came through in his time. Now the person who got the reward was Bertie Mee. Exactly the same thing,

you've got to say, happened for George Graham. The young players – the Rocastles, the Thomases – the people who came through for George Graham, were really Don Howe players. So you've got to be in the right place at the right time.

When Bertie came in we all said, "Oh, Bertie's the acting manager." But he was the shrewdest little character you could find. What he had, I think, was due to his military background. His organisational ability was amazing. Obviously, he knew that he'd only played to a certain level himself at Derby, so he was limited in his football knowledge, but he surrounded himself with the best.

He had first of all Dave Sexton, and when he moved on there was Don Howe. The reserve-team manager was Steve Burtenshaw, who was brilliant. The most difficult job in any club is reserve-team manager. For the youth team, we had Brian Whitehouse, and then he brought in George Wright as the physio. When he moved on there was Fred Street – top quality people.

In the strictest sense of the term, Bertie Mee had had no experience of football management when he took over at Arsenal in 1966, but he

Bertie Mee "was a great man-manager, a delegator. He chose the best people to work with." according to George Armstrong. When he joined Arsenal, Mee had no ambitions to get into football management, but his achievements were remarkable.

was rich in wisdom, totally aware of what makes a footballer, an expert in man management and fitness, and his advice was eagerly sought by those in the highest levels of the game. Following his mentor, Walter Winterbottom, he lectured on coaching courses, and he brought the training of footballers and the treatment of their injuries into a new era. He first joined Arsenal as physiotherapist in 1960.

It was my ambition to work for Arsenal, and, of course, my ambition came about. I had had the ambition since the early part of the war when I got my physio qualifications, and I was looking to come back into football. It is true that I went into the Health Service for various reasons, and then the opportunity arose for me to come to Arsenal.

Tom Whittaker had then died, and Billy Milne was the "sponge man". George Swindin had taken over as manager. There was a board decision

that Arsenal had to go for the top people, and, at that time, they were employing Ron Greenwood whom I knew well from the coaching courses, and it was Ron who said, "Why don't you approach Bertie Mee?"

I was working in Camden Town as a rehabilitation officer at that time and still running my courses for the FA. Arsenal came to me and said, "What about it?" And I said, "Make me an offer, and I'm there." Because I was getting very frustrated for various reasons, mostly financial. I was married by then, and when I found it difficult to buy my wife a winter coat I felt that it was time to move on.

I succeeded Billy Milne, and Ron left after I had been there a couple of months. He was offered the job at West Ham. I knew Ron well, but I didn't know George Swindin well. I stayed on as physio for six years, from 1960 to 1966. I was the equivalent of what had been called a trainer. I upgraded the job to physiotherapist, and the whole of the football scene was upgraded because people then followed Arsenal. Swindin was there two years, then Billy Wright came in, and I knew Billy well. He stayed from 1962 to 1966, and then I took over.

It didn't really make much difference to me who was manager. I got on with my job. I was respected, and I think they found me helpful in as much that, unlike the prima donnas of today whom I read and hear say, "I'll declare myself fit on Saturday," there was no question of that with me. I said, "I will tell you when you are fit." The managers appreciated that. Players were kept under close control from that point of view, plus the fact that my philosophy was you work harder when you're injured than when you're fit, which is now commonplace in football. There was no question of coming in for treatment in the morning and then "off" in the afternoon. They came back in the afternoon, and, if I thought it appropriate, they came back in the evening.

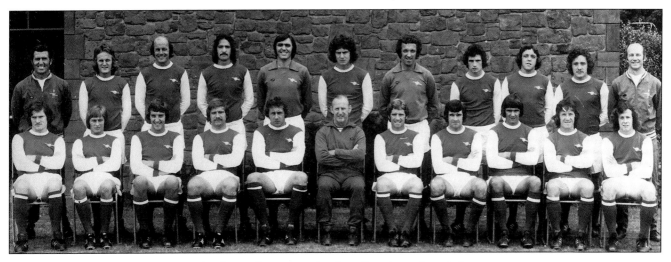

George Armstrong remembers clearly Mee's policy regarding injuries.

> He was serious and conscientious about his job. We never had a full treatment room. He didn't tolerate injuries. Today, most players have a little knowledge about injuries, which is a dangerous thing. If you were injured with Bertie, you had to work hard.

Bob Wilson, too, recalls that the goalkeeper's fear was not of the penalty but of being injured through neglect under Bertie Mee, and the boss finding out.

> His secret was his organisation. He never allowed anybody to stray out of line, and you knew it. He would even fine you for going out in the sun. If we were in Cyprus or Bermuda or somewhere, when we went on these tours round the world for three weeks at a time, which they never do now, and you got too much sun, he would fine you.
>
> He would fine you if you didn't wear shin pads, and you got a leg injury. I never wore pads. I hated wearing pads, and so when I got rattled across the shins a couple of times I had to say, "Oh, it's all right." That was the sort of guy he was, a brilliant organiser.

Bertie Mee did not expect to be offered the manager's post at Highbury when Billy Wright left, but he was confident that his work before, during and after the war had given him experience that was preparation for the task.

> I was surprised when I was asked to become manager. I had no ambitions in that direction when I first went to Arsenal, but, having been with George Swindin for two years and with Billy Wright for four, I knew in my heart of hearts that I had been involved in management in the wider sense of the word. I was a teacher for five years, teaching physiotherapy. Obviously, I had ideas of how I would do things, and when the board, the chairman, came to me and said, "What about having a go at management?" I said, "Well, if that's your wish, chairman, let's have a go for a year, and then I'll sort myself out and decide if it is something I wish to carry on with."
>
> I realise that the appointment must have taken many people by surprise, but I was better known by the coaches and managers of that period. They knew me from having worked with them at Lilleshall. We had started at Carnegie College, Leeds, in 1947. Then we went to Bisham for a year, which wasn't satisfactory for various reasons, and then we moved to Lilleshall. I used to go there every year and run a two-week course for these trainers and coaches.
>
> Changes generally were needed at Arsenal when I took over. For example, we were running four teams at the time – first team, Combination side, Metropolitan League team and the South East Counties side. When I used to go in as an "observer" of the discussions as to who we were going to retain and who we were going to let go at the end of the season it just amazed

Arsenal staff at the start of the 1975-76 season. Back row (left to right): Bobby Campbell (coach), Brian Hornsby, Terry Mancini, John Matthews, Jimmy Rimmer, Brian Kidd, Geoff Barnett, Trevor Ross, Richard Powling, Wilf Rostron, Fred Street (physiotherapist). Front row: Pat Rice, Alex Cropley, Sammy Nelson, Eddie Kelly, John Radford, Bertie Mee (manager), Alan Ball, Peter Storey, Peter Simpson, George Armstrong, Liam Brady.

me to hear the third team trainer, and the manager, obviously, because he had the ultimate responsibility, say, "We'd better keep him otherwise we'll be short of players for the third team." And I said, "Well, if he's not good enough, why do you want to sign him?"

So the first thing I did when I became manager was to cut out the third team, the Metropolitan League side, because we wanted to sign players who would be good enough for Arsenal. The club had the tradition of carrying a lot of players, but much of the staff was dead wood. If you look back historically, you'll find very few of them made it into the first team.

The philosophy of approach I adopted as manager had been built up during the war years at convalescent depots where it was necessary to get people fit to get them back into the army, into service. That was the priority, and the same principle applied to football. You had to work full-time to get fit. I had this policy when I was the physiotherapist, a policy supported by the managers, and I dictated the policy when I was manager. I would say when the players came back, not when they wanted to come back. I ran a regime. I said, "You will be in at 9.30 in the morning, before the others arrive, and you will leave for lunch at 12.00 and be back at 2.00, and I'll release you at 4.00-4.30 in the afternoon." I like to think that they respected that they were being treated like professionals and looked after in a professional way. They were well paid, and they accepted the discipline.

One built on that relationship. I think it would be unfair to mention the names, but two players came to see me on separate occasions – one had told the other – and said, "Look, boss, could you help us?" I said, "Sure, what's the problem?" And they said that they had been trying for a family for five or six years and had had no joy, and was there anything they could

do. I said, "Certainly, I will get you referred to a fertility clinic." And both of them have now got grown-up children.

When a player comes to you with that sort of request it is an important personal problem. The philosophy in which I had been brought up is what is called the holistic approach. You deal with the person as a whole, not just his injury or disability or his sickness. That approach evolved within the club, and there was also the disciplinary side, which was very necessary.

We'd done the Double, but, inevitably, there are barrack room lawyers, and they have to be kept under control. One barrack room lawyer was sent off, and I fined him two weeks wages, which I could do, but which I couldn't deduct from his salary without permission. So I called him in and said, "Look, I'm fining you two weeks wages, but I can't do it unless you give me permission." He said, "You're not having my permission. You're not fining me for that." I said, "OK, you've given me a problem." He said, "I'm sorry, but that's how it is. You're not going to deduct from my wages." I said, "All right, I'll have to deprive you of privileges." He said, "You can do what the hell you like, but you're not fining me."

He goes back to the dressing room, and the captain gets hold of him and says, "What did the little so-and-so say then?" He said, "Nothing. He's deprived me of privileges." The captain said, "Didn't you ask what they were?" He said, "No." So he said, "Well, you'd better go back and ask him. He's got something up his sleeve."

He came back after about half an hour, knocked on the door, and I told him to come in. He asked, "Can I have another word with you boss? You said you were going to deprive me of my privileges. What do you mean by that?"

I said, "Well, let's see. How many complimentary tickets do you get?"

He said, "Six. You're very good, very generous."

I said, "Well, they'll go. How many tickets do you get for the England-Scotland game?"

He said, "You're very good. You always give me two."

"For the Cup Final, how many?"

He said, "I'll pay the fine."

That's a true story, and there is another disciplinary story. At that time, long hair and beards were becoming fashionable, and when they returned for training three or four were ganging up against me, just trying it on as they do. And four of them had got beards.

I said, "Yes, rather nice. Pity you're not film stars. You're footballers. I pick my team in a fortnight's time. It's entirely up to you, but nobody with a beard will play for Arsenal." Needless to say, they went right through to the Friday team selection, and then the beards were off.

I had no illusions about the type of player I wanted when I took over. I wanted eleven George Armstrongs and eleven Frank McLintocks. Frank had been bought by Billy Wright, and George had come as a youth player, seventeen years old. There is an interesting little story there.

Dai Rees, who we knew well because we used to play golf at South Herts, always had the run of the board room, and, indeed, with my permission, the run of our dressing room. He used to come in because he was very good with players, and, after we won the Double, I said, "Dai, who would you take in your Ryder Cup team?" He said, "That's a good question." And he thought for a minute and then he said, "Take George Armstrong. Take Frank McLintock." In other words, the qualities that Dai wanted in his Ryder Cup team, people who would graft and work and become team players and not prima donnas, were what he wanted and I wanted. You couldn't get eleven like that, but you could get eight or nine. Then you relied on your senior pros so that if someone kicked over the traces,

they were just taken on one side by a couple of the seniors who would say, "Look, you'd better pull your finger out, or else!" And so discipline came from within after a time.

Don Howe was brought in as a player by Billy Wright. Don was invaluable as a senior pro, and then he broke his leg, but he had so much to offer. My first appointment as coach was Dave Sexton, and then Dave was offered the Chelsea job and left. Don was recovering from his broken leg, and I said, "Don, what about coming in as chief coach to replace Dave?" That fitted in with his scheme of things. He was 32-33 years old, and there was a very big question mark on his career prospects. That's how Don came in, and we went through to the Double. Then Don, understandably, wanted to paddle his own canoe. He was offered the West Brom job, and, quite naturally, he wanted to have a go himself, and he took it.

I left most of the coaching to Don Howe. That is what a dual situation is all about. Management in those days was, and still is, that your number-one fitted into one of two categories. He was either, as in my case, an over 40 who'd been through the mill in more ways than one and understood people, and who was supported by a very good technical coach indeed who could have a go, could shout his head off if need be. Then I could go in and pick them up. You could have the reverse situation – a young manager supported by a 45-year-old who, again, had been through the mill. You made your choice.

Bertie Mee showed both courage and perception in appointing Don Howe to the coaching staff at Highbury, for the former England full-back had never held such a position before and he was of unknown quality as a coach, but Mee's great strength was his ability to judge people His assessment of Howe's capabilities showed how acute was his perception. For his part, Howe was one who was not surprised by Mee's strength and success as a manager.

Billy Wright brought me to the Arsenal. He was manager in 1964, and, in my early days, when we used to play for England, he was from Wolverhampton and I was from West Brom so that when we came down from the Midlands to play for England we became good friends. I'd got to a point in my career where I had been at West Brom all my life, starting as a ground-staff boy, as they were in those days, at the age of fifteen, and I needed to move on. I needed something different, and, as it was, Billy bought me, and so I started my career at Highbury.

I had been here only a couple of years when two things happened. Results didn't go too well for Billy, and he was sacked, went on his way, got into television, and, at the same time, I broke my leg. I broke my tib and fib and had to have a plate in – I've still

Don How, another former Arsenal player and coach, who was appointed caretaker manager in December 1983 and had his position confirmed before the end of that season. Howe asked to be released in March 1986, having failed to bring major honours to Highbury. But he had been part of the set-up which won the Double and by his own admission was "a coach not a manager".

got it – and I was 30 years of age then, and I knew for a fact that my physical ability was gone. It wasn't my age. It was my leg, and I knew I'd never be as good as I had been. Bertie had taken over from Billy Wright and asked me if I'd like to be coach to the reserve team, and I said yes because I wanted to start coaching.

I'd always wanted to coach. In my early days, when I first got into the England team, Walter Winterbottom was the England coach, and he was also in charge of coaching for the FA. He was the director of coaching, and he always used to say to the England lads, "You'd be better players if you were to take your coaching qualification." And he used to say it every time we got together.

Gradually, he made an impression on my brain, and, in the end, I did my qualification. First of all, I did my prelim, and then I did what they call the full qualification, the full badge. It was nerve-racking. All of a sudden, you are standing up telling other people how to play when all the time you've been on the other side as a player looking at a manager telling you how to play, and now it's in your hands. It's a very daunting experience, especially when you're doing your coaching assessment. People come in and watch you and say, "Yes, he can coach" or "No, he can't". It was as bad as playing for England at Wembley. I was just as nervous.

I was with the reserves for a year, and Dave Sexton was first-team coach, and Dave was very ambitious and successful, and he got the Chelsea job. Bertie then lifted me to first-team coach, and I started taking the team, and that was 1968. I think Bertie took a chance really. I'd never coached a first team in my life. He'd seen me coach the reserves, I suppose, but he took a chance that I could do the job.

I wasn't surprised that Bertie was such a good manager. He always had an air of authority even when he was the physio. He was a leader of men, and you knew for a fact there would be good discipline within the club when he took over. He clamped down on the discipline, which definitely helped the players. They didn't like it, but it helped them.

I used to think that Billy Wright was too nice to be a manager. Super fellow, great man, and I got to know him well. We came from the same part of the country, and we travelled a lot together. We even shared rooms when we were with the England team, and I got to know him very well. He was a very nice man. The aggression he showed on the football pitch was because he had this ability to switch on to playing. When it was a tough game against someone he could be a very hard, good player. He'd become a centre-half in those days. He changed from a midfield player to a centre-half, a little bit like we did with Frank McLintock later on. He was a great centre-half and a great England captain, but when he stepped on to a football pitch he was a terrific competitor. He wanted to win, and he wanted to win badly. He was a great player, but, as a manager, there's no doubt about it, he was too nice a fellow. He knew the game, obviously, but I think he found it difficult to tell players what he sometimes had to tell them.

Like Billy Wright, Frank McLintock was converted to centre-half. He had been an aggressive right-half, and he was a natural leader. He wanted to talk on the pitch, and he liked doing a lot of talking off the pitch. Great lad. We lived next door to each other so I knew him inside-out, and we talked about it, and we decided to give it a go. He was quite happy with it. If he hadn't gone along with it, we wouldn't have done it, but he was quite happy. We converted both him and Peter Simpson from midfield players, and then we started to play because we had these players with ability who could play it out from the back, and that was the start.

Frank was really a great leader. He was part of the motivation, and we had a set of players come together, which happens to you every now and then, who wanted to win, and they wanted to win for each other and they wanted to win for the club. There was no great planning, but there was a little bit of thought and a lot of luck.

I was different to Dave Sexton as a coach. He had different ideas on the game from me, was very successful as a coach, and the players loved him. I used to work with him, and we were all very sorry to see him go, but I was given the job, and gradually I changed things. Dave liked man-to-man marking at the back. I liked zonal marking. We had different ways of looking at the game. Gradually, the players came round to my way. It took a while, but they came round to my way. Once they got to playing my way, then the usual thing – when you're trying to preach something about football as a coach you need to win as well, because if you don't win, they won't believe. And we started to win so they started to believe, and it all started to go for me. But it wasn't all my doing.

In the first place, Bertie was a terrific manager because the discipline within the club was first-class. The players knew they couldn't step out of line, and Frank McLintock, whom I've mentioned, was an outstanding captain. Then you had people like George Armstrong, George Graham, Peter Storey, Bob Wilson – great pros. They wanted to win at football. They weren't just here to play football; they were here to win at football. They showed that in what was then the Fairs Cup, the night we beat Anderlecht.

I left Arsenal after the Double year. I just felt it was right for me to move on. I mean you can't do much better than the Double, can you? I wanted to put myself on the line, and I went to West Brom as manager. I found it a very difficult job because I was a coach; I wasn't a manager. Suddenly, I found myself dealing with things I hadn't dealt with at Highbury because Bertie had dealt with them.

After two years, we got relegated, but I still think I did quite a good job there because we started getting good young players like Bryan Robson. In those days, West Brom were as good a development club as any. I went there as a schoolboy and got into the England team, and they were very good at bringing kids through. All right, I wasn't very successful there, but what is success? Is success getting results or building a club? In terms of building a club, we were successful, but success differs from club to club. I've got to say the board were terrific to me. I was there three years, and I didn't do anything in terms of results, but I think I did a lot in terms of the future of the club, and the board were very fair to me. I had no complaints when they got rid of me.

Bertie Mee was in no doubt that many of the players he inherited when he became manager of Arsenal were not of the quality, in ability or attitude, that he recognised as being necessary to take the club to the level of achievement that was both required and expected. He was uncompromising in his approach, and George Armstrong recalls that the players soon knew exactly where they stood, particularly at the end of the 1968-69 season, the year in which Arsenal finished fourth in the League and lost to Swindon Town in the Final of the Football League Cup.

I was surprised when Bertie took over, but Bertie was a great man manager. He got respect, and he was strong. We went up to Everton – it was when Don had just joined him – and I think if we had won, we would have finished second or third, but we went out there, and it was just like eleven shirts. We lost 1-0.

We came back to the hotel, because we stayed overnight in Liverpool, and we had dinner. I'll always remember that Frank McLintock stood up and knocked on the table because this was the end of the season when we'd lost to Swindon in the League Cup.

Frank said, "Well, boss, on behalf of the boys, I want to thank you and Don. It's been the best season we've had since I've been here. We reached the League Cup Final and did well in the League." And he went on.

And it seemed a lifetime before Bertie stood up to reply, and then he said, "Frank, you started, so I'll finish it. Some of you won't be here next year." And he steamed into us, and, to be fair, he got rid of certain people. He said, "I want people who can win – win!"

And, God bless the little fellow, he was right.

Mee had already begun his restructuring of the side just as he had restructured the club and the coaching staff.

My first signing was Bob McNab, and I had to work hard on him for quite a time. I had a lot of time for him and his approach, and, eventually, I will always remember, in the office, I said to him, "Well, Bob, we've sorted everything out. You've agreed to sign. Is there anything else?"

He said, "Yes, as you know, I've had discussions with Bill Shankly, and I think I'd like to let him know."

I said, "Of course, shall I get him on the phone?"

He said, "I'd be grateful if you would."

So I got Bill, and I said, "I've got Bob McNab here. He'd like to talk to you."

Bill said, "Put him on! Put him on!"

Bob took the phone and said, "I won't beat about the bush, Mr Shankly, I've had talks with Bertie Mee at Arsenal. I'm with him now, and I've agreed to sign for Arsenal."

I could overhear, and I heard Bill reply, "You couldn't bloody well play in the first place, McNab!"

Bill was a little bit hurt that I'd beaten him to McNab, but he had taken Geoff Strong from us.

Bertie Mee was for ever striving to achieve blend and balance on and off the field. He and Don Howe complemented each other, and all learned to respect the strength and discipline that Mee brought to the club. He re-established the dignity and pride of place of Arsenal in the football world, and he finally laid the ghost of the Thirties. As one of his players remarked of that great side of the past, "They never did the Double, did they?' George Armstrong played under three managers at Highbury, was a manager himself in the Middle East, and has returned to Highbury to work under another three managers, so his assessment of Bertie Mee is based on the richness of experience.

All the great managers have great coaches or assistants with them. I think it comes in twos. Bertie was a great man-manager, a delegator. He chose the best people to work with. I remember when I was in Kuwait speaking to Dave Mackay, one of the great Spurs side, and Dave believed you could only manage if you'd played at a certain level, and he asked me about Bertie.

I said, "Dave, you would have loved him. He knew everything about you as a person. He would never tell you how to play, but his strength was his management."

And I really believe that, because he had such respect for other people. I could be driving down to Highbury with him and chatting casually, but, as soon as we got to the club, the hat came on. He was the boss, and I think that's right.

I was sad to see him go, but, at the time, it was probably right for him. You can do anything too long, but I just feel that Arsenal failed when they didn't find a position for him.

Like George Armstrong, Bob Wilson has remained close to the club, and, having served under Wright and Mee, he has worked as goalkeeping coach with Neill, Howe, Graham, Rioch and Wenger.

Bert was incredible. All the way through it was staggering. He was a little guy, and he could be fairly serious. He was never aloof, but he didn't show passion if you played well, which was difficult for me in goal. I'm a passionate football man even now.

Ray Parlour came up the tunnel after we'd beaten Manchester United 3-2 at Highbury, and we've got a

manager at the moment whose passionate about football, I'm certain, but he doesn't show his passion, and Ray Parlour came up the tunnel, and I said to him, "Ray, that was brilliant!" I thought he was the best player, and I got hold of him physically – it's the way it was with Don Howe – and I said to him about three times, "That's brilliant! Do you realise you played better than Scholes, Beckham and Giggs." And he looked at me, but that's how I need to be.

So I found that aspect quite difficult with Bertie because even if I had a blinding game, he wasn't hands on. With Don, it was different. Don would be hands on if you played badly. I can still feel Don's face up against mine yelling and screaming. But we all of us took it. We accepted that.

The only time I saw Bert lose any control was with the strain at the end of the Double season when he came in and gave us our plans for what we'd be doing in the last two weeks of the season, and the paper was shaking, and I realised how it had got to him.

There was something else that he and Don did in the run-in to that season when we'd suddenly gone from twelve points behind Leeds to getting level with them, and we were still in the Cup at the quarter-final/semi-final stage. They had a meeting in the dressing room at Highbury, and they said, "Look, you've got a chance here, if you dedicate yourselves for the next twelve weeks of your lives, of making history. If you want to go off the rails and fall below it…?" And he gave us the option, and one of the statements within it was "even at the expense of your family".

Deep down, I questioned that, because nothing should be more important than your family. The priorities became quite clear – "If you want to go in the record book…?" Because that is the great thing about it. You read any book on the history of the game, and they have a list of the Cup-winning sides and the championship, and your name is there until the day you die and your grandchildren die, and so it goes on.

One of Bertie Mee's biggest signings was Alan Ball from Everton, but, in some ways, the signing marked the beginning of the breaking up of the great Double side, which Pat Rice feels came prematurely.

Personally, I think the Double side broke up too soon. I think that had we kept together for another year or so and just introduced our own young players, who knows what would have happened, but there again Bertie had to make decisions one way or the other. Who is to say that with Bally coming in we may have done it again? The second year we got to the Final and lost against Leeds, and we came fifth in the League, and the year following that we came second. You never can tell. Bobby Campbell arrived as coach, and the club was looking for better players. It wasn't long after that that Rix and Brady and O'Leary and that lot came through.

George Armstrong wonders if the cry for "more flair" from the media had any influence on Mee's decision to sign Alan Ball. Arsenal won magnificently in 1971, but, as with Graham's side later, they did not always receive the praise that was their due, but Mee was sure in his own mind of his actions.

Certainly I feel that side broke up too soon, but it was happening then. There were offers to players to further their careers. Frank went to Queen's Park Rangers, and that happened with two or three other players.

I don't regret signing Alan Ball, I think. I signed him because we wanted players of his calibre. Obviously, I'd seen him in the World Cup Final, and if you asked me whose performance out of all the players put a glint in your eye, it was Alan Ball's performance on that day. And I thought – you'll do for me. He was an absolute one hundred per center. He had a lot of ability as well so that I had no regrets on that basis, but then, later on, his father started coming into the picture and influencing him. Then it

was time to move on, and that was that.

I finished with Arsenal in 1976. I was 58, and it was getting too difficult to drive myself. Motivation goes. I'd done it, achieved most of what I'd hoped. You need a change of environment. I went to Watford and enjoyed helping to build that organisation.

I had no say in naming Terry Neill as my successor. There was no reason for me to be involved. Terry had had his experience and knew the ropes and never turned to me. I won't deny that Cloughie rang me up on occasions and said, "Look, I've just won the championship. You did it two years ago. What do I do now? How do I get them to do it again?" And others contacted me – Bobby Robson, Dave Sexton and quite a few others but Terry didn't. That didn't surprise me. He had his own problems. He had to break with the past. After all, what I had learned from Wright and Swindin had mostly been negative.

Terry Neill remains one of Northern Ireland's most capped players. He was with Arsenal from 1959 until 1970 and was captain of both club and country, and he was one of the youngest of Arsenal skippers just as he was the youngest of managers when he took over at Hull City June 1970, at the age of 28. His success at Hull was twofold in that the club came close to winning promotion, and he proved adept at public relations. He was one of the first managers to make his sides trot to the centre of the field before kick-off and salute the crowd, a gesture unknown until the Seventies.

As well as being player-manager of Hull, he had been manager of the Northern Ireland side and chairman of the Professional Footballers' Association. In 1974, he succeeded Bill Nicholson as manager of Tottenham. In this respect, he followed another Arsenal favourite, Joe Hulme, who managed Spurs in the late Forties. Terry Neill was popular at Tottenham, and it was, perhaps, logical that he should be invited to return to Arsenal as successor to Bertie Mee. Almost immediately, he paid a huge fee to bring striker Malcolm Macdonald from

Newcastle to Highbury, and he later broke the club record when he signed Brian Talbot from Ipswich. He also signed Pat Jennings from Spurs when all thought his career was at an end. It was a stroke of genius. Jennings gave Arsenal eight years of wonderful service. His problem was that he could never come to terms with managing players who had once been his colleagues on the pitch, and too many disagreements had too public an airing. He was unfortunate, too, in that Macdonald, "Super Mac", was forced to retire through injury after scoring 42 goals in 84 League games for Arsenal as well as ten goals in nine Cup-ties. Luck also deserted Terry Neill in that he took Arsenal to three FA Cup Finals and a European Cup-winners' Cup Final in the space of three seasons and saw his side lose three of those matches. His stewardship also coincided with the departure of Brady and Stapleton, but he made Pat Rice captain and brought Don Howe back to Highbury for his second spell as coach.

I came back to Arsenal when Terry Neill was manager. I was up at Leeds at the time. I'd been at West Brom, and I then went off to Galatasaray in Turkey. I did about three or four months there. I didn't want to go abroad. I had a wife and a young family at the time, all at school, but I got to know the chairman of Galatasaray very well. He was a great fellow, educated at Cambridge, and he said, "I know you don't want to leave home. I understand that, but will you come and travel backwards and forwards and help us out?" And so, for a few months, believe it or not, I commuted to Istanbul. I used to go out on Monday morning, come back on Sunday night, have a week off, and then go back again. I used to travel PanAm in those days, and they got to know me, and I got to know them, and I did that for three or four months.

Then I got a phone call from Jimmy Armfield who was a big friend of mine. We were always vying for the right-back spot in the England side, but we're still big mates and speak to each other regularly. He'd got the Leeds job and asked me if I wanted to join him as coach.

I had been there a couple of years when I got a phone call from Terry Neill saying that they wanted me to come back to Arsenal. I thought about it, and, at that time, I was living in Wolverhampton, and I was going backwards and forwards to Leeds, and I thought I might as well go back to Arsenal. I accepted his offer, and it was a terrific offer. I was a young man with a young family, and I needed the money so I came back.

We put the bits of the team together, and we got to three Cup Finals, and it was a similar situation – Terry looked after the discipline and organisation of the club, and I did the coaching. What I would say about most of the managers that I've been with is that they've given me my head on the coaching side, and I've been lucky in that respect because there are not many managers who would allow you to do that. They want you to be the coach, but you become BBC fellows – balls, bibs and cones – and the manager does the work. I was never that, and I am grateful for it.

Terry and I got on well, and we got to those Finals so it was another successful time for Arsenal. Liam Brady was a great leader, and we had people like Graham Rix, David O'Leary, Frank Stapleton – we had a great young team.

Brought into the team to provide the power and the energy in midfield was Brian Talbot who later went into management with West Bromwich Albion, in Malta and, now, with Rushden and Diamonds. He is appreciative of Neill for bringing him to Arsenal and for what he tried to do in his time as manager.

A lot of the lads criticised Terry Neill, but I would never criticise him. One, he brought me to the club. Two, I always thought he did his best. I know I'm the other side of the fence now. I'm a manager, and it's a very hard job. You appreciate that the longer you go on doing it. Terry brought in a fantastic coach, Don Howe. In my opinion, the best coach in the country. When you're working with the best you shouldn't judge the manager as a coach.

I'd say give credit to the manager for bringing him in. Terry was a good front man – good with the press, good with the board. When I realise now what you've got to do with the board… I mean when I look back now to my time with West Brom, I didn't go to a single board meeting. I don't mean to be rude to board members, but some of them haven't got any idea about football and getting a good team.

Terry could smooth things out all round, and was good with family problems. My wife was ill one Christmas, and we had three matches. Don said I'd got to be there, but Terry was more understanding and said, "Take some time off, and then you can play later." Don is obviously very

intense, very demanding, and I think there has got to be a balance. I think Terry was a good manager, and I'm disappointed that he's not involved somewhere today. He turned down one or two jobs when he finished, and I think he probably now regrets it. It's not a bad record to have been manager of both Tottenham and Arsenal.

I think a manager can lose his grip if he stays at a place too long. You've got to keep your hunger for the game. Graham Taylor is a good example. I worked with Graham when I left Arsenal to go to Watford, and I think he would be the first to admit that we didn't see eye to eye. I didn't like the way he played the game. I think the game should be played on the grass, passing the ball, looking good to the eye. Graham wanted to get results, and there's a way of doing that. You've got to get the crosses in the box and the ball forward early. Graham Taylor has never lost his enthusiasm, and now he's back, he's still got the same hunger. Some others lose it. It's the same with players. Some go on until they're 35; others pack up at 30.

Graham once said, "You can't always change the manager, but you can change the players." And look at his teams – I looked at them a lot when I went there in '85 – he changed his teams in different divisions. He wanted success, so his turnover of players was tremendous. He was bringing in new players all the time because you get used to the manager's ideas.

I think Ron Atkinson is a good manager. He gets the board to spend their money to get a good team round him who enjoy it. His man management is first-class. If there's a problem, he calls you into the office. You have a cup of tea with him and sort it out. But whereas I call Don Howe a coach, Graham Taylor a coach, Terry Venables a coach, Arsène Wenger a coach, Ron Atkinson is a manager.

I know George Graham a bit. He is a very clever man, a very clever tactician. He gets blood out of a stone. I don't know Arsène Wenger, but he comes over very well in the press and on television. He definitely looks and plans for the future. Arsenal are

George Graham is saluted by his players after the Gunners lifted the League championship. His success as a manager surprised several of his team-mates from the 1971 Double year, because he had shown little interest in pursuing that side of the game.

playing some beautiful football under him, and the crowd love it, but, in the end, what the fans want is to see you win something. There was a lot of criticism of how Arsenal played under George Graham, but he won six trophies. He won everything while he was there.

Terry Neill left. Don Howe, by his own admission a coach and not a manager, had a brief period in charge, and then came George Graham. The sadness of his departure from Arsenal, and the reasons for that departure, are still fresh in the memory. There are wounds which are still to heal, but, in what was achieved, Graham's period as manager was a golden age in the history of Arsenal Football Club. That he ever became manager of Arsenal took those who knew him by complete surprise, and Bob Wilson is the first to admit that he was among the sceptics.

George Graham's great success as a manager did surprise me. In our time, I took my full coaching badge when I was in the reserve side and had come down from Loughborough University, about 1965, 1966. I took my full badge then.

When I left the club we used to have this group around the coach. There'd be Alan Ball, and we'd be arguing tactics; and you knew the ones who were going to be managers. We argued why we hadn't done this and why we'd done that, but George's interests were what were the latest fashions and where were the best places to eat. It was the last thing you'd expect of George Graham, to be a manager. Then he suddenly got the bug.

He caught the bug really from Terry Venables because he was going to run a pub, and Terry said, "Don't waste yourself there. Have a go at running my youth team at Crystal Palace." And he went, and he got the bug.

So he did his apprenticeship, and he learned even more at Queen's Park Rangers where he did the reserves. From Queen's Park Rangers, he went to Millwall as manager, and everyone began to say, "He's a shrewd cookie

this guy." And suddenly, he's got the Arsenal job.

I think the real proof now of how good he is as a manager is what he's doing at Leeds where he's thrown out all the old players and they're near the top of the League. He's a shrewd cookie. You can't win what he did without being.

Like Bob Wilson, Pat Rice played with George Graham, the "stroller" in midfield in Bertie Mee's great Arsenal side.

George Graham took over from Don, and the first year was a little bit difficult because he had his own way of doing things, but after he'd been here for a year, he was absolutely brilliant. He just let us get on with it, myself and Terry Murphy. There was no interference. He supported the youth team very well. His success as a manager surprised me because, as a player, you would never have thought of him in a million years as being a manager.

George Armstrong was equally surprised.

Without a doubt it surprised me that he became a good manager. I'd have lost my mortgage if I'd said he would make a top manager. We grew together, and he's no different now to what he was then. He may be different as a manager. He ran the club. I learned a lot of things from him. The discipline was excellent. That's why the players were good. People say "boring", but if you're successful every week, you can't call it boring.

My first year back was the year we won the title and lost only one game, 1991, and they never got the credit for what they did. I don't think Arsenal have ever had credit for their success in the past, even in my time. It became a joke with us. If Manchester United were playing Liverpool in the Cup, say, and we were playing somebody like Swindon Town, we'd be on Match of the Day, because they were always hoping there'd be an upset. But that used to make us stronger so did the "lucky" tag.

George was a part of the Double

side, and he must have learned a lot from Bertie Mee. The spirit in that team was phenomenal. We only had fifteen/seventeen players, and the whole team – manager, coach, physio – were a unit. We used to go away for a weekend – Blackpool, Bournemouth – and Bertie Mee used to say, "Let your hair down, but when you come through that hotel door remember who you are." And if ever we had a lad who'd had one too many, nobody ever knew about it, because the rest of us would say, "Get hold of him, and get him into bed." In those days, the press were better than they are now. Now, they're diabolical.

It was sad the way George left, but the FA gave Arsenal no option. I think if you asked the fans, they would say they were grateful for all he did, but it was probably time for George to go anyway.

George Graham brought John Jensen to Highbury, for which the Dane is eternally grateful.

He was a great manager. I have a tremendous amount of respect for him, personally and professionally. He made Arsenal a great team by making sure that we were a team. Every player on the staff was made to feel part of George Graham's plans. There was no hierarchy, and we all respected each other as players and were made to realise that everybody in the club had a part to play. Tactically, he was brilliant, and the record shows that he brought the best out of all of us.

Graham was not without his problems, and he and the Arsenal fans did not always see eye to eye over Anders Limpar, the Swedish international, who became a tremendous favourite at Highbury. Bertie Mee understood Graham's problems.

He had his problems with Limpar who was another of those who only produced when he felt like it. He didn't produce consistently. When the chips were down he didn't produce. No, I would understand George's problem there, and I think there was a personality clash. What the public sees

is not always the real thing, and managers cannot always change players.

I used to lecture to bank managers and other groups of businessmen who were interested, for motivating footballers is no different from motivating a staff in a bank.

If Graham, like all managers, had problems, he also had the desire and the means to bring the best to Arsenal. Not only did he sign Anders Limpar, he brought Lee Dixon, David Seaman, Nigel Winterburn, Ian Wright, Steve Bould ("a brilliant defender, the most underrated in English football" in the opinion of John Jensen) and Alan Smith to Highbury. Smith was bought from Leicester City, won thirteen England caps and scored more than 100 goals for Arsenal. Nobody could ever calculate the number of goals that he created for others, but none will ever forget his contributions at Anfield in 1989 and in Copenhagen in 1994.

George Graham was the manager all the time I was at Highbury. He got sacked the day I went in for an operation on my knee, and I never played under Stewart Houston as caretaker manager. When Bruce Rioch came I'd retired so George was manager all the time I was there.

I think he was a very good organiser of the team. He knew what he wanted off each player. He knew what you could do, what your peak performance was, and he would demand that from you every week. If you fell short, he would have a go at you. Sometimes you felt he was asking too much, but he said, "I know what you can do, and I want you to do it every week." You can't do it every week, but he would try and push you to do that. Even in training, he expected a standard. They were a very good bunch of lads, and they responded, but he had organisational flair and good motivational skills. If you weren't performing, you knew that he'd let you know about it at half-time. He was very good at putting things right at half-time. He could see things weren't going right and what was wrong, and he'd make changes. He was tactically astute like that.

He chose his players well. He went very fully into the character of a player to make sure he'd fit into the team, off the pitch, in the dressing room. Would they fit in or would they rough about? Did they have a big ego? He didn't want that. He was careful about things apart from ability.

George only left out Anders Limpar when he wasn't playing well. Anders was brilliant his first season or first half of that season, the championship season. Then he had an injury or something, and that set him back, and he stopped performing like he had been. In the subsequent two seasons, he was really very patchy. He could do something brilliant, but some games you would look over, and you could really see he was not fit and his heart wasn't there. I wouldn't blame George for the way he treated Anders. He knew what Anders could do, and Anders was falling well short of it. I know crowds want to see people like him on the pitch, and when he got dragged off time and again you could understand the frustration, particularly as we weren't playing well, and there was a lack of creativity in the team.

We stopped becoming a threat in the League because we weren't good enough basically. We still had the defence, but if Wright didn't score, Arsenal didn't score. We became a great Cup team. We could win 1-0 easily, but in the League we were hopeless. George used to say he was looking for players but they weren't available, but we just couldn't score for a few years. I think you should buy players after you've had success. When we won the League he bought David Seaman and Anders Limpar, and we won again, but he really didn't buy anyone except Wrighty after that. I think that's where he went wrong. He thought he'd got enough. You always hope young players will come through. Ian Selley was a good

footballer, but he had such a quiet personality. He didn't assert himself enough.

I think George was sad that he had to sell David Rocastle. Rocky says his knee is OK, but they thought he'd never be the same after his injury. He'd been in and out the side in '91, but he was an Arsenal lad through and through, his whole heart was at Highbury, and George knew that. But he never did anything once he left Arsenal. It's unfortunate the way things develop.

In the case of Michael Thomas, he lost it a bit. He'd come up from the youth level, and it is hard to get on top wages. He didn't want to sign another contract so George sold him, but Micky wasn't showing top form. Again, George was sad because he knew that Micky was such a great athlete and could have done a lot more.

If the manager has the same players, it is impossible for him to keep motivating them. George had players who'd been with him there eight or nine years, and we'd heard all he'd got to say at half-time, full-time and beforehand. And that's when he went wrong, I think. He couldn't motivate the players any more. They say you should either change the manager or the playing staff. Neither happened, and he got stale. Perhaps you can do any job too long. At the end, I think he was angry. He used to berate players like he'd never done before, and we didn't know the reason why, but, looking back, I think he was so angry because he knew what was going to happen. He was annoyed with himself really.

He was passionate about the Arsenal. He collected memorabilia, and I've seen his study with all his prints and pictures. That was why I was so shocked when it all came out, when it was alleged that he had done something that would sully the name of Arsenal. I couldn't believe it because he always used to preach to us,

"Remember who you are and who you represent." He drummed that into us from day one, and then the rumour came out, and I said, "He wouldn't do that. He wouldn't shame the name of Arsenal." That's why I was so surprised.

Perhaps George Graham's greatest gift to the Arsenal was his establishing the great back four, now part of football legend, but he also brought music back to Highbury. In the Sixties, with the Beatles and Rolling Stones at their zenith, the Metropolitan Police Band always included the Arsenal song in their programme. It was sung to the tune of *Anchors Aweigh!* And one cannot remember a word of it. It certainly never impinged itself on the minds of the supporters, for, by 1971, the Double year, Arsenal were in search of a Cup Final song with which to counter the heavenly choir of Liverpool.

The solution was:

'Good old Arsenal. We're proud to say that name. While we sing this song we'll win the game.

It was sung to a tune, and, in a manner, which suggested the Last Night of the Proms. It retains a certain nostalgic aura, but it hardly commands a fondness in those concerned with music or lyrics. The record sold well, but few would play it today.

As *Good Old Arsenal* became a museum piece so the club was songless until the period of 1-0 victories of which Alan Smith has spoken. It was then that *One–nil to the Arsenal*, vocal by Ian Wright, surged through Highbury, and, astonishingly, the chant has found its way to Italy and other parts of Europe.

None has quite been able to imitate the great back four although reference to the Arsenal defensive formation was made in one of the very best films of recent years, *The Full Monty*, in which a group of unemployed former steel workers are desperately trying to master a routine to use in their planned striptease act. They are having the unhappiest of times, for, when one steps forward, the others cannot grasp the timing of when to join him in line. Suddenly, all becomes clear when one of the group realises that this is the Arsenal offside trap. The first man forward is Tony Adams. He raises his arm. All fall into place. They are at last in time with the music.

If Arsenal's role in *The Full Monty* is not quite as significant as it was in *The Arsenal Stadium Mystery*, it still shows that the club has regained the power to enter the public consciousness.

Lee Dixon was a founder member of the back four.

I learned a lot from George Graham. I've got much to be thankful for to him in bringing me to the club, and I think the hours he spent on the training pitch with the back four paid off. We've all been together now for ten years, and I think the hours we spent, sometimes a bit tedious, sometimes a bit boring, doing the same old thing, drilled into us the way he wanted us to play in the back four. I certainly learned a lot about defending from him. I was a young, naive, bombing full-back when I came, and I like to think I've kept some of those qualities but also improved myself on the defensive side of the full-back's job, which is paramount really. I learned an awful lot from him, and if, eventually, I went into coaching, I'd take a lot of his ideas on to the training pitch with me.

He was Arsenal through and through, and he learned a lot from his predecessors, and he's passed that on to the back four we've got now. I'm sure that if Tony goes into management, he'll have his ideas as well as George's in his mind, and it's the same with me. I try to do a bit of coaching with the kids at a local football club. They are seven or eight years of age, but you can soon get things into them, like lines you should be holding, and they soon pick it up.

Working with George interested me in coaching, and I think I've got something to offer from a defensive coach point of view. We don't do an awful lot of that in English football. It tends to be one coach for everything. I think we could perhaps take a leaf out of American Football. The way they do things. Obviously, they have a lot more players, but they tend to coach in areas rather than the whole team. Newcastle tried it with Mark Lawrenson, and I think, certainly, a couple of days a week where you specifically coach defenders is necessary. It's not always the case where the coach is a defender so he might not know the certain way of doing things. So perhaps I might become a defensive coach.

It would be idle to suggest that George Graham's departure, and the FA's judgement on an illegal payment that was the principal reason for that departure, did not hurt both the club and it supporters. In typical Arsenal manner, the whole affair was conducted with as much dignity as was possible and with the allowance for the sadness, and gratitude, felt on all sides. There was no hasty rush to fill the managerial post, and Stewart Houston took charge for the rest of the season and took Arsenal to the European Cup-winners' Cup Final, but John Jensen's assessment of Houston is probably an accurate one.

Stewart Houston was a more light-hearted personality. Always there if you needed him, and always the one to make you feel good if things were not going well. Of the three managers I played under at Highbury, he was the comedian, yet I felt that even though he was the manager, he was never going to get the job on a permanent basis.

That proved to be true, and Bruce Rioch, who had done well as manager of Bolton Wanderers, was named as George Graham's successor although his tenure of office was to be brief. The job he came to was no sinecure. As George Armstrong insists, working at Highbury has traditionally been a family affair, right from the days of Bertie Mee, and even before.

I was sick when Bertie left, but you either change yourself or you change the players. That was the problem I had in the Middle East because I couldn't buy players. But Bertie and Doris were at every function. She shook hands with the players and knew them. It was a family affair.

I was in Burma when Bruce Rioch was appointed, but I contacted him straight away. I wanted to know where I stood, but I've always found him a very honest man, and he said he wanted me to stay, and he increased my salary.

He is very passionate about the game, but there was so much happening at that time that I wasn't surprised when he left. You're never going to get a manager who is liked by all the players, and, like school-teachers, those who are the strongest disciplinarians and most disliked are often the best. Not all my players like me, especially when I drop them. Bruce was a strong character, maybe a little bit military in his way, but I didn't mind that. He didn't tolerate fools, but that's the man.

Bob Wilson feels that Bruce Rioch tried to establish good habits at Highbury, but perhaps the time was not quite right.

He had a military background. We already knew that. He was quite a complex character, I found. He was a huge family man. If a player had a problem at home, he'd say, "You get off home, son. Your family comes first." And that I liked, but he also had a brusque side to him, particularly in dealing with the press. He could put people down a bit, but the great thing about Bruce when he came was that he wanted to do it his way.

He came from Bolton who played with real style, and they played the ball on the floor. Everything I ever saw Bruce do in training was to play the game á la Pele, the beautiful game. He didn't want the ball hoofed. He didn't want percentages and probabilities. He wanted the game to be played on the floor – pass it, pass it. He was a Cloughie man. If you ever asked Brian his secret, he would say, "If a player can't pass between point A and point B, I'll never have him." It was the whole basis of his play. OK, he used to suck people in and hit them on the break, but when he hit them on the break it was the precision of passing that did it.

Bruce Rioch saw that and took it on board. It was very unfortunate the way it all happened. He obviously didn't endear himself to people, but I liked the way he believed football should be played.

Rioch was fortunate in one way in that, shortly before the confirmation of his arrival, Arsenal had signed former England skipper David Platt and Dennis Bergkamp, the Dutch international and a player of world class, who was quickly to be recognised as one of the greatest players to wear the red and white and one of the most popular in the club's history. He feels he owes a debt to Bruce Rioch.

He was probably the typical English manager with a lot of spirit in training and in his talks before games, but, in a way, off the pitch, he was a very friendly manager. He taught me a lot about English football so it was a good thing coming to England when he was manager. He helped me a lot.

Pat Rice, too, is thankful, and his promotion under Rioch was to have a profound effect on the fortunes of the club as a whole.

I owed it to Bruce Rioch for moving up the ranks, without a doubt. What happened was that he wanted to bring in Tom Whalley as youth team coach, and he asked me if I would come up and assist him and Stewart Houston, and I said yes, and that's how it happened.

John Jensen is a third man who pays tribute to Bruce Rioch, but he is also aware of the difficulties that the ex-Bolton manager faced in coming to Arsenal.

He was a very humane manager, and I have the greatest respect for the way in which he allowed me to leave Arsenal. This, for me, underlined the greatness of the club, and the type of person Rioch was.

He tried to change the side tactically, above all else by playing three in defence, and this did not altogether work. I think the players had grown used to Graham's system, and this could not be changed from one day to another.

Lee Dixon has sympathy for Bruce Rioch and the position in which he found himself.

Things were a little bit different under Bruce Rioch. I felt a little bit sorry for him. It was not the ideal

situation for any manager to take over, and I think he was fighting a losing battle in following in George's footsteps. A lot was expected, because we had a bit of time without George, and Stewart and Pat had taken over. He was on a hiding to nothing really.

Maybe he'd have done it differently if he'd had a fresh start. He'd have mellowed a little bit. Another time, he might have been a bit more successful although we did finish fourth, qualified for Europe, not a disaster by any means. At the time, the atmosphere seemed to be a waiting before the next manager came. It didn't really set off with fireworks, and the season just petered out. I think they realised not long after he got the job that the club had made a mistake, and he wasn't the man for the job. Maybe Bruce Rioch thought that as well.

When George Graham departed there had been constant speculation in the press that Bruce Rioch would succeed him. When Rioch left there was no obvious heir apparent. Suddenly, we began to hear of a certain Arsène Wenger, who had been born in Strasbourg, was

an economics graduate, spoke five languages, had been manager of Monaco when they were champions of France and was now coaching in Japan. Monsieur Wenger was in a similar position to the one in which Bertie Mee found himself when he became manager of Arsenal in 1966: he was known to coaches and managers, but the general public, the football followers were, for the most part, ignorant of his reputation and achievements.

It gradually became apparent that Arsène Wenger was to become manager of Arsenal, but his arrival would be delayed because, refreshingly, he was concerned to honour his contract with Grampus. Arsenal signed two players before his arrival. They were both French. Rémi Garde came from Strasbourg, and Patrick Vieira, a twenty-year-old mid-fielder, was with AC Milan. The press poured scorn. Garde? Vieira? Who? It was not to be long before they discovered "who".

Arsenal won at Blackburn when Arsène Wenger arrived, but there had been the disappointment of losing to Borussia Mönchen-gladbach in the UEFA Cup. A place in Europe was the new manager's priority as he began to impose his own authority on the side, and that was achieved when Arsenal finished third in the Premier League, beaten into second position by Newcastle on goal difference.

Wenger had captured the imagination of the public. He was courteous, intelligent, and Arsenal had started to play football of great beauty. It was the shape of things to come. There were departures, and there were new signings – Manninger, Petit, Grimandi, Wreh, Anelka and Overmars, the Dutch winger, a famed and thrilling prospect. How did the established players like Lee Dixon take to this French manager and his new ideas?

Mr Wenger was a breath of fresh air. He inherited a team that certainly had an older section in it, myself included, and perhaps we were at a stage in our careers when we needed something to kick-start us up again. Coming to the end of the George Graham era, it was a type of change one way or the other, whether he'd change the team or go himself. I don't think it is any secret that he said he was thinking about leaving anyway before the unfortunate circumstances that happened.

The players needed a fresh start; someone has come in who has changed things so radically, from match preparation to what we do before and after training, the training itself, the food we eat, everything was changed. It wasn't done over a period of time; it was done straight away. So we didn't have a lot of time to think about it. It was either sink or swim.

From his point of view, he was fortunate, perhaps, that he'd got a bunch of players, some youngsters and some older heads, who wanted to try something different. He might have come a bit earlier, perhaps, when we were the know-alls of 28 or 29 years of age, the age when you think you know everything and have done everything, and maybe then we wouldn't have changed so easily. We knew that we'd got, perhaps three or four years left in us as a team, and some of the lads, myself included, were coming to an age when you start to think, "How long can I keep going?" So I think we were open-minded and said if anything can give us an extra year playing for a great club like this, then let's go for it.

He concentrates on what we are going to do rather than spend time worrying about the opposition. I think since he's been here we've watched one video of the opposition. He's very much into the idea that you can't predict how the other side are going to play. You've just got to concentrate on your own game, and he tries to put that into our thinking before games.

"A breath of fresh air" was in keeping with the developments, physical and administrative, that were taking place at Highbury. The majesty of the stadium was reflected in careful and intelligent layers of responsibility. Advantageous to Arsène Wenger was that a highly-skilled communications department had been set up before his arrival. It is, as we have mentioned, under the guidance of Clare Tomlinson, a graduate in history from Leeds University who had worked in a voluntary capacity at Tottenham, had been involved with fund raising for the Football Trust, from which the redeveloped North Bank had benefited, and had been with the FA as a media relations officer. Her expertise in dealing with the media was to take pressure not only off Wenger but off members of the administrative staff. It was all part of a streamlined Arsenal which was to prove receptive to Arsène Wenger and his ideas. He soon proved adept with the press. He was recognised as a man of charm, calm and control. Although the calm, as Dennis Bergkamp notes, could be one of his greatest assets.

Arsène, of course, is more or less the European style of manager. He is very calm, and he is very focused on rest and keeping the team ready for the next game. He is very intelligent, of course, very good with words and very experienced as well, so it's very good. He is not the type of manager who raves and rants at you at half-time. If he does it, he does it in his own way. Every manager will get mad at times, but he does it in his own way. And you really take it to you, because when a calm person gets mad you really feel it.

Arsène Wenger himself has considered Pat Rice, his right-hand man, as one of his greatest assets, for the former Arsenal and Northern Ireland captain has been invaluable in assisting the Frenchman to avoid any of the pitfalls that English football might present.

The workings and thinking with Monsieur Wenger is completely different from how an English coach would do it. I've learned a lot from that. I've had to adjust because he's a coach in his own right. He virtually does all the coaching, and Boro Primorac and myself assist him in that.

His ideas are no different from mine. At the end of it all, the game is about putting the ball in one end and keeping it out of the other. It is also about having good players and motivating good players, and it's

Arsène Wenger captured the imagination ...he was courteous, intelligent, and Arsenal started to play beautiful football. According to Lee Dixon, "Mr Wenger was a breath of fresh air."

When he first came I was certain he was an original thinker. I am now not quite so sure, but he has studied football like a scientist. I say to people that he's like a professor – sometimes he's like an absent-minded professor – but first and foremost, he's a very nice man, truly a really nice man. I think his handling of the media is exemplary. I think he's the best handler of the media I've ever seen, whether things are going well or whether things are going badly.

What I think he's done is studied both the art and history of football. I think he's studied nutrition, diet and what makes an athlete almost to university standard, but the art of what he has done is in bringing those, together with a very ordinary track record as a player, and convincing players, not just young kids, but that half a dozen in the Arsenal team who are over 30. I think that Steve Bould and Tony Adams are more of athletes now than they have ever been in their careers. Lee Dixon and Nigel Winterburn, they're smaller guys so they're more athletic, but to get these people to believe in the nutrition, the diet and the stretching which he does, and to believe in his form of training has been amazing to watch. And, of course, he loves football to be played in a certain way.

You will never, ever, have Wenger hitting aimless long balls. He just would not allow it. I see it day after day, the way he drills them. It's pass, pass, pass.

With George Graham, it wasn't always pretty. It wasn't like Arsenal are playing now when you sit thinking that this is a joy to watch, but with George Graham, we won everything. Of course, in the end, we've got to see, with Wenger's way, if that wins you anything. He's got to win something.

about having a good team and team formation and discipline and spirit, and I think that's one thing that's always been recognised at this club.

Bob Wilson assesses the impact that Arsène Wenger has made at Highbury:

As a person, the longer I have lived, the more I love original thinkers.

And then came 1998.

The Beautiful Game

THE season began at Leeds on 9 August 1997, with Adams, Dixon and Keown missing for a variety of reasons, and Emmanuel Petit, Gilles Grimandi and Marc Overmars making their League debuts for Arsenal. The match was drawn 1-1 with Ian Wright scoring, and when he netted twice against Coventry City, at Highbury, on the Monday, he drew all the attention for he now needed just two goals to beat Cliff Bastin's club record of 177. The media and the Arsenal faithful held their breath in anticipation, but it was the Dutchmen, Overmars and Bergkamp, who now took centre stage. Bergkamp, although handled roughly by the Southampton defence, scored twice at The Dell, and Overmars notched his first goal for Arsenal in a 3-1 victory. Four days later, at Filbert Street, Bergkamp scored a hat-trick, but his three goals of varied brilliance did not give Arsenal the points although they led 2-0 at one time. Leicester scored three goals in the last six minutes, and three goals came in the last minute. The Arsenal defence was not at its best, and the inspiration of Tony Adams was being sorely missed.

There was a goalless draw against a quite dreadful Tottenham side who were down to ten men by half-time, but the following Saturday, Ian Wright scored three times as Arsenal beat Bolton Wanderers 4-1, and the Highbury crowd stood in homage to the effervescent striker who had begun his Arsenal career six years earlier with a hat-trick against Southampton and now, on 13 September 1997, had become the leading goalscorer in the club's history.

Eight days later, at Stamford Bridge, Nigel Winterburn drove the ball past de Goey, the Chelsea goalkeeper, from some 30 yards, with two minutes remaining, to give Arsenal a 3-2 win. It was a magnificent shot, and it gave Arsenal just reward for a fine display. Bergkamp had scored two excellent goals, and Tony Adams had returned to add more solidity to the defence and to bring his own dimension of leadership. Arsène Wenger recognised the importance of this win. Chelsea were in very good form, challenging at the top of the table, and this was the first encounter Arsenal had had with one of the top sides.

Bergkamp was playing magnificent football. In the BBC's Goal of the Month competition for August, he had filled the first three places, the first player ever to do so, and, at Highbury, he was deified. The word "great" may be overused, but, whether Dennis Bergkamp was born great, achieved greatness or had greatness thrust upon him, the word undoubtedly is the only one that can be used to describe him. In the words of the Ipswich Town manager, George Burley, "Dennis is something special."

He scored his eighth League goal in as many matches, another sublime effort, when West Ham were beaten 4-0 at Highbury, but the real joy of that match was the performance of Marc Overmars who, first the time, displayed his real talent to the Arsenal faithful.

There was disappointment at Goodison Park where Arsenal again surrendered a two-goal lead and allowed Everton to claim a point, but, the following week, the Gunners were rampant against Barnsley. The Yorkshiremen, who had not played a League game away to Arsenal for 82 years, began brightly, but their sweeper system lacked cohesion, and they suffered in consequence. Bergkamp, picking up the ball just inside the Barnsley half, moved forward, shrugged off an attempted tackle and curled the ball into the top left-hand corner of the net from 25 yards – so calm, so controlled, so exquisite. He added a second, wonderfully, executed goal, set Parlour up for the third, and, with substitute Platt and Ian Wright scoring in the second half Arsenal won 5-0. Having won six and drawn four of their first ten games, Arsenal led the Premiership. The only blot on their season had been elimination from the UEFA Cup by PAOK Salonika, a defeat which had stunned all in the club, but that was being driven from the memory by the entertaining, attacking football being played by the side who, quite clearly, had the championship in their sights. And then, suddenly, everything started to go wrong.

There was a dire contest against Crystal Palace at Selhurst Park which ended with no goals and five Arsenal players booked. One of them was Dennis Bergkamp. The booking meant that he would miss three matches, including the vital home game against Manchester United, at a time when he was at peak form. He considers it as the worst moment of his time at Highbury. The booking against Palace came for dissent, and while one would never condone ill discipline, one feels that Bergkamp was being given scant protection by several referees. The press were unanimous in condemning the way in which Benali of Southampton had shadowed and shirt-tugged Bergkamp in the match at The Dell in August, but Benali had gone unpunished while Bergkamp had been shown the

yellow card for retaliation in a moment of frustration.

If the match at Selhurst Park had been poor, the game at home to Aston Villa was an even more desultory affair. Again it was goalless, and Arsenal seemed bereft of confidence and of ideas. Bergkamp was closely marked, Wright appeared to have lost all his sparkle, and Petit, who was establishing himself as a potent force in midfield, was sent off. There had been Arsenal protests at a caution to Bould, and, as referee Durkin waved the protesters aside, Petit raised his hands. Did he push the referee or did the referee run into him? Mr Durkin thought the former, and Petit was shown the red card.

The following weekend, with Bergkamp serving the first match of his suspension, Arsenal travelled to Derby and lost 3-0. They were, for the most part, totally outplayed. The defence looked leaden, Wright's verve and inspiration had seemingly deserted him, and newcomers Boa Morte and Anelka looked short of class. But Anelka, for one, was to prove the critics very wrong indeed.

Without Bergkamp, without Petit, without a goal for 270 minutes was hardly the preparation that Arsène Wenger would have wished before Manchester United came to Highbury on Sunday, 9 November 1997. United were top of the League and contending strongly in Europe. They had top quality international

Derby County's gangling Costa Rican striker Paulo Wanchope scores against the Arsenal at Pride Park and there is nothing that Tony Adams or Nigel Winterburn can do about it. Ian Wright missed a penalty that day in November 1997 and the Gunners went down 3-0. A League and Cup Double at the end of the season was not even a dream at that stage.

players sitting on the bench, and the odds were heavily in their favour. What transpired surprised the most faithful of Arsenal followers just as much as it excited them.

Ray Parlour was growing in stature with every match, and he, Patrick Vieira and David Platt outfought Manchester United in midfield as Marc Overmars sprinted forward threateningly, cutting deep into the United defence. After one surging run he produced a shot which was a blocked, but the ball broke loose and Anelka swivelled on the edge of the penalty area and beat Schmeichel at his near post with a low, hard right-footed drive. It was the young Frenchman's first goal for Arsenal, and, in the coming months, he was to give further evidence of the prodigious talent which Arsène Wenger had recognised and brought to Highbury.

United, as ever, were a threat, with lightning breaks and brisk, accurate passes which took them the length of the field in seconds, but they fell further behind to a goal from another Frenchman, Patrick Vieira. Parlour's corner from the right was only partially cleared, and the ball fell to Vieira on the edge of the penalty area. There were several United players in attendance, but Vieira hit a shot of such ferocity that it swerved and dipped over Schmeichel's head and into the roof of the net. In the celebrations, Vieira was injured, did not return for the second half and missed the next four matches.

Perhaps Arsenal were still celebrating when, unmarked, Sheringham headed in a cross from the right. Pallister was injured and replaced by Johnsen, but United drew level before half-time. Again Sheringham was the scorer. A weak clearance was touched on by Giggs, and Sheringham hit a left-foot shot across Seaman into the far corner. Blackburn were to score an almost identical goal at Highbury just over a month later.

It seemed that Arsenal had run out of steam. Bould came on for the injured Vieira, and Grimandi moved into midfield. With eleven minutes to go, Wreh replaced the tiring Anelka. United had already brought on the dangerous Solskjaer in place of Giggs, but the middle of the field was now firmly in control of Arsenal, with Parlour covering every inch of Highbury and making men like Scholes and Beckham look second-best. It was Parlour who put

Wright clear to slip the ball to Wreh who, with the aid of a deflection from Gary Neville, seemed to have won the match for Arsenal only for Schmeichel to claw the ball away while he was sitting on the ground. With seven minutes remaining, Arsenal had a corner on the left, in front of the North Bank. From a point somewhere in the region of the penalty spot, David Platt leaped above Beckham and, with a twist of his neck, headed the ball into the far corner above and beyond Schmeichel and Phil Neville. Highbury exploded. This was one of the memorable goals, and it reopened the title race, moving Arsenal to within a point of United.

Thrilling, dramatic, it may have been, but it was a false dawn. There was defeat at Sheffield Wednesday and at home to Liverpool, and no goals and no hint of form. November had ended as badly as it had begun, but December began with a vital win at Newcastle. Wright's goal drought ending when he headed in Bergkamp's gentle cross from the left, and, momentarily at least, faith was restored, but then came an horrendous defeat at home to Blackburn. Overmars had given Arsenal the lead when he lobbed Flowers as the goalkeeper advanced, but Blackburn scored three times in the second half, and Tony Adams, in particular, looked far from his best. Troubled by injury which had affected his form, he was out of the side for more than a month for special treatment.

The pressure now on Arsène Wenger was intense. The press urged him to move into the transfer market and buy players. Others suggested that the French connection was causing problems, that all was not well at Highbury. As we have already evidenced, the honeymoon with some fanzines and some fans was over. We live in an age which demands instant results. Wenger responded to criticism and hysterical advice with characteristic wisdom and calm. He said that he preferred to remember that Arsenal had been a very good side in October, that good players do not suddenly become bad and that he had confidence that they would soon reassert themselves. Manchester bookmakers had less faith in Arsenal than Wenger had and were willing to concede that United had already claimed the title.

On Boxing Day, there was a somewhat bizarre victory over Leicester City. David Platt headed home Bergkamp's free-kick in the first half, and Arsenal went two up early in the second when Walsh lobbed his own 'keeper in spectacular fashion, but, with little more than minutes remaining, a silly back pass left Seaman in trouble. The goalkeeper attempted to dribble his way out of the penalty area, was dispossessed and Lennon put the ball into an empty net. The last ten minutes saw Arsenal struggling frantically for survival. Two days later there was a 1-1 draw at Tottenham in one of the less memorable of derby games.

The Cup now intruded. There was a less than impressive performance at home to Port Vale who, at the time, were struggling at the bottom of the First Division and could not score goals. The trouble was that neither could Arsenal. In extra-time in the replay, Bergkamp seemed to have sealed victory with another spectacular effort, but Port Vale equalised, and, in the end, via a penalty shoot out, Arsenal went into the fourth round where Middlesbrough were disposed of more easily.

In the League, confidence seeped back in spite of the absence of Adams and the fact that Wright was facing all sorts of injury problems. Overmars twice cut inside to score outstanding goals against Leeds. The Yorkshire club, very much title contenders at the time, were beaten more soundly that the 2-1 score line suggests. There was a 2-2 draw at Coventry where the home side equalised from a penalty and Vieira was sent off for arguing, but Southampton, a team in form, were destroyed at Highbury where Adams notched one of the three goals on his return to the side. Hughes scored twice as Chelsea were beaten at home, and, with Manchester United dropping points, the title race was open again.

Injuries and suspensions had taken their toll. Seaman and Bould, who had played mightily in the absence of Adams, were out as was Wright, but Manninger and others reached new heights. With a much-weakened side, Arsenal beat Crystal Palace 1-0, the goal coming from a magnificent volley from Gilles Grimandi. It was his first in English football. Palace were also beaten in a Cup replay, the two sides meeting three times in ten days, so that Arsenal were now second in the League and in the last eight of the Cup where they would meet West Ham.

In the League match at Upton Park, neither side could score, but this, as it transpired, was Arsenal's last bad performance of the season. West Ham were beaten in a penalty shoot out in a Cup replay at Upton Park, but attention was now firmly on the League.

The away match against Wimbledon had been abandoned in December when the floodlights had failed, and it was rescheduled for 11 March. Wenger chose Wreh ahead of Anelka, and the Liberian responded by hitting a splendid goal from twelve yards after accepting a pass from Overmars. Wreh had suffered much criticism when he first appeared in the side, his ability at the top level strongly doubted, but, again, Wenger's judgement was to be totally vindicated in the closing weeks of the season. Wimbledon, never an easy side to beat, were defeated by Wreh's goal, and Arsenal went to Old Trafford the following Saturday morning, knowing that victory over Manchester United would put them just six points behind the reigning champions with three games in hand.

Arsenal went to Manchester without Seaman, Platt, Bould and Wright, all of whom were injured. United, too, were weakened by injury and suspension, but the accepted view from the start of the season had been that, whereas Manchester United were strong in depth and were always able to replace one international with another, Arsenal had no such luxuries. In the closing weeks of the season, this proved to be a false premise as men like Manninger, Wreh and Anelka came of age, displaying outstanding ability and admirable temperament, while United discovered their squad to be less technically accomplished than had been anticipated.

There were more than 55,000 packed into Old Trafford, and most of them believed that they would see United confirm their status as England's best and end Arsenal's last lingering hope of stealing the title, although recent form gave no substance to that assumption. Such a belief was further undermined as, from the start, Arsenal were more assertive, more confident, more menacing and more skilful. The midfield of Parlour, Vieira and Petit had matured during the season into a potent force, boundless in energy, tigerish in the tackle and creative in purpose. They quickly asserted their dominance. Like Bergkamp in his first season with Arsenal, Overmars had taken some weeks to settle and he had also been troubled by an ankle injury, but his confidence had grown with every match. He had begun to move inside more often, beat men with his speed and trickery, shown that he possessed a powerful and accurate shot and had recovered all the magic that some had thought had been taken from him by a lengthy lay-off through injury during his time with Ajax. It was Overmars who gave the first indications this was to be Arsenal's day.

Opposed by reserve full-back John Curtis, he attacked with pace, went past the defender on both the outside and inside and caused havoc in the United defence. The Dutch winger burst between Curtis and Gary Neville but hit the side netting with his shot. He surprised Schmeichel with a delicate chip which missed the far post by inches, and he ran Curtis ragged. Surging in on goal, he was brought down by the young full-back. It was a blatant penalty in the eyes of all but the most committed of United fans and of referee Alan Wilkie. Parlour was set free by Bergkamp but missed a golden opportunity, and the half-time whistle went with Arsenal well ahead on quality and control but with no goals to their credit.

Alex Ferguson had switched Phil Neville to attempt to deal with Overmars, and, seven minutes into the second half, he replaced Curtis with Thornley, a naturally left-sided player. United improved, but the famous back four, with Adams and Keown at the heart, gave not an inch, and Vieira and Petit, ever offering support in defence, were quick to set the attack in motion. Behind them, Manninger, a Highbury favourite in his first season, did all that was asked of him.

A quarter of an hour into the second half, Petit put Overmars clear with a delightful chip – a tactic that the intelligent and charming Frenchman was to employ with great success in the coming matches – and Schmeichel committed himself early. Overmars lifted the ball over the goalkeeper only to see it bounce wide. Wenger brought on Garde for Parlour, and Anelka for Wreh. Almost immediately, Garde tested Schmeichel with a fierce shot as he bore in on goal from the right. United, too, made changes, introducing May and Solskjaer after injuries to Phil Neville and Johnsen. It was while they were regrouping that Arsenal struck.

Keown cleared a long ball out of defence to Bergkamp whose headed pass to Anelka was nodded into the path of Overmars. The winger headed the ball forward, sprinted away from any challenges and slid the ball past Schmeichel as he came out. It was a well-deserved goal for both Arsenal and Overmars. With ten minutes remaining, United pressed forward, but Adams, Manninger and the rest surrendered nothing. Schmeichel himself came forward, but this brought near disaster, for Bergkamp got control of the ball outside the Arsenal area, and the Danish goalkeeper lunged at him, but succeeded only in damaging a hamstring. Bergkamp coolly took the ball upfield, and minutes later, the whistle blew.

The quality of Arsenal's performance was rapturously received in the press and by millions who had watched on television. Arsenal had now been beaten only once in their last eighteen matches while United had won only four of their last thirteen matches in all competitions, but, as Alex Ferguson said, the pressure was now on Arsenal. They had 54 points to Manchester United's 60. United had seven games to play, four of which were at home; Arsenal had ten games to play of which five were at home and five away. On top of that, Arsenal faced a Cup replay at West Ham three days after beating United.

We have noted that Arsenal beat West Ham on a penalty shoot-out, but the victory came at a cost. Dennis Bergkamp was shown the red card for an elbowing offence, which meant that he would miss the semi-final against Wolves and the League matches against Bolton Wanderers and Newcastle United. Arsenal had suffered in his absence in the autumn; and now they were to lose the services of this inspirational footballer in the spring climax to the League campaign. He said his temporary farewell in style, converting Overmars's pass for the only goal of the match against Sheffield Wednesday. Overmars was again in stunning form, and Wednesday were outclassed for much of the match.

On the Tuesday evening after beating Wednesday, Arsenal travelled to Bolton who had been playing well in their desperate effort to retain their place in the Premier League. Two minutes after the interval, Hughes and Petit combined on the left and the ball was pushed inside to Wreh who was some 30 yards from goal. The striker struck a shot of tremendous power into the corner of the net which left Branagan clawing at space. Wreh was later replaced by Bould after Keown had been sent off for a second bookable offence. With Seaman, playing his second game after return from injury, in his best form, Arsenal repelled everything that Bolton threw at them, and they were now just three points behind Manchester United.

In the Sixties, a film was shown time and again on television of Leeds United players exchanging some fifteen or sixteen passes between them as they kept possession of the ball. In 1998, it became commonplace for Arsenal to do that except that the combination inevitably ended with a man being released for a quick thrust down the wing. Against Wolves, in the semi-final Villa Park, a breathtaking exchange of passes criss-crossed the field only for the final thrust to find Parlour, on the right, marginally offside. It happened in the second half, and by then Arsenal were a goal in front, and the difference in class between the two sides was becoming embarrassing. The First Division side had tried to disturb Arsenal's rhythm with a physical approach, and they did threaten down the left wing where Grimandi, deputising for the injured Dixon, had occasional difficulties against Froggatt, but, apart from Goodman once following through on Seaman in the first half and punching the ball out of his hands in the second, the Arsenal goal was rarely threatened. Wolves had pressed hard at the start of the last 45 minutes, and Keown sustained a facial injury and was replaced by Bould, but Arsenal soon took control again.

The goal had come in the twelfth minute. Vieira latched on to a loose goal-kick by Segers, shrugged off a weak attempt at a tackle as he surged forward menacingly before freeing Wreh on the right. To his winning goals against Wimbledon and Bolton, the Liberian added the winning goal in the semi-final, driving the ball across Segers into the far corner before celebrating with his famous somersault. Later the same afternoon, Newcastle beat Sheffield United to earn the right to meet Arsenal in the Final. The pessimists among us recalled history. In 1932 and 1953, Arsenal had been in pursuit of the Double and had lost to Newcastle in the Final, but the class of '98 were

Wenger's Wonders, and the world, and the style had changed.

Manchester United came from behind to beat Blackburn Rovers, but dropped points at home to Liverpool on Good Friday. The next day, Arsenal met their Cup Final opponents, Newcastle, at Highbury. There was a fright for the Gunners early on when Steve Bould got into difficulties and pushed the ball back to Seaman who, under pressure, picked it up. Arsenal formed a barrier on the goal line as Barton touched the indirect free-kick to Shearer. The centre-forward's fierce shot was blocked by the line of red shirts which charged forward, and the danger was cleared. Adams might have scored for Arsenal, and Anelka showed his enormous talent when he touched the ball past Given. The Frenchman appeared to have no chance of reaching the ball, but his phenomenal pace enabled him to catch it by the byline, only for him to touch it against the post. He was more fortunate four minutes before half-time when he accepted a pass from Wreh, side-stepped Pearce and scored cleanly. Nineteen minutes into the second half, he scored again. Petit, Vieira and Parlour had total command of midfield as Newcastle sought only to defend, and it was Parlour who surged down the right, beating three men before crossing to Anelka who was left with the easiest of chances. Eight minutes later, Vieira brought the ball out of defence, powered his way into the Newcastle half and from fully 30 yards hit an unstoppable drive into the roof of the Newcastle net. A late consolation goal by Barton took none of the gloss off Arsenal's victory. Against a side concerned only with survival, they had been rampant and had excited with the sweetness of their passing and the passionate strength of their commitment.

If one thought the win over Newcastle was impressive, the victory over Blackburn Rovers at Ewood Park on Easter Monday was awesome. Bergkamp returned after suspension and lifted Arsenal to another dimension. Inside two minutes, his name was on the scoresheet. A throw on the right, a Blackburn defence with their minds still in the dressing room, and Bergkamp was gliding in on goal to put an unstoppable shot, low past Fettis. Within the next twelve minutes, the game was decided. A clearance by Seaman allowed Bergkamp and Anelka to bemuse the already tattered

Blackburn midfield. Bergkamp emerged with the ball, and, as Parlour raced through in the inside-right position, the Dutch master delivered a perfectly-weighted pass which Parlour took in his stride to score. Next, Petit, shaping to take an in-swinging corner on the right, spotted Bergkamp unmarked and slipped the ball to him. A powerful shot rebounded off the goalkeeper, and Parlour banged it back in the net. The fourth epitomised the outstanding quality of Arsenal's football. A long pass out of defence by Winterburn left the Blackburn defence static on the halfway line as the ball passed beyond them. Anelka was some five yards behind two defenders when the pass was made, but he raced past them, took the ball in his stride and, reaching the penalty area, dummied the goalkeeper before slipping the ball into the net. The defenders were still in vain pursuit, and we had exhausted the superlatives.

Blackburn pulled a goal back in the second half. Sleet swirled around the ground. Overmars might have had a hat-trick. Bergkamp shot over an open goal to disprove the belief that he was immortal. 4-1 to the Arsenal who now stood one point behind Manchester United with two games in hand.

Wimbledon had long posed problems for Arsenal at Highbury, but superstition and lack of belief no longer found a place in the Arsenal psyche. The generally tough opponents, who had not lost at Highbury since 1987, were shredded in the first eighteen minutes. Within twelve minutes, Adams had headed in from a corner. It was the first goal Wimbledon had conceded in five matches, and the ball was in the back of their net again five minutes later when Anelka set up Overmars who left Michael Hughes stranded before putting a left foot shot past Sullivan. Almost from the kick-off Arsenal scored again. Anelka broke quickly from just inside his own half, drew Blackwell and pushed the ball to Bergkamp who struck his 21st goal of the season. In the second half, a flowing move that involved Seaman, Bergkamp, Overmars and Anelka ended with Petit driving home his first goal for the club. Wreh, coming on as sub, notched the fifth and celebrated with his customary acrobatics. On the same day, Manchester United drew at home to Newcastle, and Arsenal led the table by one point. And they still had two games in hand.

The following Saturday, Arsenal were at Oakwell, entertained by the gallant Barnsley who had fought so hard in the closing stages of the season but were destined for a quick return to the First Division. The Barnsley supporters were a credit to football, but their spirits were lowered by another sublime strike from Bergkamp who curled the ball beyond the goalkeeper in his accomplished fashion. From that point, there was only going to be one winner, and Overmars confirmed victory in the second half.

Four days later, Arsenal were at home to Derby County. Just as they had done in the away fixture earlier in the season, Arsenal missed a penalty, Poom saving Bergkamp's kick. Worse followed as Bergkamp suffered a hamstring strain when he over-stretched for the ball. The man who had been voted Players' Player of the Year and Football Writers' Player of the Year, and who had done so much to bring Arsenal to the point of glory, was to be denied a place in the climax to the League season and in the Cup Final. This was a cruel blow. Petit scored with a rasping drive to beat Derby who never mounted a serious attack in return, and if Arsenal could beat Everton, at Highbury, on Sunday, 3 May, they would be champions. At one time, they had stood thirteen points adrift of Manchester United.

Having reached this point by playing some of the most fluent and entertaining football imaginable, Arsenal did not disappoint at the last. They took the lead when Adams jumped for a corner and so disconcerted an Everton defender that he headed the ball in his own net. The passes crossed and recrossed the field tracing delightful patterns, and, with half-time nearing, Petit was flattened by a vicious tackle. As he lay by the players' tunnel, Overmars gathered the ball, outstripped a leaden defence and beat Myhre with his shot. Overmars added another brilliant, individual goal in the second half. Platt – what a wonderful luxury to have as sub – replaced the injured Petit, and Wright and Bould, who had given so much to the cause and so much to the club, were brought on for the closing stages of the party. Wright was to be denied a goal, but not the championship medal which had long been his ambition. The final goal was to go, appropriately, to Tony Adams. Steve Bould, his faithful colleague in the back four, was operating in midfield and lobbed a beautifully judged pass over the Everton

Ian Wright, Marc Overmars, Martin Keown and Dennis Bergkamp couldn't look happier after the win over Everton which confirmed Arsenal as Premiership champions.

defence, and there was Tony Adams galloping free. He took the ball in his stride and thumped a left-foot shot past the 'keeper. It was the perfect ending. No man has ever been more dedicated to a club. Few men have been able to match his strength of character in overcoming unjust criticisms and in surmounting personal problems. His place among the greatest of Arsenal players and captains is assured.

Highbury erupted in joy. The trophy and medals were presented. Bob Wilson ran gleefully on to the pitch, and at least one part of North London was in ecstasy. The two remaining League matches were an anti-

The sign says it all – Arsenal are the 1997-98 Premiership champions and players, management and coaching staff all join in the fun at Highbury.

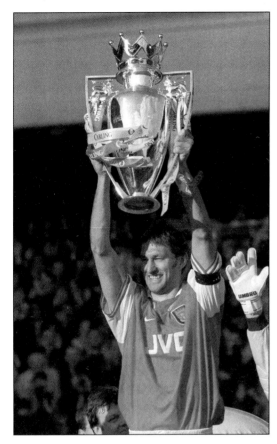

Left: Tony Adams and Newcastle's Alan Shearer and Temuri Ketsbaia chase a loose ball during the 1998 FA Cup Final.

Far left: Arsenal skipper Tony Adams lifts the Premiership trophy. For Adams in particular the triumphs of 1997-98 were an outstanding achievement after his own personal difficulties.

Marc Overmars fires the ball past Newcastle goalkeeper Shay Given to give Arsenal the lead at Wembley. And celebrates his goal.

but the England skipper hit the post, and there were to be no more chances. Anelka settled matters with one of those bursts of speed that took him clear of the defence and with a shot that left the goalkeeper helpless. And so Arsenal completed the second Double their history.

The quality of their play was to bring from

climax, and attention was now focused on Wembley and 16 May.

It is rare for a Premier League side to beat another Premier League side three times in one season, but that is what Arsenal had to do if they were to complete the Double. They did it comfortably. It was not a great Final. Newcastle adopted something akin to a scorched earth policy. They had neither the wit nor the ability to match Arsenal, and, for the most part, their most dangerous player, Shearer, ploughed a lone furrow up front. Arsenal should have taken the lead when Parlour severed the Newcastle defence and crossed from the right to Anelka who headed over an open goal, but the goal was not long in coming. Vieira, with those long legs wrapping round the ball in the tackle, and Petit, deft, strong and wise, had taken possession of midfield, and Parlour was playing with the energy and vision that had seen him make 1998 the year that he developed from lively runner to a footballer of international quality. It was Petit who set up the first goal, lobbing the ball gently over the full-back for Overmars to avoid any challenge with disdain and push the ball past the advancing goalkeeper. There was one moment of horror in the second half when Keown fell over the ball and left Shearer a free run on goal,

Ray Parlour and Nicolas Anelka, scorer of Arsenal's second goal, go to congratulate each other.

Tony Adams raises the FA Cup and he and his Arsenal team-mates acknowledge the roar of the Wembley crowd.

Arsenal Double-winning team parade through the streets of North London.

Emmanuel Petit leads the celebrations at Islington Town Hall. Other Arsenal players are Lee Dixon, Ian Wright and Marc Overmars.

older supporters like Len Grimsey, writer and sports fanatic, fulsome tributes.

I've always been a devotee of the Male/Hapgood side as the best of Arsenal, but this crowd were marvellous.

For once, the press were unstinting in their praise of Arsenal. Not only had Wenger and Rice and Armstrong and the rest taken the side to the League and the Cup, they had silenced the jibes of "lucky" and "boring". They had given us the beautiful game as it should be played.

At a press conference two days before the League game against Newcastle, Arsène Wenger began by complaining with good humour that he did not like the English weather, that he didn't like wind. Perhaps we may borrow an Irish wish for him – "May the wind be always at your back."

Towards the Millennium

WHAT of the future? A magnificent new training centre is being developed in a quiet part of Hertfordshire near London Colney. There will be indoor and outdoor facilities of which even Herbert Chapman could not have dreamed. A stadium big enough to hold all those clamouring to watch Arsenal presents greater problems, but supporter Andy Charalambous offers one solution.

The answer must be to move down the road to King's Cross, a hundred-acre site where we could build a stadium that holds more than 50,000, reduce the prices, fill it every week and recapture some of the lost generation. It would only be a couple of tube stops down the line, and there would be room for parking plenty of cars. With modern technology, we could actually dig up the front of the East Stand and take it as a whole to King's Cross, half-a-mile down the road.

It wouldn't worry me or anyone else that we left Highbury. This club has grown and developed and achieved things through moving itself to strategic places. It started as a poxy little club in Woolwich, playing on the common. It moved to another common, had a bit of success and then moved right across London to Highbury and achieved greater success. Moving a mile down the road to a state-of-the-art stadium with room for all the people who want to watch us, and ample parking space, is just a logical development. It's been done in Milan. It's not breaking tradition. It's moving house. You move house when you want to move to a bigger and better house. You take your bits with you, your kids and your fans and the rest. It would even raise the area of King's Cross. We could still use the same restaurants and get there in time. It's a stone's throw from where we are now. There is a marvellous picture of Arsenal just after the war with 80,000 people in the stadium and not a car in sight, but things have changed, and we have to change with them.

Indeed, things do change, as I hope this book has shown, but some things remain. I shall continue to park in Blackstock Road and meet fellow supporters in Il Cavaliere before the match and talk about last week and ponder on today. Then I shall walk to the ground, eagerly but apprehensively, buy a programme and take my seat. I will live in constant fear that the opposition will score every time the ball is down our end; and I will never see a goal coming when we are on the attack. It has always been like that.